FOREIGN MILITARY INTERVENTION
IN AFRICA

For Tom, in the hope that he may see a more peaceful Africa

FOREIGN MILITARY INTERVENTION IN AFRICA

KEITH SOMERVILLE

Pinter Publishers, London
St Martin's Press, New York

First published in Great Britain in 1990 by
Pinter Publishers Limited
25 Floral Street, London WC2E 9DS

British Library Cataloguing in Publication Data

A CIP catalogue record for this book is available from
the British Library.

ISBN 0-86187-890-6

First published in the United States of America in 1990

Scholarly and Reference Division
St. Martin's Press, Inc., 175 Fifth Avenue, New York, N.Y. 10010
ISBN 0-312-04727-4

Library of Congress Cataloging-in-Publication Data.

Somerville, Keith.
  Foreign military intervention in Africa / Keith Somerville.
    p. cm.
  Includes bibliographical references.
  ISBN 0-312-04727-4
  1. Africa--Foreign relations--1960- 2. Africa--Politics and government--1960- 3. Intervention
(International law) I. Title.
DT30.5.S64 1990
960.3'2--dc20
                                                                    90-8370
                                                                       CIP

Typeset by The Castlefield Press Ltd, Wellingborough, Northants in Ehrhardt 10/12 point.
Printed and bound in Great Britain by Biddles Ltd.

Contents

Acknowledgements

This book is the result of the collation of ten years' research on different aspects of political, military and economic development in Africa and on the prevalence of foreign intervention in African affairs. The material is derived from a number of research trips to East, Central, Southern and West Africa and from the speeches, writings and broadcasts of African political leaders and from innumerable secondary works and commentaries on African affairs. Much has been collected during research for other books, articles, radio programmes or lectures.

It would be impossible to thank or make reference to all those who have contributed through their comments, advice and encouragement, particularly as many gave their help unwittingly in interviews for articles or radio broadcasts. But among those to whom I am indebted are Dr Karen Dawisha of the University of Maryland, for over a decade of encouragement and advice; David Morison, editor of *USSR and the Third World;* Stephen Ellis, editor of *Africa Confidential;* Martin Plaut of the BBC African Service; Sean Moroney of Africa File; Heather Bliss and Iain Stevenson of Pinter Publishers; Marcelino Komba; Joan Baxter, formerly of CBC and the BBC in Ouagadougou; Liz Blunt, BBC West Africa correspondent; and Gerald Bourke, the *Independent's* West Africa correspondent.

There are many politicians and diplomats who have given time to answer questions on various aspects of foreign military intervention in Africa. Many have given interviews in confidence and that confidence will be respected. Those that I can mention include: Witness Mangwende, formerly Foreign Minister and now Information Minister in Zimbabwe; William Ndangana and Mayor Urimbo of the ZANU Central Committee; Ndabaningi Sithole, former President of ZANU; Ben Mkapa, Foreign Minister of Tanzania; Hage Geingob, Theo-Ben Gurirab, Hidipo Hamutenya and Peter Manning of SWAPO; Obed Asamoah, Ghana's Foreign Secretary; Colonel Assassie, coordinator of the Ghanaian Committees for the Defence of the Revolution; Jean-Leonard Compaore, Minister for Territorial Administration, Burkina Faso; and Thabo Mbeki, Head of the International Department of the ANC.

On a more personal note, I must thank members of my family for their support, encouragement and patience during the writing of this and other works. My brother-in-law Michael Anderson, his wife Eija and their two children, Risto and Elisa, provided me with a comfortable and relaxed haven (not to mention extensive supplies of cold Guinness) during a hectic trip through West Africa. My mother has been an endless support. But most of all I must thank Liz and Tom for putting up with me and making me laugh when I felt like throwing the word processor out of the window.

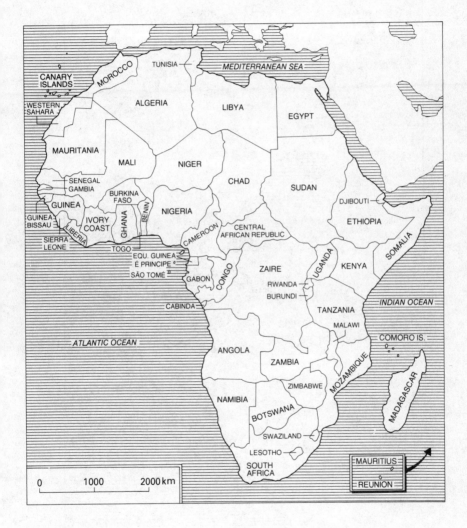

Map 1 Africa

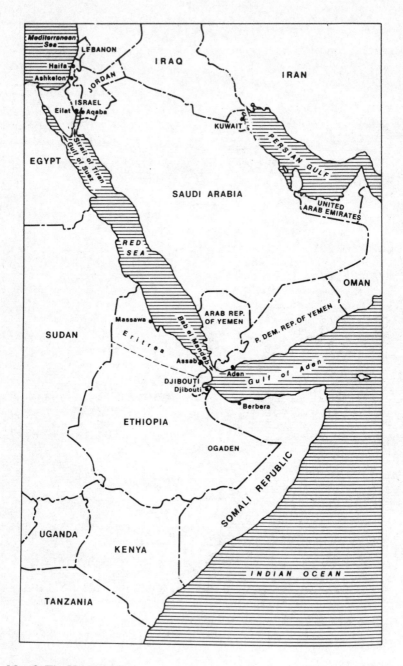

Map 2 The Horn of Africa
Source: Bogdan Szajkowski, ed., *Marxist Governments: A World Survey,* London, Macmillan, 1981.

Introduction

It is now over three decades since the decolonisation of Africa was embarked upon. By 1960, a large number of colonies had achieved full statehood amid unparalleled optimism about the future. But those thirty years have not seen the peace, prosperity and progress hoped for by so many Africans. Instead they have seen war, famine and misery. Not a year has gone by when a war has not been in progress on the continent. The wars have ranged from short-lived border clashes, such as the Burkina-Mali war of December 1985, to the bloody Nigerian civil war and the two decades of conflict in Chad. The wars have destroyed efforts at economic, social and political development and have given Africa an undeserved reputation for political strife and violence. They have also opened the way for foreign military intervention.

Many of the wars fought since 1960 have not just been between competing African states or rival movements within states, they have also involved outside powers, whose presence has escalated, prolonged and frequently prevented the conclusion of the conflicts.

Foreign intervention has been a fact of life in Africa since the early days of decolonisation in 1960. Hardly had the Congolese flag been run up the flagpole in Leopoldville (now Kinshasa) than Belgian troops seized control once more, alleging that mutinies against Belgian officers forced them to step in and restore 'order'. French troops were used to support the new governments in Senegal, Congo (Brazzaville) and Gabon in 1960. By the end of the first decade of independence, Africa had seen interventions by the Belgians, UN forces, the French, the British, the Cubans and the Israelis; the Soviet Union and China had shown their interest in military developments in Africa by engaging in army building programmes in various independent states.

By the end of the next decade, Chad, Ethiopia, Angola and Zaire had experienced large-scale interventions by foreign armies and had witnessed war on a scale previously seen in Europe, Asia and the Middle East but not Africa – tank battles were fought in the Ogaden desert and Cubans fought South Africans and European mercenaries in Angola.

As we enter the 1990s, some aspects of foreign military intervention appear to be receding. Peace agreements have led to an end (for the time being) to the war in Chad, to the phased withdrawal of Cuban forces from Angola and of all South African forces from there. Thousands of foreign troops remain in Africa, but their combat role has been much reduced. Yet, there is the ever present threat of new wars or the reopening of old ones, and it cannot be doubted that Libya would be ever ready to send its men back into Chad if it felt the need and that the French and Cubans would be willing to intervene once more if requested to do so by an African ally.

But what is the cause of foreign military intervention? Is Africa so weak militarily and politically that it must call on or be the target of foreign armies? Is conflict so endemic and African states so incapable of finding solutions that external involvement is a necessary means to bring wars to a conclusion? Whatever the answers, it is clear that for most Africans, the presence of foreign troops is unwanted, is a threat to sovereignty, to development and to peace. One African political scientist has written that 'prolonged military intervention by the imperialist powers in the affairs of African countries is the most important single threat to peace, development and security' (Nnoli in Hansen, 1987, pp. 221–2). If it is such a threat, then why has it continued and why have so many countries called on foreign powers to intervene?

This study aims to identify why foreign intervention has been an ever present factor in Africa since independence. Previous studies have looked at the motivations of those intervening in Africa (Klinghoffer, 1980; Lemarchand, 1988; Chipman, 1985; Luckham, 1982) or at the implications for regional security (MacFarlane, 1983–84), but not at the root causes of intervention.

To answer the question of why foreign intervention has remained a feature of the African political and military landscape, this book follows the history of foreign intervention from the Cameroon and the Congo to the latter stages of the Chadian war and the Cuban role in Angola. With thirty years and at least twenty examples of intervention to cover, it is obvious that a full history of each and every example will be impossible within the confines of a single book. The major cases of intervention will be looked at in depth, including an examination of the background to the conflict which brought about intervention. In the opening chapter, an attempt will be made to set the scene for post-independence intervention by running through the major hangovers of colonialism and through the rather hasty process of decolonisation. From there, the narrative will proceed via the Congo, the East African mutinies, the start of Africa's liberation wars, the first Sudanese civil war, the first shots in the struggle in the Horn, the war in Chad, the conflicts in southern Africa following the end of Portuguese rule and the weakening of the white minority regimes, the second and bloodier phase of the wars in the Horn, Libya's intervention in Uganda, France's in the Central African Republic, the desert war in the Western Sahara, destablisation in southern Africa and the second round in the Sudan. The penultimate chapter will examine why so many states have been motivated to intervene. In the final chapter suggestions will be made as to why intervention is still rife and why, despite the current peace offensives in Africa (themselves foreign-backed), foreign armies are still likely to be seen in Africa in the coming decade.

Readers wishing to go deeper into the conflicts in individual states or regions are directed to the footnotes and to the bibliography.

1 The colonial legacy: a recipe for conflict

In the decade between 1957 and 1967 over thirty African states came into being. Fifteen years later, the number of independent countries on the continent had passed fifty with only Namibia, Reunion and the Western Sahara still to achieve statehood (a nationalist struggle was of course still continuing inside South Africa, but it was a fight for democratic rights and against racism rather than for independence). Many states were granted independence after a token nationalist campaign, some after riots and repression and others after brutal wars of national liberation. But whatever the path to freedom, the countries of Africa grasped at the prize with enthusiasm and high hopes. Africans sought self-rule, freedom from foreign control and, perhaps above all else, dignity. But did they achieve these aims?

Self-rule they have, if one counts the formation of a government, the enacting of laws, international recognition and the membership of international organisations as the criteria for self-rule. Yet even the running of their own economies, the organisation of their armed forces and the results of their domestic and regional conflicts are decided or at least influenced by foreign powers. This suggests that they are not free of foreign control; states outside sub-Saharan Africa all too frequently intervene militarily in Africa's affairs, sometimes invited in, sometimes not. And in such conditions, what of dignity? Many Africans believe that they have sacrificed their dignity or lost it in the face of constant interventions in their affairs by the Western powers, the socialist countries or states from the Arab world. Often African leaders have been forced to appeal to their former colonial rulers to send back the troops which once ensured colonial rule in order to defeat rebels, to maintain domestic order or to fight or deter an aggressor. Some leaders have approached allies outside Africa to gain support to fight foreign intervention or to fight an aggressor from within the continent. Worst of all, many states have had to watch foreign troops invade their lands uninvited and most certainly unwanted.

So what happened to the brave new world envisaged by each African state on its independence day? Has foreign military intervention in Africa rendered independence meaningless? Or was that independence flawed from the start?

Colonial rule and decolonisation

Colonial rule was imposed on Africans agains their will and for the benefit of the coloniser not the colonised. Effectively it was a system created and maintained by the threat or the use of force. Michael Crowder sees violence, and frequently the use of massive force out of all proportion to need, as a basic characteristic of the colonial system – 'the colonial state was conceived in violence rather than by negotiation. This violence was often quite out of proportion to the task in hand, with burnings of villages, destruction of crops, killing of women and children, and the execution of leaders' (Crowder, 1987, p. 11). The military force used by the European colonial armies was unrestrained by the standards of war in Europe and was an ever present factor under the colonial system. It was used to build a political and economic system where might was right. Political power and the control of economic resources was in the hands of those who could wield the greatest force. Few African politicians have failed to learn this lesson – drummed into them as it was by the wars of conquest, the wars of 'pacification' against indigenous uprisings and the repression of the pre-independence nationalist movements.

The people of Africa were too divided and too weak militarily to defeat the European powers which partitioned the continent, though they resisted the process from the first wars of colonial occupation to the lowering of the imperial flag on independence day. But resistance was not enough to prevent the partition of Africa at the Berlin conference of 1884–5 or the signing of the Berlin Act on 26th February 1885. The act set the boundaries of most of today's states and, as Professor Uzoigwe of the University of Calabar has stated, 'in a broad sense, African history in the post-1885 period is a legacy' of the act (*Africa Now*, March 1985, p. 27). The arbitrary creation of colonial boundaries divided ethnic groups and lumped others together in inherently unstable aggregations. Ethnic and community conflict existed in Africa before Berlin, but after the conference structural violence based on ethnic and regional competition was ensured in any future states based on the colonial borders. The pre-colonial African system 'characterised by migration, fragmentation, incorporation, exchange and war' (Timothy Shaw in Shaw and Heard, 1979, p. 361) was abruptly changed by foreign conquest into a collection of states whose shape, balance of forces and population had little if any similarity to what had been evolving prior to external intervention. Ethnic conflict, secessionism, irridentism and border conflicts became inevitable. The seeds were sown for countless national and international disputes that would give outside powers endless scope for manipulation and intervention in independent Africa.

It is hard to argue with former Uganda Justice Minister Grace Stuart Ibingira when he says that one of the major causes of post-independence political and military instability in Africa was 'the total failure of colonisation to combine within a given colony ethnic groups with compatible characteristics; instead the colonial frontiers were drawn purely on the basis of alien strategic and economic interests' (Ibingira, 1980, p. xi-xii). These alien interests frequently led the colonial power to manipulate competition or conflict between ethnic groups within a colony to entrench imperial power and weaken African resistance. In Uganda, the pre-colonial fight for power between the Baganda and neighbouring communities was utilised by the British – the well organised Baganda state became an agent of British colonialism in return for the retention of some political and economic power. This, as is all too clear from the recent history of Uganda, sowed the seeds of ethnic rivalry and national disintegration within Uganda. The rivalry was exacerbated by the British practice of recruiting its colonial troops from among non-Baganda peoples of north and north-west Uganda, notably the Kakwa and Lugbara.

Uganda is but one example of the creation of an artificial 'national state' housing previously hostile, or at best unconnected, communities whose differences were then worsened by divisive forms of administration. Nations were formed by force and colonial dictat rather than by the more long-term processes which had led to the rise of the modern nation-states of Europe. It had taken centuries for Britain, France, Germany and Italy to develop into their late nineteenth-century forms – yet at the stroke of a pen in Berlin, a host of African 'nations' came into being. No attempt at nation-building ensued under colonial rule, but on independence the new states were expected to ape the political, social and economic examples of their former colonial rulers. In fact, rather than encourage the growth of national feelings, colonial policies were specifically designed to prevent ethnic communities from coming together; colonial powers adopted the 'tactic of divide and rule . . . by so doing they [introduced] . . . into the African body politic a cancer called ethnicity, or 'tribalism' as they preferred to call it' (Uzoigwe in *Africa Now*, March 1985, p. 29). Conflict existed before imperial rule, but as a factor in the evolution of a state system in Africa not as a cancer within individual African states.

Secessionism, irridentism and border conflicts were also a natural development of the boundaries drawn by Africa's foreign masters. Contemporary Africa has 103 examples of borders which are the subject of dispute between neighbours, are a cause of secessionist or irridentist conflicts or arbitrarily divide distinct ethnic communities. Hereby causing political, social and economic dislocation (*Africa Now*, March 1985, p. 37; and Asiwaju, 1985, pp. 1–3). One only needs to think of Somalia's disputes with Ethiopia, Jibuti and Kenya; Ethiopia's secessionist problems in Eritrea; and the Libya-Chad dispute over the Aouzou Strip to realise the ramifications of the straight lines drawn across the map of Africa by European statesmen.

The colonial state was little more than an area of land and a disparate group of people thrown together for the purposes of enrichment of the metropolitan states or to prevent that state's competitors from adding to their empires. Only ten current African states bear any resemblance to pre-colonial African polities and few of the states have populations that until independence shared anything but the experience of colonial exploitation and oppression. As the Zairean writer Nzongola-Ntalaja has noted, few modern African states have a homogenous cultural identity. Most 'comprise a mixture of peoples without a core cultural tradition around which others may coalesce' (Nzongola-Ntalaja in Hansen (ed), 1987, p. 64). The struggle of African nationalists for independence helped build something approaching a national identity, but as events have shown, it is one thing to unite to fight against a common enemy and another to unite to build a nation, especially within the space of barely three decades.

The cultural, ethnic and religious differences which were evident in the colonial entities were added to by political and economic policies which favoured one community or one region over another. The existence of valuable natural resources in a particular area of colony usually led to greater infrastructural development and provision of employment in that area and neglect of less economically favourable parts of the country. In Chad, for example, the south was given far more attention and received far more investment than the north – this was paralleled, not surprisingly, by closer French links with the southerners and the development of a small, educated southern elite and a southern-dominated army. Nzongola-Ntalaja has identified the raison d'etre of colonial policies which were frequently regionally rather than nationally orientated within a particular colony:

The north–south cleavage in Chad and Sudan is primarily a function of the colonial political economy. For the colonialists, it was only those regions which were economically useful that were to witness the development of the infrastructure and that of supportive social services such as education and health. In the Sudan, it was the north, with its historical and economic links with Egypt, that was deemed useful to British imperialism . . . the French imposed two separate administrations in the two cultural zones of Chad. For the French, the Chad utile (or useful Chad) was the southern region, where the cultivation of cotton, the major export crop, was made compulsory in 1926 (Hansen (ed), 1987, pp. 75–6).

Chad and Sudan are particularly vivid examples of the regionalisation of colonial territories. They split very definitely into north and south, with one region being favoured, developed and an indigenous elite allowed to form, and the other region being neglected economically and often ruled more or less by the military, this certainly being the case with northern Chad (Thompson and Adloff, 1981, pp. 6–8). In both countries (as will be shown later), the era of independence saw the handing over of power to the elite group or class in the favoured region of the country, with the 'backwater' areas being unrepresented in government and effectively subject to a government from a different regional, ethnic and cultural system. Civil wars and external military involvement have followed directly from the dual policy pursued by the metropolitan power and the effective continuation of that pattern following independence.

Nigeria, also to suffer a devastating civil war, was ruled by the British in a manner that encouraged regionalism rather than nationalism. Certainly, nationalist politicians emerged and parties were formed calling for independence, but they developed along regional rather than national lines, for the most part. One major reason for this was the 'dual mandate' system of rule instituted under the guidance of Lord Lugard. The northern emirates were governed under a form of indirect rule which left much of the authority of the emirs intact. The eastern and western regions were ruled more directly and although they had greater access to education, European influence and wage labour, they had less autonomy and their pre-colonial structures did not survive in the way that northern polities were able to. As calls for independence became louder after the Second World War the British gradually increased the role of Nigerians in the colonial administration. But this again was on a regional rather than a national basis, and with the north lagging behind the eastern and western regions. Nigerian political leaders were appointed to regionally based legislative councils, not to a Nigeria-wide council. The 1951 and 1954 constitutions promulgated by the British recognised the overall unity of Nigeria but still fostered regionalism. The latter constitution set up the eastern and western regions as internally autonomous states within Nigeria – a status not accorded to the north until immediately before independence. When independence was actually achieved in 1960, the parties competing for power were regional parties, 'each led by a leadership which could make no real claim to represent an all-Nigerian nationalism' (Davidson, 1978, p. 237).

These patterns of divisive rule were established throughout Africa by the British, French, Portuguese and Italians. They claimed to be forming nations, but only bequeathed the shell of a nation to each African state. Their administrative policies ensured that there was no embryo nation inside the shell. Where embryos began to grow and to develop under the impetus of nationalism, they were frequently aborted by repression or distorted by attempts to split nationalists along ethnic, religious or cultural lines.

A variety of tactics were used to thwart the nationalists. In French West Africa, the main nationalist grouping was the Rassemblement Democratique Africain (RDA). A territory-wide organisation, it was led by future African Presidents such as Leopold Senghor of Senegal and Felix Houphouet-Boigny of Cote d'Ivoire. The RDA was made up of parties and politicians from the whole of French West Africa. It had strong links with opposition parties in France, at first the Communist Party and later the Socialists. The French colonial authorities were concerned at the advances made by the RDA and its component parties. Houphouet-Boigny was seen as a particularly key leader and the French government made strenuous efforts to destroy his power base and render him harmless. In 1949, an offensive was launched against his Parti Democratique de la Cote d'Ivoire involving the detention of activists and the breaking up of party meetings and rallies. A few dozen Africans were killed and hundreds imprisoned during the crackdown (Davidson, 1978, p. 253). When this failed to break the will of the PDCI and the broader RDA, underhand methods were attempted to defeat PDCI candidates in local elections. Houphouet-Boigny tried to avoid outright confrontation by moving away from the Communist Party and towards an accommodation with the colonial government. Nevertheless, the colonial authorities did their best to destroy him and the RDA by covert means. As Patrick Manning has recounted in his work on Francophone Africa, 'the administration falsified elections during 1951 in Niger, Soudan [Mali], Ivory Coast [Cote d'Ivoire] and Guinea' (Manning, 1988, p. 144). They also forced PDCI supporters to pay higher taxes in order to coerce them to end their support for Houphouet-Boigny (ibid., p. 145).

Unlike the British system of ruling the colonised states individually, the French ruled their territories as large colonial units rather than separate colonies. This meant that there was the opportunity to create extensive, multinational states in which no particular region would dominate and which would have large enough markets to develop viable economies and be of sufficient weight to prevent easy domination by the former colonial power. But once the French realised that a large, independent African state could better resist its blandishments, they decided to split French West Africa and Equatorial Africa into separate statelets. Thus when independence came, it came to small, economically unviable mini-states rather than to a large federation with extensive human and material resources. And the French eventually found allies for this balkanization approach in leaders like Felix Houphouet-Boigny. While Senghor of Senegal wanted a large French-speaking federation in West Africa, Houphouet-Boigny decided that he and Cote d'Ivoire would be best served by splitting up the West African territory. His view was based on the comparative wealth of Cote d'Ivoire compared with other parts of the territory and on his own political position: he could be President of an independent Cote d'Ivoire but could not bank on being the overall leader of a greater French West Africa. His decision to support Paris led to the development of close, cooperative relations between Houphouet-Boigny and successive governments in France. Senghor accused Houphouet-Boigny of 'being an instrument of France [in] balkanizing Africa' (Mazrui and Tidy, 1984, p. 81).

The splitting up process started in 1956 with the division of French West Africa and French Equatorial Africa into separate states. Under the new system, individual states gained some internal autonomy, but France maintained control of law and order, the military and the police. Eight states were formed in West Africa and four in Equatorial Africa. The decision of the main African nationalist leaders in the French colonies to go along with the division and to accept the borders imposed by imperialism led to the creation of a system of small states in West and Central Africa lacking homogenous populations, sufficient markets or resources for a viable economy (Green and Seidman, 1968, p. 33) and minute armies dependent on the metropolitan power.

It was against this background of repression, cheating in elections, manipulation of tax and other regulations that nationalism gained force in Africa. The dynamic force in the nationalist movement was the petty-bourgeoisie. This was both because they had received some education and were therefore in a position to campaign effectively and spread their message and also because they had an economic base from which to operate (many nationalist leaders were traders, prosperous farmers, teachers, doctors or civil servants). They also had the most to gain, as they hoped to replace the colonial rulers and to gain the economic prize of independence. Many saw their political and economic futures as being bound up closely with the outgoing colonial power and with multinational companies from the former colonial state. More radical leaders, Kwame Nkrumah in Ghana and Sekou Toure in Guinea, wanted to create a fully independent Africa yet they too had to operate in the environment created by the metropolitan powers.

Although they wanted to gain economic as well as political independence, the radicals saw the quickest path to freedom as the immediate granting of independence, thus Nkrumah's famous slogan, 'Seek Ye First the Political Kingdom'. But Nkrumah was very well aware of the threat posed to Africa's security by the creation of a mass of small, weak states. After his overthrow by elements within the Ghanaian armed forces (with the moral and perhaps material support of Britain and the USA)'. Nkrumah wrote that the colonial powers gave states independence only to replace direct rule with neo-colonial rule. The latter form of control being 'based upon the principle of breaking up former large united colonial territories into a number of small non-viable states which are incapable of independent development and must rely upon the former imperial power for defence and even internal security' (Nkrumah, 1968, p. xiii). And certainly, it will be seen the extent to which new states were compelled by circumstances to rely on the military and police assistance of their former rulers.

The speed with which independence came to many African states, often with under a decade separating the start of serious nationalist activity and the hauling down of the colonial flag, was in many ways a serious handicap to the emerging nations.

The nationalists called for immediate independence. Yet they were unprepared for it. Even the best organised and most militant nationalist movements were small and lacking in administrative experience and, most importantly of all, a pool of educated cadres who could be expected to fill posts in the government, the civil service or within the party itself. Education had been poor under most of the colonial regimes and few Africans had been allowed to rise above the lowest rungs of the civil service or the armed forces – in the Belgian Congo, for example, on independence there were no Congolese officers in the army, all the officers were Belgians.

The nationalist movements had been able to mobilise opposition to colonial rule, but they were not well established enough to have a presence throughout the states in which they operated and were in no position to generate policy ideas, act as a channel of communications from the grassroots level to the government or to explain party policies (where they existed) to ordinary people. Frequently, the move from nationalist struggle to freedom had been so swift that parties and leaders had been unable to draw up the most basic of agendas for government action. The leadership of the nationalist movement throughout the continent was concentrated in the hands of a small, educated elite, frequently professionals such as doctors and lawyers, but often businessmen and traders, who saw independence not just as freedom from foreign rule but the chance for Africans to succeed to the positions enjoyed by their colonial counterparts or to become the middlemen between independent Africa and the foreign multinationals which operated there. Basil Davidson, the leading writer on African history, summed up the situation accurately when he wrote that the African business interests which came to dominate many nationalist parties were 'the commercial tail that wagged the political dog . . . their object was not to change the system by getting national independence, save in its political overlay, but to convert the system to their own advantage' (Davidson, 1978, pp. 215). The bourgeois nationalists wanted political and economic power, but were content to maintain close links and economic and military dependence on the former colonial powers. Many believe that the middle-class nationalists who frequently became the first rulers of independent countries, connived with the colonial powers in the splitting up of Africa into artificial states with meaningless borders and became the pioneers of the neo-colonial relationships which maintained the influence of the metropolitan powers over the military, political and economic affairs of Africa (Nzongola-Ntalaja in Hansen, 1987, p. 62; and Davidson, 1978, p. 215).

But those who were to lead Africa into independence frequently had little experience of government. Prior to 1945, few if any Africans had played any administrative role except perhaps traditional chiefs or a few of the elite who took part in local government. And in many Africa states 'not a few inhabitants exercised the right to vote for the first time at the elections that brought their independent governments to power' (Crowder, 1987, p. 14).

The end of the colonial era saw the handing over of the trappings of government to the new states, but frequently real administrative control remained in the hands of European civil servants or army officers. Many African armies were officered almost entirely by Europeans even several years after independence. Furthermore, the armies had been established and trained to be instruments of domestic control rather than national armies devoted to the defence of sovereignty. And very few of the armies handed over to African governments were truly national. Under imperial rule, the armies in the colonies were generally recruited from particular ethnic groups rather than from a broad range of the populations. This was deliberately done to provide a unified force that could be used as a prop for foreign rule. The groups chosen for recruitment were often the most backward and the least politically-conscious segments of the population. Grace Ibingira believes the British followed this policy very carefully in his own home country of Uganda as well as Nigeria and Ghana – 'the British deliberately based the colonial army in each territory on a narrow ethnic base among the least-developed and hopefully least politicised groups, systematically omitting other groups, especially those from the more developed areas' (Ibingira, 1980, pp. 263–4). The French and Portuguese followed very similar policies. In Congo (Brazzaville), the French found their soldiers from among the Mbochi and Kouyou of the north, while the better educated Lari and Vili and other Bakongo peoples of the south dominated the African business sector and the African portion of the civil service. The dangers of this split have been identified by Radu and Somerville: 'while Lari and Vili youths studied at the French lycees in Brazzaville. Dakar and France, ambitious young Mbochis and Kouyous ended up as the dominant majority in the colonial army and at military academies. This pattern became dangerous in a country without a national consciousness or traditions of inter-group solidarity or cooperation' (Radu and Somerville, 1989, pp. 160–61).

The legacy of division left by the colonial era is one that has had very direct and dire consequences for the stability of independent Africa. In some countries, the destabilising effects of the inheritance made themselves felt within weeks of independence. The inherent flaws in the political, military, social and economic institutions laid Africa open to continued interference and manipulation by external forces.

Independence: the first faltering steps

The late 1950s saw the emergence of the first African states to be freed from the shackles of colonialism. Ghana started the process in 1957 and Guinea followed in 1958. But it was in the first four years of the 1960s that the trickle of independent states became a positive flood. The opening year of the decade saw the formation of fifteen new Francophone states and the independence of the giant of Africa, Nigeria. By the middle of the decade, the majority of the continent's states were free.

These years were ones of exuberant celebration and great hopes in Africa. In Martin Meredith's words. 'African leaders stepped forward with energy and enthusiasm to tackle the problems of development and nation-building, boldly proclaiming their hopes of establishing new societies which might offer an inspiration to the world at large' (Meredith, 1984, p. xiii). Lamentably, all they inspired in many foreign powers was the desire to intervene in African conflicts or to reassert old relations of dominance.

African leaders and nationalist movements had mobilised tens of thousands of their countrymen in the struggle for independence, they fondly hoped that these thousands would be similarly united in the quest for economic development, political stability and the welding together of new nations. They also hoped for the disinterested assistance of the developed world and their former colonial masters. That the latter was unlikely could have been seen in the French reaction to the decision of the people of Guinea to opt for independence rather than membership of a wider French-speaking community led from Paris (effectively colonialism under a more modern garb). Following the urging of the nationalists led by Ahmed Sekou Toure, the people of Guinea alone among the Francophone states (though poll-rigging by the French in Niger may have prevented a second state from choosing freedom) rejected the French proposal for internal autonomy within the French community. De Gaulle reacted like a spoilt child. He agreed to Guinean independence in 1958, but ensured that Guinea's inheritance would be a poor one. French economic aid and personnel were withdrawn. The departing French personnel wreaked havoc with the economy. Telephones were ripped from the walls in government offices (Manning, 1988, p. 149); all government files and records were burnt, offices were stripped of their furniture, light bulbs were taken from lights, army doctors took all medical supplies when they left, the French police smashed all the windows in their stations and Sekou Toure found that all the crockery had been smashed in the governor's house (Meredith, 1984, p. 102); even the law books had been taken or destroyed in the Ministry of Justice library (Crowder, 1987, p. 15). Such were the actions of a major European power when thwarted by the will of the people of Africa. It set a marvellous example of how to react to a negative vote in an election.

Not all colonial powers went to the extent of deliberately wrecking the infrastructure, but few left the new states in a position to fulfil their hopes. Politically, the divide and rule policies of the colonial era and the lack of opportunities for the gaining of political and administrative experience prior to independence were a major drawback. Militarily, the armies of the new states had been recruited in an unbalanced way and had been trained to be instruments of domestic control rather than national armies, few had a large African officer corps, and many had no African officers. Economically, the new states were often too small to support domestic industries and had little opportunity to shrug off dependence on their former rulers: 'political independence for African states did not automatically alter their export-oriented economic structures, characterised by a low growth of output and a high profit drain which combine to limit economic reconstruction and industrial development . . . no African state is economically large enough to construct a modern economy' (Green and Seidman, 1968, pp. 21–2). And the borders of the states meant nothing in terms of ethnic, political or economic geography – Africa's frontiers were a recipe for secessionism and irridentism. Overall, Africa was ripe for rebellion, interstate conflict and foreign intervention.

And it did not take long for the negative factors to exert their influence over the attempts of the new states to mould themselves into nations. To cite Basil Davidson once more, the

jagged edges in the relations of a mosaic of communities and nationalities overlaid by colonial rule came thrusting to the surface. Regrouped within the nation-state that was still the colonial state, old and less old troubles and ambitions shook and rattled at its feeble institutions, broke through its constitutional defences, trampled on its frail procedures and made nonsense of its preaching certitudes (Davidson, 1978, pp. 294–5).

Cameroon and Congo: a pattern is established

Many of the conflicts in post-independent Africa emerged from the mess of contradictions foisted on Africa by foreign rule, but some were a continuation of conflicts that had started under colonial rule.

The first military conflict to plague a new state was the rebellion in Cameroon. France had ruled the territory under a UN mandate (inherited from the old League of Nations). As the territory moved towards independence, conflict grew between the French authorities and the most radical of the nationalist parties, the Union des Populations du Cameroun (UPC), led by Um Nyobe and Felix Moumie. From the start, the UPC saw its task as the achievement of economic and social emancipation as well as political freedom. This angered and worried the French, who wanted to hand power over to a more compliant, capitalist-orientated African leadership. From 1954 onwards, when Governor Pre arrived in Cameroon, stern repression was used against the UPC and every assistance was given to the more 'cooperative' nationalist groups. Eventually, the French banned the UPC and pushed it into a guerrilla struggle. The UPC's leaders and cadres took to the forests and set up liberated zones from which to fight the

French and their allies. The UPC was based in the south, so the French sought allies from the Muslim north. They promoted the political power of the northerners while using massive military force against the guerrillas. In 1958, Nyobe was killed in a clash with a French patrol, leaving Moumie to lead the rebellion. This he did, though without conspicuous success. However, the UPC kept up the fight successfully enough to force the first government of Cameroon to rely on French military units to continue the fight against the UPC.

Many Francophone states (and some former British colonies) became bases for foreign troops, but only Cameroon actually had a war between an indigenous political movement and the former colonial power actually in progress as independence was granted. This was hardly an auspicious start for Cameroon or for Africa as a whole. It meant that the new President, Ahmadu Ahidjo, was from the start dependent on the French for the security of his government. After independence, the UPC escalated its struggle, forcing Ahidjo to go cap in hand to the French for more military aid – at one stage five French battalions were actively involved in the war with the UPC (Mazrui and Tidy, 1984, p. 215). Although joint Cameroonian and French forces, under the command of a Frenchman, General Brand, were able to control the revolt and reduce it to little more than an irritation within eight months of independence, the UPC continued fighting until 1972 (partly due to aid from radical African states and, at times, the USSR and China). One reason for the decline of the UPC after 1960 was the assassination of Felix Moumie in Geneva in late 1960; some believe that the French security services were responsible for poisoning him, though this has not been proved conclusively (see Karl Van Meter in Ray *et al*, 1980, p. 28).

Cameroon's war was little publicised at the time, but was important because of the precedent it set for the continued presence of foreign combat troops in Africa and their use in fighting domestic rivals to the government. It was no accident that it was the French who were involved in the first post-colonial military conflict. They had assiduously drawn up rigid agreements for military cooperation (on French terms) with all their ex-colonies with the exception of Guinea. These mutual defence or military assistance agreements often involved the stationing of French troops and naval or air force units in African states or the provision of officers and training teams for the armies of the new states. The most far-reaching agreements were with Cameroon, Senegal and Cote d'Ivoire, the states still most closely aligned politically, militarily and economically with the French and the states which have most often been staging posts for French military operations elsewhere in Africa (Tordoff, 1984, p. 75).

If Cameroon set an early if unrecognised precedent for foreign military intervention, it was Congo-Leopoldville which really ended any illusions that Africa was ridding itself of external interference and foreign troops.

The Congo debacle: Africa's conflicts internationalised

Of all the colonies on the continent, the Belgian Congo was undoubtedly the least prepared for independence when it came and had the shortest period between the advent of nationalist activity and the granting of independence. Despite claims to the contrary by the Belgians, the Congo had hardly been a model colony. In the late 19th and early 20th centuries there had been horror among other European colonial powers at the brutality of Belgian exploitation of the region. None of the imperial states were exactly caring or gentle in their treatment of colonial subjects, but the Belgians were particularly harsh. The cutting off of hands and feet as punishments for failure to work hard enough or for insubordination was commonplace and caused such an outcry in Europe that the Belgians were forced to moderate their policies.

No real attempt was made to provide education for the people of the Congo and in the years after the Second World War, the territory had few African civil servants or professionals and no African officers in the Force Publique – the police force cum army maintained by the authorities. Those Congolese who had received an education, and they were few and far between, had usually done so at mission schools. Even as other colonial rulers were preparing their possessions for independence and cultivating an indigenous elite (small and insufficient for the purposes of governing a country as they inevitably were), the Belgians just continued their policy of total neglect of the future.

The first real stirrings of nationalism, if they can be called that, came in the early 1950s. In 1950, a number of educated Bakongo came together to form the Association pour la Sauveguarde de la Culture et des Interets des Bakongo (Abako). In the beginning it was essentially a tribal organisation aimed at protecting the cultural identity of the Bakongo people of lower Congo (the Bakongo people were spread between the Belgian and French Congos and Angola). It didn't take on an overtly political role until 1956, by which time it was being led by Joseph Kasavubu. But even when it started to campaign for independence, it remained a Bakongo and not a national group. As Thomas Kanza, the son of Abako's Vice-President during the pre-independence period, has explained, the organisation called for immediate, total and unconditional independence, but 'its conception of the nation was limited to the area of the lower Congo'. Kasavubu even had dreams of reuniting the Bakongo peoples of the two Congos and Angola (Kanza, 1972, p. 33).

Many of the other groups which emerged at this time were ethnically or at best regionally based. In the province of Katanga, a regionally-orientated group, the Confederation of Tribal Associations of Katanga (Conakat) grew up with the strong financial and political support of the giant Belgian mining concern, Union Miniere, which was the main exploiter of the vast mineral resources of Katanga. Conakat was led by Moise Tshombe, he had no national aspirations as far as Congo as a whole were concerned, but saw his future as the leader of a breakaway Katanga. He was encouraged in this ambition by Union Miniere, by Belgian officers of the Force Publique and by political groups in Belgium. Tshombe was also in regular contact with the US government through the US consulate in Leopoldville (Kanza, 1972, p. 140).

The only really nationalist minded groups were the Mouvement National

Congolais (MNC) of Patrice Lumumba (founded in the capital in 1958) and the Parti Solidaire Africain (PSA) of Antoine Gizenga and Pierre Mulele. They both had national rather than ethnic or regional aims and called on all the peoples of Congo for unity. However, they did not have nationwide support and suffered from internal dissension, often along ethnic lines. Thus, prior to independence, Baluba members of the MNC from the Kasai province split away from Lumumba to form a breakaway MNC led by Albert Kalonji.

The political scene was hardly an encouraging one from the point of view of national unity or or party organisation. The existing parties were small, dominated by a few individuals and with little in the way of organisation or political experience. There were few educated Congolese capable of organising national parties and the Belgians held no territory-wide elections prior to the immediate pre-independence ones. The only elections the Congolese experienced before the one in which they chose their first leaders were local ones held in 1957. The holding of local rather than national polls encouraged the ethnic/regional bias in the parties (Manning, 1988, p. 150).

Parties such as Abako and Conakat, had close links with Belgian interests or with the Americans and lacked a national as opposed to an ethnic identity. Conakat, in particular, was heavily reliant on Belgian support. Although Thomas Kanza was clearly on the opposite side to Tshombe in the Congo conflict, he is right in identifying the fact that 'the Congolese separatists in Katanga were dependent, ideologically and financially on the mining companies. Their political moves were dictated by the Europeans who made common cause with them, and the colonial officials who simply obeyed whatever directives came from Brussels' (Kanza, 1972, p. 136). And Conakat, Abako and the Kalonji wing of the MNC worked closely and received support from American diplomats in Leopoldville. As a member of Abako, Kanza attended meetings with US diplomats at which they made clear their concern for the future of the Congo and their desire to ensure that American interests were safe. Kanza said that it emerged from discussions with the Americans at which he was present that 'the American government was not opposed to African nationalism, provided that it did not do anything to counter American capitalist interests. Washington would not tolerate nationalism that was neutralist, but fight against any nationalism with communist leanings' (Kanza, 1972, p. 139). The Americans obviously took the view that freedom was OK for Africa as long as it was within parameters set by Washington – Africans would not be allowed the leeway to choose a path of development for themselves. The origins of foreign interference are clearly present in the close US monitoring of the run up to independence in Congo.

The Soviet Union was less closely involved. It only really 'discovered' Africa in the late 1950s and so was badly placed to make friends among the new and aspiring nations. The few Soviet diplomats in Africa had few contacts in Congo and the only links between Moscow and the Congolese nationalists were via the Belgian Communist Party, a party which Stevens and Kanza judge to have been riddled with Belgian agents (Stevens, 1976, p. 12; Kanza, 1972, pp. 140–41).

The early activities of the nationalist parties put little pressure on the Belgians and up to the beginning of 1959 they had made no moves towards preparing for independence; there was no attempt at administrative or economic decolonisation to clear the way for eventual political independence (Manning, 1988, p. 151). Unlike in British and French colonies, the Belgian Congo saw no growth in consultative or legislative bodies in which Africans could participate and no growth in the recruitment or advancement of African civil servants or army officers.

But the picture changed dramatically in January 1959. A sudden spontaneous outburst of violent opposition to Belgian rule occurred that shocked the Belgians into immediate and over hasty efforts to pull out of the Congo. The riots broke out on 4th January in Leopoldville. The immediate spark for the violence, in which the Force Publique killed 50 Congolese and wounded over 200, was the banning of an Abako meeting. But the events had been preceded by an upsurge in activity by Abako and Lumumba's MNC. In December 1958, Lumumba attended the All-African People's Conference in Accra. There he discussed Congo's problems with the Ghanaian leader, Kwame Nkrumah, and with leading nationalists from all over the continent. He returned more certain than ever that his appeal must be a national one and that Congo's independence should be part of a Pan-African process of gaining freedom and uniting the continent. This made him an anathema to the Belgians (and one might add the Americans) and distanced him even more from groups like Abako and Conakat. On his return from Accra he called on the Belgians to give Congo its freedom as a right and not as a gift. He held a number of public meetings and stepped up the campaign for decolonisation. Abako also escalated its calls for independence and prepared for a campaign to call for an end to colonial rule. A public meeting was scheduled for 4th January 1959. When it was banned by the colonial authorities, Abako supporters rioted in Leopoldville. No Belgians were hurt but the Force Publique were severe in their repression of the riots. Disturbances followed in towns around the country.

At first the Belgians reacted by seizing the whole Abako central committee – Kasavubu went into hiding but gave himself up after a week. The leadership was charged with inciting racial hatred. But on 13th January, the Belgian government suddenly announced that it would grant Congo independence. Although welcome to Congolese nationalists, the announcement was abrupt and indicated Belgium's total lack of concern for an orderly and planned transition to independence. That the Belgians did not release the Abako leadership for two months was a further indication of this unplanned approach.

The announcement of impending independence (no date had been set at the time of the first Belgian announcement), led to heightened political activity and regional-ethnic conflict between the different political movements. Lumumba went into top gear in trying to develop a truly national movement, while Kasavubu and Kalonji concentrated on entrenching themselves firmly among their ethnic compatriots (Kasavubu spent a lot of time in Brazzaville, capital of the French Congo, cementing an alliance with the Bakongo leader there, Fulbert Youlou). In Katanga, Tshombe gave every impression of preparing for secession.

The Belgians still did nothing to aid the Congolese to take over the government of the country. They did not embark on Africanisation of the civil service or army and gave no help in devising a political system that would help in moulding a new nation. In December 1959, they organised elections, but these were local rather than national and were boycotted by Abako, MNC (Lumumba), PSA and MNC (Kalonji) candidates.

The first serious move towards arranging a proper independence process came with the convening of a round table conference in Brussels on 20th January 1960. This was to set the date for independence and work out the constitutional framework for a Congolese government. Unfortunately, the Belgians did not approach in a spirit designed to give the Congolese movements an equal opportunity to contribute. Prior to the conference, Lumumba was charged with a number of minor criminal offences (most observers, such as Thomas Kanza, believe he was framed) and told to appear before a court in Stanleyville on 21st January (the day after the opening of the conference in Brussels). He was convicted by the court and imprisoned. Only energetic lobbying in Brussels by MNC leaders obtained his release. He arrived at the conference table six days into the discussions.

The outcome of the conference was a decision to grant independence on 30th June and to have a Belgian-style constitution with an executive President and a Prime Minister responsible to parliament. As the conference only ended on 20th February, the Congolese had just five months in which to organise themselves to run the country. They were not helped by the results of an economic conference on Congo held after the political discussions. It resulted in a Belgian stranglehold over Congo and the maintenance of the power of the huge mining company Union Miniere. Kanza described the conference as 'sheer treachery on Belgium's part; its results stand as a monument to Belgium's shame in her determination to give Congo an independence poisoned and truncated from the first' (Kanza, 1972, p. 95). The power of the Belgians over the economy, the massive influence of Union Miniere, the lack of trained Congolese to man the civil service and command the army and the attitude of those Belgians who were to continue in the administrative and military institutions were to add to the disarray of the Congolese political forces in ensuring that independence would mean conflict and misery for the Congolese.

The elections held prior to independence produced no clear winner, though Lumumba commanded the strongest group of supporters in the national assembly. After considerable inter-party bargaining and manoeuvring, Kasavubu was chosen as President with Lumumba as Prime Minister and Minister of National Defence; Thomas Kanza became minister responsible for relations with the United Nations. Agreement on a division of power between Kasavubu and Lumumba had only been made possible by the intervention of African leaders (including Kwame Nkrumah); the two men were fiercely opposed to one another and hardly a stable team to lead Congo to independence.

Congo became independent on 30th June 1960. But from the start the government was weak and divided. It had immediate trouble with the Belgian administrators and officers who remained in control of the civil service and the army. Prior to independence, the Belgian commander of the Force Publique,

General Janssens, had made clear his total opposition to Africanisation of the officer corps. He had openly told the country's new leaders that 'everyone must be of service according to his merits and abilities, rank depending on ability rather than on skin colour. The replacement of the Belgian command must be effected from below and gradually' (Kanza, 1972, p. 179). Radical Congolese perceived him and his officers as intent on maintaining effective control of the country despite the political changes underway. This perception was heightened by a strange Belgian decision to reinforce its troop contingent in Congo in May 1960 – new units were flown to the Kamina base in Katanga and the Kitona base in lower Congo. Thomas Kanza says that after the army mutiny and the Belgian intervention, it was discovered that before independence, Janssens had drawn up a plan to seize control in the event of 'trouble' that would have 'paralysed the political and civil authorities in the Congo and brought the whole country under military control by the Force Publique, aided and supported by the troops from Belgium now in those bases [at Kamina and Kitona]' (Kanza, 1972, p. 179). The problem of the army was compounded by the continuing control of the security and intelligence services by a Belgian, Major van der Waele.

The euphoria generated by independence was very short-lived indeed. Outraged by the high-handed and unchanged attitudes of their Belgian officers, on 4th July troops at Camp Hardy, near Thysville, started threatening their officers and then broke into the armoury. The next day a number of Belgian officers were beaten by the soldiers. On 6th July, Kasavubu and Lumumba visited the base to calm the soldiers down (Legum, 1961, p. 108). Lumumba announced a promotion of one grade for all Congolese soldiers. But the presence of the Belgian officers remained a destabilising factor as the soldiers 'were not going to put up with having their organisation, now the Congolese National Army, remain indefinitely under the command of the same colonial officers. They had the same grudge against the Belgian officers as . . . politicians and civil servants had against the Belgian colonial officials' (Kanza, 1972, pp. 1985–6).

Lumumba's attempts to stop the mutiny in its tracks failed. Troops revolted against their officers throughout Congo and attacks on Belgian civilians were reported. On 8th July, troops rampaged through the capital and violence broke out in Matadi and the lower Congo, led by soldiers and Congolese policemen.

By 10th July, the Belgian troops and officials had had enough. The Belgian units stationed in Congo stepped in, ostensibly to restore order, but effectively to take control of the country. Under the independence agreement with Congo, the Belgian forces stationed in the country could be called in by the Congolese government to restore order, but could not act of their own volition. Their action on 10th July, clearly supported by the Belgian government, was a clear violation of the agreement and as such was open interference in Congo's affairs.

The initial intervention was followed on 11th July by the occupation of the capital by Belgian paratroops and the deployment of around 10,000 Belgian soldiers around the country (Legum, 1961, p. 110; Meredith, 1984, p. 142). On the same day, Moise Tshombe declared the secession of Katanga, with Belgian backing. Belgian military units were stationed in Katanga and gave their full backing to the secession. The Belgian soldiers disarmed Congolese troops in the province and expelled them. As one eminent journalist who was an eyewitness to the events wrote at the time 'it was difficult to avoid the impression that the Congo was being taken over by the Belgians and their allies' (Legum, 1961, p. 110).

Lumumba and Kasavubu were in Kasai province on 11th July and in their absence the Deputy Prime Minister, Gizenga, asked the American Ambassador, Timberlake, to pass on a request to his government for military assistance to the Congo to end Belgian intervention. Gizenga, acting on written instructions from Lumumba made an official protest to Belgium and demanded an end to its interference in Congolese affairs.

The request to the Americans, for a total of 3,000 troops, was turned down and the American government suggested that the Congolese approached the UN. This they did via Ralph Bunche, the UN Secretary-General's special representative in the Congo. The call for UN aid to end the Belgian military actions was made on 12th July. There was a delay of two days between the request and the UN answer and in that time, Gizenga, on behalf of the government, asked Ghana to provide military assistance. The Ghanaians agreed but decided to coordinate their actions with the UN. To hasten UN action, Kasavubu and Lumumba sent UN Secretary-General Dag Hammarskjold a telegram stating the need for UN forces to protect Congolese 'national territory against aggression of metropolitan Belgian troops . . . the help we ask should be given solely by a UN force of soldiers from neutral countries, not of the USA' (cited by Kanza, 1972, p. 206). By this time, Lumumba was concerned that the Americans tacitly supported the Belgian action and could not be trusted to give real help to Congo. While still awaiting a UN answer and in the wake of the US refusal to help, the President and Prime Minister sent a message to the Soviet Union asking it to be ready to help Congo 'if the Western camp do not stop their aggression against our sovereignty'.

The appeal to the USSR was condemned by the Belgians and the Americans and the former started spreading rumours in Leopoldville that Russian troops would be used to disarm the Congolese army and to take control. This led to the rough handling of a Soviet delegation visiting Congo to attend the independence celebrations and to arrange the opening of diplomatic relations. The Soviets were forced to leave the country because their safety could not be assured.

The call to the Soviets proved to have been unnecessary, as on 14th July, the United Nations Security Council accepted a plan put forward by Hammarskjold calling on the Belgians to withdraw and agreeing to 'provide the government [of the Congo] with such military assistance as may be necessary until, through the efforts of the Congolese government with the technical assistance of the United Nations, the national security forces may be able, in the opinion of the government, to meet fully their tasks'. The resolution required UN forces to maintain law and order but did not mention specifically obtaining a Belgian withdrawal or the reimposition of Congolese rule over Katanga.

The UN airlift started soon after the Security Council decision, but Lumumba was dissatisfied with the pace of assistance and was as a result very receptive to an offer by the Soviet leader Nikita Khrushchev on 16th July to send 10,000 tons of food aid and other unspecified help (Stevens, 1976, p. 14). The Soviets did back the UN operation, though, and along with Britain and the USA played a major logistical role. But the failure of the UN to move quickly enough for the Congolese, led to another appeal to the USSR. Lumumba and Kasavubu warned Bunche that if the Belgians had not withdrawn by 19th July, they would ask for Soviet troops to help end the intervention. As nothing had changed by that date, the Congolese Council of Ministers appealed to Moscow and to Afro-Asian countries 'to send their troops to the Congo . . . to evacuate peacefully Belgian troops . . . to contribute to the maintenance of order in the Congo . . . to prevent all external aggressions' (Stevens, 1976, p. 15). The Council of Ministers added that all foreign troops would be withdrawn from the Congo once the Belgians had left and order had been restored. But the call angered the Western powers, who blamed Lumumba. If they hadn't been plotting his downfall before, they certainly did so now and openly sided with Kasavubu and with Joseph Mobutu, who had been put in charge of the Congolese armed forces. Kasavubu and Mobutu opposed Lumumba's radical approach and were very amenable to Western pressure and blandishments.

Although Lumumba accused the UN of acting too slowly, 3,500 troops of the UN force had arrived by 17th July and by the end of the month they had been deployed in five out of six provinces, the exception being Katanga (Meredith, 1984, p. 143). The deployment led to the withdrawal of the Belgians. But this did not satisfy Lumumba, who wanted the UN forces to move against Katanga. So he continued to press for Soviet aid. This was forthcoming in the form of 100 trucks and sixteen Ilyushin transport aircraft (Kanza, 1972, p. 275). The aircraft were based at Lumumba's home town of Stanleyville. They were used to fly Congolese troops to Kasai province, which had declared its secession from Congo on 8th August. The sending of troops to Kasai rapidly ended Albert Kalonji's secessionist attempt, though over 1,000 Baluba were killed when the troops moved in to reimpose central control; many Baluba accused the government of deliberately massacring Baluba tribesmen during the operation (Legum, 1961, p. 123).

In addition to sending trucks and aircraft, the USSR dispatched 300 technicians to maintain the equipment and a medical team. In August, Gizenga signed a military assistance accord with Mikhail Yakovlev, the Soviet Ambassador in Leopoldville – though little came of the accord because of Lumumba's subsequent downfall and assasination.

The provision of Soviet aid led to a worsening of the already bad relations between Lumumba and the Americans and, even more unfortunately, between Lumumba and the UN Secretary-General, who seemed to take the American view that by seeking Soviet aid, Lumumba was bringing the cold war into the crisis and undermining the UN effort.

Although the Soviet assistance enabled Lumumba to retain control over Kasai, it was not of overall benefit as the Soviet Union was unable or unwilling to involve its own troops or to project sufficient power in a regional conflict to help an ally win a decisive advantage. Instead, Lumumba's call for Soviet aid, perfectly legitimate as it was in terms of international law and given his earlier request to the United States, served only to alienate further conservative elements within Congo and the UN and the Western powers. The USA was particularly alarmed at Lumumba's relations with Moscow (Weissman, 1974, pp. 81–3) and recommended to his opponents that they try to overthrow him; this suggestion was backed by increasing CIA activity in the country in support of Kasavubu (Meredith, 1984, p. 147).

Urged on by his own opposition to Lumumba and the evident support of the USA, on 5th September, Kasavubu announced that he had dismissed Lumumba from the post of Prime Minister. Lumumba refused to accept this decision, which was not in line with the constitution, and obtained a parliamentary vote ousting Kasavubu from the presidency and reinstating Lumumba. This led to a constitutional impasse, as neither man had sufficient power to subdue the other and the legal situation was incredibly confused, with neither leader having a cast iron constitutional case against the other.

The stalemate was broken after ten days when the chief of staff of the Congolese armed forces, Joseph Mobutu, effectively seized power. Mobutu had the tacit support of the Americans and was willing to work with Kasavubu. The latter retained the post of President, but Lumumba was held under house arrest and deposed as Prime Minister. In reaction, Lumumba's supporters set up a rival government in Kisangani (Stanleyville). Lumumba tried to escape from house arrest but was captured and taken to Katanga, according to Kanza on the advice of the Belgians (Kanza, 1972, p. 320), but according to other observers (Meredith, 1984; and Young, 1986), the Americans were at least indirectly involved. In Katanga, Lumumba and a number of his colleagues were murdered by Tshombe's forces.

The government crisis had further complicated the UN role. Its forces were there to maintain law and order on behalf of the legally constituted government – but which was the legal government? Even before Lumumba's assassination, Hammarskjold had put his weight behind Mobutu, Kasavubu and the more conservative elements, having become exasperated with Lumumba. Many African states accused the UN of taking sides in the domestic conflict and of supporting the Americans and Belgians against Lumumba.

The government split, between Leopoldville and Stanleyville was paralleled by an army split. Part of the army remained loyal to Mobutu, the chief of staff, while many of the troops rallied to General Lundula, a distant relative of Lumumba's who had been appointed commander-in-chief after the mutiny. Mobutu was able to retain control over Leopoldville and western Zaire, but the Lumumba supporters were in command of the region around Stanleyville. But Mobutu was in a stronger position as he was supported by the UN and by a 'clandestine transfusion of funds from the CIA' (Young, 1986, p. 132).

The confused situation continued until August 1961, when a new government under Cyrille Adoula was installed. He had the post of Prime Minister, while Kasavubu remained President and Mobutu remained the real source of power. Adoula received the support of parliament and as a result the rival government in Stanleyville withered away and its members reached a compromise with Adoula or went into exile and prepared for rebellion.

During this whole period, the UN took no effective action to regain control of Katanga and Tshombe's regime remained in power supported by Belgian troops on effective secondment from the Belgian armed forces and by mercenaries paid for with funds from the mining companies operating in Katanga. UN units had made attempts in September and December 1961 to end the secession but had not carried them through to a conclusion because of the willingness of the Katangese gendarmerie and Tshombe's mercenaries to fight. It was not until December 1962 that the UN forces finally took military action to bring an end to the secession of Katanga. After a brief UN offensive, the secession was brought to an end on 14th January 1963.

But the end of the secession did not bring peace. Many of Lumumba's supporters were still intent on regaining power and on ousting the Kasavubu/Adoula/Mobutu government. The main leaders of the Lumumbists were Gizenga, Gaston Soumialot, Pierre Mulele and Christophe Gbenye. They received support from radical African states, China and, according to some reports, the Soviet Union (McLane, 1974, p. 168). Mulele's forces were active in Kwilu province and those of Gizenga, Gbenye and Soumialot in the Kivu and Stanleyville regions. By August 1964, the rebels controlled almost a third of the country. The rebellion had brought down the Adoula government and led to the appointment of Tshombe, of all people, as Prime Minister in July 1964. Tshombe succeeded in strengthening the national army by recruiting his former Katangese gendarmes to fight the rebels and by obtaining Belgian military aid and funds to pay for mercenaries.

Tshombe's attempts to regain control of the country were heavily backed by the USA. According to Stephen Weissman, the USA was closely involved in the Congo throughout the five years from independence to the crushing of the rebels in 1965. Most of the involvement was clandestine and conducted by the CIA, though he points out that 'covert action and planning focused mainly on direct combat operations and were coordinated with overt US and Belgian military assistance' (Weissman in Ray *et al.*, 1980, p. 163). Through the CIA, the Americans supplied financial assistance, helped to recruit mercenaries and sent pilots and counter-insurgency instructors to directly help the Congolese army. The CIA sent Skyraider jet fighters and B-26 bombers to the Congo to help the government put down Soumialot's revolt and hired exiled Cubans to fly the bombers (Lemarchand, 1976, pp. 11–16). When there were rebel successes in the east in the spring of 1964, the USA, via the CIA, sent T-28 fighters, C-47 military transport planes, helicopters and 100 military 'technicians' and a number of counter-insurgency advisers to the government forces (Weissman in Ray *et al.*, 1980, p. 163).

On the rebel side, there were persistent rumours that Soumialot's force included Chinese troops. Mulele had visited Peking in 1962 on behalf of Gizenga's Stanleyville government (on whose behalf Soumialot was fighting) and received financial and other material assistance, but there is no evidence that any Chinese troops assisted Soumialot or any of the other rebel units. The only serious attempt by a socialist state to intervene on the side of the rebels came in 1965, when Che Guevara and an unknown number of Cuban troops volunteered to aid the rebels. They tried to reach the rebels, who by then had lost Stanleyville, but failed (though Young believes that some of the Cubans did fight alongside the rebels – Young, 1986, p. 135). Rather than return to Cuba, they moved into neighbouring Congo-Brazzaville, where they were welcomed by Massemba-Debat, who asked them to train a militia and the armed forces. The Cubans also took on the role of assisting and training the Angolan MPLA liberation movement which was based in Congo-Brazzaville (Radu and Somerville, 1989, p. 166).

But the little foreign aid that was given to the rebels was insufficient to enable them to hold out for long against the Western and mercenary-backed forces led by Mobutu. When a number of European hostages were taken by the rebels holding Stanleyville, a combined Congolese–mercenary force advanced on the rebel capital and a large force of Belgian paratroopers was dropped on the town. The aim was both to rescue the hostages and strike a decisive blow against the rebels. The successful offensive against the rebels was organised by the Belgians and the Americans, the latter providing vital logistical support; the Belgians were flown to Stanleyville in US C-130 aircraft. The capture of Stanleyville was the death blow to the rebels' chances of seriously threatening the Leopoldville government. Some rebels remained in remote forest and mountain areas of eastern Zaire, but the danger to the central government was over. After the main rebel threat was eliminated, elections were held. In character with the fragmented nature of the political system, 223 parties contested the elections and no clear result emerged. Instead there was a fight for power between Tshombe and President Kasavubu. The result – as during the Lumumba–Kasavubu conflict in September 1960 – was that Mobutu seized power. But this time, in a military coup on 24th November 1965, Mobutu took power himself rather than holding the ring for Kasavubu. He was at least able to restore some semblance of order and to dispense with the need to rely quite so heavily on UN and mercenary forces, though he did remain dependent on American and Belgian, and later West German and French, military aid.

The Congo was a brutal lesson to Africa of the dangers of foreign military intervention. But it was a lesson that all too few benefited from. The Congo disaster, to borrow the title of Colin Legum's book, was one precipitated by the disorganised and self-interested way in which Belgium thrust Congo into independence while retaining effective control of the military and of vital sectors of the economy. Once the crisis had developed, political leaders from the right and left and from all the conflicting ethnic and regional groups sought foreign aid to advance their causes given their fragmented and weak nature. For five years, the Congo was dominated by civil war and the intervention (much of it unwanted) of foreign forces.

Coup and counter-coup: the foreign role

The Congo was the most dramatic, brutal and highly publicised example of foreign military intervention in the immediate post-independence period, but it was far from being the only or the only case in which a newly-formed African government requested external military assistance. Both the French and the British answered calls from former colonies for the sending of troops to restore order, put down mutinies or stage counter-coups to bring the original government back to power.

The French were best placed to respond. When they granted independence to the states of West and Equatorial Africa, they tied them closely to France through defence or military cooperation agreements. These involved not only the provision of arms, training or even seconded officers to the government concerned but also the retention of military bases. In Chad, the whole of the northern half of the country remained under French military control until 1965 (five years after independence). Defence agreements were signed with Central African Republic, Chad, Congo, Gabon, Senegal, Madagascar, Cote d'Ivoire, Benin (then called Dahomey), Niger, Mauritania, Togo and Cameroon. Guinea and Mali refused totally to any continuing military connection with France, while Upper Volta (later Burkina Faso) obtained the dismantling of French bases and refused to sign a defence agreement but did agree to give France overflying rights and to provide transit facilities for French forces (Chipman, 1985, p. 7). The French government made no secret of the use of the bases and the defence agreements as a means of maintaining its influence over the new states and their armies. The French were also able to continue recruiting for its own army in many of its former colonies and to retain the services of those recruited prior to independence. John Chipman has calculated that there were still 58,500 troops in Africa in 1962, though they were reduced in stages to 6,400 by 1970 (Chipman, ibid.). But the withdrawal of French forces was balanced by the creation of a French Force d'Intervention whose primary role was to give military assistance to former colonies and to back up the Forces d'Outre Mers which were stationed in Francophone African states.

The French troops symbolised France's continuing influence over its former possessions in Africa, but the forces were more than just a symbol. As already noted, they played a major role in fighting insurgents in Cameroon in the period immediately before and after independence. French forces also gave assistance to the government of Mauritania in fighting insurgents – as in the case of Cameroon, this was a low-level conflict inherited directly from the French. French troops were fighting alongside the Mauritanian army until 1963. French forces were deployed on a small scale in Congo, Gabon and Niger in 1960, in the immediate aftermath of independence, to help the new governments maintain law and order.

In August 1963, the French were called upon directly to intervene in Congo-Brazzaville by the beleaguered President, Fulbert Youlou. His unstable regime was seriously threatened by a general strike and rioting over the poor state of the economy and the total failure of the government to do anything effective about it. The three days of riots became known as Les Trois Glorieuses. Despite the severity of riots, the Congolese army (which was led by French officers) refused to become involved. Youlou appealed to De Gaulle to send in the French forces based at the Congolese port of Pointe Noire, but the French President refused (Radu and Somerville, 1989, pp. 163–4).

Earlier in 1963, the French had refused to send in troops when serious public disturbances followed the assassination of President Olympio (perhaps because the French were convinced that the army commander in Togo, Gnassingbe Eyadema, was capable of dealing with the situation and of protecting French interests). It was therefore surprising that the French chose to intervene so quickly in Gabon in February 1964 to reinstate President Leon M'ba.

M'ba had been overthrown by a military coup after trying to exclude opposition candidates from the forthcoming election. When sections of the army removed him from power he appealed to France for help. The French, keen to retain their influence in the potentially rich state, acted swiftly, and sent in troops from Congo-Brazzaville and Chad. They put down the coup instantly and restored M'ba to power (Meredith, 1984, p. 180). His restoration led to Gabon's increased dependence on French support and the permanent basing of French military units there (they remain there today). According to Karl van Meter, the operation to put M'ba back in power resulted in Gabon becoming one of the main French bases in Africa and the centre for covert military and secret service activities in Africa (Karl van Meter in Ray *et al.*, 1980, p. 29).

The Gabon intervention did lead, though, to a temporary toning down of French military operations in Africa. An outcry in France over the role played by French troops in deciding the political future of a supposedly independent state forced De Gaulle to hasten the withdrawal of French troops from Africa (Chipman, 1985, p. 9). He also became less willing to engage in similar operations elsewhere in Africa. In 1965 and 1966 there were coups in Benin, the Central African Republic and Upper Volta, but no French intervention was forthcoming. It may have been that the ousted leaders did not appeal to France or that France believed that its interests would be best served by the new regime.

The British military role in Africa was on a more modest scale than the French, but troops were used in support of African allies in the first decade of independence. Britain, like France, had retained military links with many former colonies. Few of the colonies served directly as British bases but Britain did provide officers, training and equipment for the new armies. Even radical Ghana relied for many years on a British officer, General Alexander, to lead its national army. British units enjoyed training facilities in Kenya and played a major role in setting up national armies in Kenya, Tanzania and Uganda. And it was in those three states that Britain intervened in 1964.

The intervention followed an army mutiny in Tanzania on 19th January 1964. Troops at Colito barracks outside Dar es Salaam mutinied against their British and Tanzanian officers. They arrested the officers and then moved into the capital, where they seized the radio station, the airport and State House. The Tanzanian leader, Julius Nyerere, was forced into hiding. Troops at a base in Tabora followed the example of the mutineers and locked up their officers. The government tried to end the mutiny by negotiation but in the end was forced, much against Nyerere's basic instincts, to appeal to Britain for help. The insurrection by the troops was brought to an end on 25th January 1964, when British Royal Marine Commandos landed at Dar es Salaam and rounded up the mutineers.

There were immediate copycat mutinies in both Kenya and Uganda, and again British commandos were used to end them (Low, 1974, p. 188; and Meredith, 1984, p. 183). The Tanzania mutiny led to the disbanding of the army and reconstruction of the armed forces along lines more consistent with Nyerere's African socialist ideology. In all three cases, British troops were withdrawn immediately after the restoration of order. Nyerere was hardly proud of having to call in British troops to put down an army mutiny, but he denied charges that the British were gaining control again, saying: 'I am told that already there is foolish talk that the British have come back to rule Tanganyika again. This is rubbish. I asked the British government to help us in the same way as I would have asked our neighbours to help us if that had been possible. Any independent country is able to ask for the help of another independent country' (Grundy, 1968, p. 305).

Although the intervention proved successful for Tanzania and there was no resulting loss of sovereignty, over the next twenty five years, the number of interventions increased dramatically and in many cases, Africa's independence and sovereignty was frequently called into question.

2 National liberation wars: the foreign factor

Although the majority of African states achieved independence without the necessity of fighting, many had to wage long and hard military conflicts to force the colonial power to withdraw or to end white minority rule. The first major liberation war fought in the post-war period was the Mau Mau uprising in Kenya. Although this was limited mostly to the Kikuyu people and the highland areas of the country, it did take on the character of an anti-colonial struggle and was instrumental in quickening the pace of decolonisation. But the struggles which started in the 1960s against the Portuguese, the white Rhodesian regime, South African occupation of Namibia and apartheid in South Africa itself, were to be long-drawn out struggles which were to become major international conflicts.

Although arising out of the desires of the indigenous people for independence from foreign rule or the rule of a white minority, the national liberation wars of the 1960s, 1970s and 1980s became cockpits for foreign intervention. But why? Did it result from the need or wish of the liberation movements to quicken the pace of their campaigns for freedom by seeking military and other support from abroad, thus bringing new forms of intervention to the African continent? This is certainly the view taken by many Western commentators (see Greig, 1977; Seton-Watson, 1978). Such commentators and Western decision-makers have essentially adopted a critical position towards movements which have sought external military help and accused them of allowing their countries to be used as springboards for Soviet and Chinese penetration of Africa and Soviet attempts to gain control of Africa's mineral resources and maritime transport routes (Thompson and Silvers, 1979; Jaster, 1983). In 1979, David Newsom, President Carter's Under-Secretary of State for Political Affairs gave testimony to the Africa Subcommittee of the House Committee on Foreign Affairs in which he attacked 'Soviet penetration' of Africa and those governments or movements in Africa which were receiving Soviet military aid (cited by Somerville, Winter 1984, p. 308).

The adoption of these attitudes by the USA and its NATO allies frequently led to counter-interventions or the implementation of policies that put the West in opposition to African states or movements. This resulted in a further escalation of the external role in the conflicts. So how did external actors come to play important roles in Africa's wars of independence?

The Portuguese Empire and the white minority regimes

The liberation wars that started in Africa in the early and mid-1960s resulted from the refusal of the Portuguese to withdraw from their colonial possessions in Angola, Cape Verde, Guinea-Bissau, Mozambique and Sao Tome e Principe and from the refusal of the white minorities in Rhodesia and South Africa to grant full democratic and civil rights to the black majority populations (plus, of course, South Africa's continued illegal occupation of Namibia). Indigenous political and independence movements sprang up (or, in the case of South Africa, gained strength) in the 1950s and began to press the colonial or white governments for independence or for full and equal political participation. In the cases of all the territories above, the authorities reacted with repression and violence. Leaders of the liberation movements were detained or forced into exile, the movements were banned and activists were beaten or killed when they held demonstrations.

In Angola, the arrests of leaders of the MPLA (Popular Movement for the Liberation of Angola) in 1959 and 1960 led to demonstrations in the home area of one of the leaders which were brutally suppressed by the Portuguese; over thirty people were killed and 200 wounded when colonial troops fired on demonstrators (Somerville, 1986, pp. 26–7; see also Marcum, 1969 and 1978). In Zimbabwe, a succession of African movements (the Southern Rhodesian African National Congress, the National Democratic Party, the Zimbabwe African People's Union, the Zimbabwe African National Union and the People's Caretaker Council) were banned by the government. As each one was banned, those leaders who had not been detained, formed another movement to press for democratic rights. Eventually, in 1963, the banning of ZANU and the PCC led to the formation of exile movements by the nationalists and the first serious moves towards guerrilla war. In Namibia, South African repression of independence movements such as the South West African National Union (SWANU) and the South West African People's Organisation (SWAPO) led the latter to turn to guerrilla warfare to end South African occupation. In South Africa itself, the Sharpeville massacre of 21st March 1960 and the subsequent banning of the African National Congress (ANC) and the Pan-Africanist Congress (PAC) led to sabotage campaigns followed by the beginnings of guerrilla struggles. The experience was the same in Mozambique and Guinea-Bissau.

Writing during the course of Mozambique's independence struggle, the first President of Frelimo explained his movement's reasons for launching a guerrilla war, they are reasons which are common to all the liberation movements mentioned here:

By 1961 two conclusions were obvious . . . Portugal would not admit the principle of self-determination . . . or allow for any extension of democracy under her own rule . . . secondly, moderate political action such as strikes, demonstrations and petitions, would only result in the destruction of those who took part in them. We were, therefore, left with these alternatives: to continue indefinitely living under a repressive imperial rule, or to find a means of using force against Portugal (Mondlane, 1983, p. 125).

The African nationalists launched their military campaigns in highly disadvantageous circumstances. In the Portuguese territories, they were fighting a European power with a modern, well-trained and well-armed military machine. Portugal was part of NATO and was able through the organisation to obtain the latest weaponry and to gain from the military experiences of its partners. The Rhodesian government had, by African standards, a strong, though fairly small military force. Most of its officers had been trained by the British and many, including senior commanders, had fought in counter-insurgency campaigns in Kenya, Malaya and Borneo. They also had the advantage that on the dissolution of the Central African Federation (which had included Zambia and Malawi), the Federation's air force and much of its arms had been given to the Rhodesians and not split equally between the three constituent parts of the Federation. South Africa had the strongest armed forces in Africa. Traditionally linked to the British, the armed forces had been able to purchase up-to-date weapons from Britain and its NATO allies and to cooperate closely with Western defence establishments. It was only the UN arms embargo in November 1977 that ended the open importing of arms by South Africa. The nationalists had to take on modern European-style armies, armed and often trained by NATO members and retaining close links with NATO members.

Portugal gained the most from NATO membership in its military struggle against African movements. It also benefited from military support from South Africa and Rhodesia. A former Portuguese army officer who served in Mozambique told the author in 1981 that he had acted as a liaison officer taking visiting South African military delegations around the war zones and enabling them both to advise the Portuguese on their counter-insurgency tactics and to learn from their combat experience. It was also the case that former NATO officers and soldiers frequently chose to serve with the Rhodesian or South African forces and were not dissuaded from doing so by their governments (unattributable correspondence with American Vietnam veteran who served for several years with the Rhodesian army).

The Portuguese dispatched over three quarters of their armed forces to Africa to put down the rebellions. By 1970, 160,000 troops out of a total of just over 180,000 were fighting in Angola, Guinea-Bissau or Mozambique (Minter, 1972, p. 71) and the Portuguese defence budget had tripled between 1960 and 1970, reaching over $350m in the latter year. To meet this commitment, Portugal needed the full support of its NATO partners. Portuguese troops who were assigned to NATO duties were allowed to serve in Africa and other NATO members supplied arms to the Portuguese under NATO agreements, even though the agreements did not allow for the use of the weapons outside the NATO area. When questioned about the supply of forty fighter-bombers to the Portuguese air force during the course of the wars in Africa, the West German Defence Ministry replied that the sale took place on the basis of the principle of mutual aid between NATO partners. The delivery is subject to a clause agreed on between the government of the Federal Republic and the Portuguese government which states that the planes are to be used exclusively in Portugal for defence purposes within the framework of the North Atlantic pact; and of course the Portuguese were adamant that Guinea-Bissau, Angola and Mozambique were actually part of Portugal and so were included in the NATO area (Davidson, 1981, pp. 126–7).

Those forty planes were just the tip of the iceberg though. Between 1962 and 1968 (half the length of the African conflicts), the USA gave military aid to Portugal worth $39.1m and financial support amounting to $124m (military assistance in the first decade of Portugal's membership of NATO totalled over $300m). The Americans supplied over a hundred fighters and fighter-bombers to Portugal, several hundred trainer aircraft (that could also be used in counter-insurgency roles) and thirty bombers, in addition to transport aircraft, M-47 tanks, 155m artillery pieces and small arms. An American Military Assistance and Advisory Group was sent to Portugal to assist with training and the use of American weapons and large numbers of Portuguese officers who fought in Africa were trained in the USA at Fort Leavenworth (Minter, 1972, pp. 100–113). Britain, West Germany and France also played an important role in supporting the Portuguese military effort in Africa. Over and above the aircraft mentioned above, the West Germans sent the Portuguese a hundred Dornier-27 counter-insurgency aircraft in the late 1960s and supplied small arms to the army. West German intelligence officers were reported in 1969 to have been involved in the assassination of the Mozambican nationalist leader Eduardo Mondlane (Minter, 1972, pp. 128–43). French support was just as important and military supplies were paid for using a $100m loan given by France in 1967.

The policy of directly aiding the Portuguese war effort (and of tacitly and covertly helping Rhodesia and South Africa) constituted a major intervention in the liberation wars from the very start. African nationalist leaders from all the colonies involved sought Western backing during their political campaigns for independence but were brushed aside or ignored completely. The nationalist groups were not slow, particularly in Portuguese Africa and South Africa, to realise that it wasn't that NATO states were uninterested in the liberation struggles, but rather that they supported the Portuguese, the South Africans and, to a lesser extent and more clandestinely, the Rhodesians. The Americans saw the Portuguese presence in southern Africa and the stability of the Rhodesian and South African systems as bulwarks against possible Soviet expansion in southern Africa and they discounted the possibility that the Portuguese colonial system could collapse or that successful military/political struggles could be waged in Rhodesia, Namibia and South Africa. This point of view was graphically illustrated in the US policy review towards Africa carried out under President Nixon. This review, known as memorandum 39, supported the continued backing of the Portuguese and came out against any change in policy towards the rest of southern Africa (El-Khawas and Cohen, 1976). British policy under successive Labour and Conservative governments was hardly more favourable towards the African nationalists, while West Germany and France followed policies generally in opposition to the liberation struggles, France in particular. The British maintained close relations with South Africa in the military field until

1975, when the agreement for the Royal Navy's use of the Simonstown naval base (which involved arms supplies to South Africa) came to an end. Both France and West Germany supplied arms to South Africa until the imposition of the UN embargo in 1977. Since the embargo, arms from NATO states have reached South Africa through clandestine deals, while French Mirage aircraft are built under licence in South Africa.

When the nationalists launched their armed struggles it was plainly obvious that the West was supporting the enemy and therefore would not help them, even diplomatically. As a result they turned to other sources for aid. Even for those espousing socialist beliefs, it was not a matter of ideology or of favouring relations with the Soviet Union, Cuba or China. It was purely a matter of necessity.

The reasoning behind the search for foreign sources of military help or the acceptance of aid when it was offered, has been described by Ndabaningi Sithole, the first leader of Zimbabwe's ZANU movement, as follows:

Communist help has been accepted from time to time to effect the liberation of the African continent from the shackles and fetters of colonialism. Help has also been accepted from capitalist countries . . . Even if help had come from the Devil himself, African nationalism would not have hesitated in accepting it. Imagine a man sinking in a river. He cries for help. Someone stretches out a helping hand. The sinking man would not be interested in knowing whether or not the helping hand was from the West or from the East. What is material to the sinking man is that it is a 'helping hand' (Sithole, 1968, p. 187).

Sithole stressed the point in conversation with the author in April 1982. He said that as one of the leaders of the Zimbabwean nationalist movement in the late 1950s and early 1960s, he had become convinced that armed struggle would have to be used to overthrow the white minority government. In order for armed struggle to be successful, arms and other forms of assistance would have to be elicited from friendly states. African states such as Tanzania, Zambia, Egypt and Algeria were approached first. There was a limit to the help that they could give, but they were able to serve as a channel of communications between the liberation movements and the socialist states. Sithole said that in January 1963, he met representatives of China and the Soviet Union at an Afro-Asian People's Solidarity Organisation meeting in Moshi, Tanzania. By that time, a few Zimbabwean nationalists had already been sent for military training in Algeria, China and Czechoslovakia (Somerville, 1984, pp. 198–200).

The Zimbabwean example is mirrored in Angola, Mozambique, Namibia and South Africa. Having accepted the need for armed struggle and realised that the West would hinder rather than help, nationalists turned to neighbouring African states and the socialist countries, who through their ideological stance and declaratory policy had made clear their willingness to help liberation movements. For both the USSR and China, despite their ideological split in the early 1960s, there was an important link between the struggle for national liberation in Africa, Asia and Latin America and the development of what they termed the world revolutionary process. Soviet theoreticians (who often served as members of the party central committee and of official think tanks), emphasised that in the Soviet view, help to liberation movements was a means of advancing the cause of socialism as it assisted in the destruction of imperialism, weakened the overall power of the capitalist world, created links between potentially revolutionary movements in the Third World and the socialist states and shifted the 'correlation of forces' in favour of socialism (see Brutents, 1977; Ulyanovskiy, 1974; *Voprosy Istorii KPSS*, October 1975; and Dziak, 1971).

The Soviet preparedness to give material help to African movements had been declared to the world from the rostrum of the United Nations in New York in 1961 by Nikita Khrushchev in a speech demanding the dismantling of the colonial systems of capitalist states and offering Soviet support for those fighting colonialism. In February 1961, *Pravda* published an article by the President of the Angolan movement, the MPLA, Mario de Andrade, in which he described the Angolan fight for independence from Portugal. On 11th March 1961, the Soviet government newspaper *Izvestiya* published a telegram from Andrade to Khrushchev appealing for Soviet assistance. Soviet aid to the MPLA is believed to have started around this time (Somerville, 1986, pp. 28–9; see also Marcum, 1969). But it was not until 1964 that weapons in any quantities began to be supplied to the MPLA. In that year, Tanzania and Zambia became transit points for supplies of Soviet and Chinese arms to the MPLA (the FNLA and later UNITA also received supplies of Chinese arms via Zambia and also Zaire).

Guerrillas from the southern African movements and from the PAIGC in Guinea-Bissau received military equipment, medical help and some financial assistance from the USSR, the socialist bloc states, Cuba and China. These countries also provided places at military academies and training camps for liberation movement cadres. The first group of ZANU guerrillas to carry out an attack against whites in Zimbabwe had received military training in Ghana and China. The leader of the group, William Ndangana told the author in 1982 that he had been given very basic training in Ghana but more advanced education in the theory and practice of guerrilla warfare in China. Ndangana said that throughout the guerrilla war in Zimbabwe, ZANU personnel received advanced military training in China. In the early 1970s, the Chinese began to train ZANU forces (as well as Frelimo cadres from Mozambique) at camps at Itumbi and Nachingwea in southern Tanzania. Only small numbers of Chinese were sent to Tanzania to train Mozambican and Zimbabwean guerrillas, but according to former guerrillas their role was very important as they were able to prepare cadres for the task of preparing the political foundations as well as the military ones for a successful guerrilla war (interviews with Ndangana, Mayor Urimbo and George Rutanhire, Harare, April 1982; and Martin and Johnson, 1981, pp. 11–12).

The Cubans also played an active role in training liberation fighters actually in Africa. The group led by Che Guevara which made the unsuccessful attempt to aid the Congolese rebels, settled in Congo-Brazzaville, where they helped train the government forces there while also assisting the MPLA, which had established offices and training camps in Congo-Brazzaville. The MPLA–Cuban link forged during the early years of the Angolan war was one which was to prove decisive for the MPLA in its struggle for power during the Angolan civil war in 1975–6.

Although the Soviet Union did not send military instructors to assist with training in Africa, it did train guerrillas at camps in the Soviet Union as well as supplying weapons and other supplies. Given its own massive military power, it was in a position, when it chose to, to give more effective aid than China. China itself often lacked the sophisticated weaponry that many of the movements needed in the later years of their campaigns (interviews with Ndangana, Urimbo and Witness Mangwende, Harare, April 1982). In Guinea-Bissau, Angola, Mozambique and Zimbabwe, it was the Soviet provision of weapons like the recoilless 75mm cannon, which was portable, and the 122mm rocket-launcher which enabled guerrilla groups to take on the counter-insurgency forces in more than just hit-and-run operations (Davidson, 1981, pp. 190–9). The rocket-launcher, which could be used at quite long ranges, enabled groups like the PAIGC to take the offensive and to attack well-defended positions.

The Sino-Soviet split and the existence of competing movements within the colonies, meant that the Soviets and Chinese were generally supporting different movements; frequently ones that were in a state of war. The splits became polarised and so the Soviet Union and its allies ended up supporting one distinct group of movements (the PAIGC, MPLA, Frelimo, ZAPU, ANC and SWAPO), while the Chinese aided ZANU, the FNLA, UNITA and the PAC (Somerville, March 1984, pp. 102–5). Frelimo and the PAIGC, being the only successful movements in their territories, were able to get both Soviet and Chinese support.

3 Disintegration, secession and irredentism

National liberation wars and resistance by colonial regimes affected a limited number of African states in the 1960s and 1970s, but a much broader threat to stability (and therefore of foreign intervention) was presented by the lack of national unity of many states and the competition that arose between incompatible elements confined within artificial state borders. As has been seen with Congo (Zaire), some states were on the verge of total anarchy and disintegration very soon after independence. Many African countries experienced ever more severe secessionist wars, conflicts between competing regions, communities or political groups or border disputes. Others, such as Togo, Benin, Burkina Faso (formerly Upper Volta) and Congo-Brazzaville, suffered instability and frequent coups because of the failures of political leaders and institutions.

Foreign intervention did not decline as the period of independence lengthened, rather the imminent fragmentation of many countries led to more frequent and serious cases of foreign military interference. Governments seeking to hold their states together or to cling on to power sought external aid, while movements seeking secession or countries seeking to gain claimed territory looked for help from powerful allies abroad.

By the mid to late 1960s, a number of African states were in the throes of wars resulting from the above causes. In Sudan, the Anyanya movement in the south was fighting a government from the predominantly Arab and Muslim north – this was a conflict that brought in Arab support for the Khartoum government and covert Israeli support for Anyanya. In Chad, French troops were.withdrawn from the north of the country only for a serious revolt to break out that led President Tombalbaye to ask for French military aid to ensure his control of the whole of the national territory (see next chapter). In the Horn of Africa, the people of Eritrea took up arms to fight their forced annexation by the Ethiopian monarchy, while the people of Somalia sought military means of restoring what they saw as their lost territories in the Ogaden and the north of Kenya. And in Africa's giant, Nigeria, the failure of the British-imposed political system and the growing hostility between the people of the country's main regions led to a civil/secessionist war of great ferocity.

Serious ethnic hostility was evident in many of the conflicts which developed in Africa during the first decade of independence, though none more so than in Burundi, where a tragic tribal conflict left many thousands dead. The only fortunate aspect of the fighting there was that Burundi was peripheral politically and strategically and the massacres that took place did not draw in external interference.

The killings in Burundi had their origin in the ethnic make-up of the old German colony of Ruanda-Urundi. The colony contained two distinct kingdoms, as implied by the hyphenated name. In the region that became known as Burundi, the Tutsi people had ruled the majority Hutu population for over 400 years, despite making up under a sixth of the population. There was a similar situation in the Ruanda colony – the Tutsi minority lording it over the Hutu. The German colony was handed over to Belgium after the 1914–18 war, and the Belgians ruled the two kingdoms until independence was granted in 1962. The kingdoms were ruled separately and no attempt was made to merge the two regions. But neither was any attempt made to sort out a workable political system prior to independence. Instead, as freedom approached, it was clear that the Belgians would hand over power to the Tutsi monarchies, leaving the Hutu in thrall once more. But the Hutu of Ruanda (which became Rwanda on independence), were not prepared to stand for perpetual domination by the minority. When the Tutsi king died in July 1959, the Hutu revolted against the new king. In a spontaneous rising, 10,000–20,000 Tutsi were killed (most of them unarmed civilians) and over 100,000 fled south to Burundi (where the Tutsi still had firm control). The Belgians had enough trouble to cope with in Congo (Zaire) and did little to try to control the Hutu uprising, though some commentators believe that the Belgians aided the Hutu movement, the Parti de l'Emancipation du Peuple Hutu (Parmehutu), which seized power (see Oliver and Crowder, 1981, p. 248). They left as planned in 1962, handing over power to a Hutu government controlled by President Gregoire Kayibanda. In the first few years of independence he had to fight off a guerrilla campaign by Tutsi insurgents known as Inyenzi (cockroaches). There was suspicion that the Tutsi guerrillas were trained and armed by the Chinese. The Chinese were believed to be supplying aid to the Inyenzi through projects involving Rwandan Tutsi refugees in Burundi (McLane, 1974, p. 17). Although the Hutu army contained the rebellion, periodic guerrilla attacks occur and the Tutsi Union Nationale Rwandaise still claims to have guerrillas operating in remote areas near the border with Tutsi-dominated Burundi. Kayibanda was later overthrown by the army, who accused him of abuses of power, corruption and of favouring members of his own Gitarama sub-group of the Hutu from central Rwanda in making government appointments. He was overthrown in a military coup on 5th July 1973 by mainly northern army officers. The military ruler who succeeded him, Juvenal Habyarimana, still governs the country. Under his rule, economic development has been emphasised over ideology and ethnic concerns and relative stability ensured. The Tutsi minority (they make up under 10 per cent of the 6.3m population) suffers discrimination in education and appointment to government positions (though there are token Tutsi in ministerial posts) but ethnic peace has been maintained and impressive developments made with the economy. Kayibanda's and Habyarimana's successes in keeping the lid on a potentially explosive situation have prevented external interference, despite jockeying for influence by the USA, the Soviet Union and China in the 1960s and 1970s.

In Burundi, independence was achieved in 1962 with the Tutsi monarchy still in place and with a Tutsi government led by the Union pour le Progres National (Uprona). The Hutu were very much under the thumb of the minority group but succeeded in winning a massive victory in the national election of May 1965. But the Tutsi refused to give up power and the Tutsi monarch, Mwame Mwambutsa, declined to confirm the election results. The Hutu, hoping to follow the example of their Rwandan counterparts, rose in revolt in October 1965. But the Tutsi had too tight a grip on the army and the government and the revolt was repressed with great ferocity – about 5,000 Hutu being killed; the Tutsi army deliberately set out to kill educated Hutu, who they saw as a threat to Tutsi hegemony. Following the revolt, there was strife within the ruling Tutsi group, leading to the abdication of the Mwami and then the overthrow of his successor by the Prime Minister, Colonel Michel Micombero (Brogan, 1989, pp. 15–16). There was another purge of leading Hutu in 1969. But the most shocking massacres took place in April and May 1972, when a Hutu rebellion took place in Bujumbura. It is not known how many Tutsi died – though the government claimed 50,000 – but at least 100,000 Hutu were wiped out in a genocidal campaign of repression by the Tutsi army. A further 120,000 Hutu fled to Rwanda and Tanzania. The Burundi government received assistance from President Mobutu of Zaire in suppressing the revolt, chiefly because there had been reports that Zairean rebels linked to Pierre Mulele had taken part in the revolt (Brogan, 1989, p. 16). The Micombero government was later overthrown in a military coup led by Jean-Baptiste Bagaza. Under his rule, the Hutu were kept in subservience, but peace was maintained and a few token Hutu were given cabinet posts. After Bagaza was overthrown himself in September 1987, the tribal conflicts again broke out. The main fighting occurred in August 1988 after attempts by the Tutsi-dominated police and army to put an end to coffee smuggling operations across the Burundi-Rwanda border. The Hutu of northern Burundi accused the army of killing innocent Hutu and a wave of anti-Tutsi attacks took place. In return, the army turned on the local population killing at least 20,000 Hutu and forcing 50–100,000 Hutu into Rwanda. As during previous massacres, the troops sought out educated and prominent Hutu as targets for their anger (unattributable interviews with Hutu refugees in Kigali, November 1988).

But again, because of Burundi's relative political insignificance and the absence of a major power with a vested interest in the region, there was no obvious external interference, apart from international calls for an end to the killings.

Sudan: the war of the grass curtain

The state of Sudan, which achieved its independence from joint British and Egyptian (though much more of the former than the latter) rule on 1st January 1956, was born with the seeds of conflict already germinating in the thin soils of the south. Sudan has over 115 languages and dialects to match its heterogeneous ethnic make-up. But its major ethnic/political problem has been the huge, centuries old divide between the north which is mainly Arabic-speaking, Muslim and which looks for its cultural roots more towards Egypt and the Middle East than to Africa, and the south, whose people see themselves as Africans and who are animist or Christian in their religious beliefs. Prior to the colonial period, the north and south of present-day Sudan had not been linked, except through northern raids against the south for slaves and ivory (Meredith, 1984, p. 270). There was no common political culture, no common religion and no common ethnic background. Geographically, the regions were very different – the north was arid desert or dry scrub, while the south started with the huge grass plains of Bahr el-Ghazal and developed into swamp and rainforest further south. It was said that the two areas were kept apart by the 'grass curtain'.

It was only under the colonial system established by Britain (and Egypt) that an attempt was made to weld the two regions together, and this only ten years before the granting of independence. Up until 1946, the British had encouraged separate identities for the north and south and had tried to prevent the spread of Muslim/Arab influence into the south. While the north developed politically, economically and educationally, the British made little attempt to advance the people of the south. A large gulf in terms of education, administrative experience and political skill grew up to exacerbate the existing differences. The north was permitted by the British to gain a position of political dominance. Northern political parties, notably those centred around the Muslim Ansar and Khatmiya sects, began to develop in the late 1930s, but in the south, the first parties did not appear until 1953. When the British and Egyptians opened negotiations on Sudanese independence in 1953, the south was not represented.

Had the south and north been kept as two separate entities which would cooperate on a federal basis or in a state in which the south had autonomy, these problems could perhaps have been overcome. But, in 1946, the British reversed their policy of keeping the two halves of Sudan apart and joined the two together – the idea being to thwart Egyptian ambitions of taking over Sudan when Britain decided to pull out. The integration of the north and south by the British did not mean joint control of the future state or the south gaining a greater say in the running of the country, rather it meant that once the British withdrew, northern civil servants and army officers would move south to assume the positions of authority vacated by the British. British troops left the south in 1955, the year before independence. As there were few southern officers (in the southern Equatoria Corps of the Sudan Defence Force there were thirty-three officers, twenty-four northerners in the twenty-four senior positions and nine southern subordinates), the northerners took over command of the southern units of the armed forces – to the chagrin of the southern NCOs and private soldiers (Woodward, 1979, p. 153; and O'Ballance, 1977, pp. 39–41).

The anger of the southern troops did not take long to emerge. Demonstrations in the south in July 1955 against the growing northerner presence led to a decision to send northern troops south to keep order – in return, southern detachments would be moved north. The southern troops refused and a mutiny occurred at Torit. Southern soldiers attacked their officers and went on the rampage attacking northerners and their property. The mutiny started on 18th August and spread within a few days to units at Juba, Yei, Yambio, Wau, Malakal and Maridi. An estimated 366 northerners were killed during the uprising. Some of the mutineers crossed into Uganda (where most of them were captured and sent back), but some went into hiding in the bush taking their weapons with them. The end of the mutiny came after 8,000 northern troops were flown south by the British on 21st August. After the suppression of the mutiny, the Equatoria Corps was disbanded – though not before further desertions by southern troops. For a year, a ban was in force on the enlistment of southerners into the army. There were reports that the northern troops used to crush the mutiny took heavy reprisals against southern civilians and captured mutineers, increasing the antipathy between northerners and southerners – whole villages were said to have been put to the torch and thousands of southerners killed (Mazrui and Tidy, 1984, pp. 194–5).

When independence came on the first day of 1956, there was burning resentment in the south at the perceived subjugation to the north. A constitutional conference was set up after independence to draft a new constitution – it was made up of forty-three northerners and three southerners; the new Sudanese civil service of 800, which replaced the departing British and Egyptian administrators, consisted of 794 northerners and six southerners. It was all a recipe for further strife. The situation was exacerbated by the external links developed by the two communities. The north looked to the Arab world and developed close ties with Egypt, Syria and Libya, while the south looked to Africa, and particularly to Uganda, where the people of northern and western Uganda had kinship links with some of the peoples of southern Sudan. The Khartoum government's links with the Arab Middle East and its support for Arab causes – notably in the struggle against Israel – meant that the internal conflict was compounded by involvement in a wider, international struggle.

The early years of independence saw the entrenchment of northern control and growing unrest in the south. But the unrest lacked a focus as no one party or ethnic group predominated. The southern Sudanese had only begun to develop a group identity when the British merged the two parts of Sudan in 1946. This identity was a mixture of race, culture, religion, geophysical environment, history, education and 'the very existence of the Arab Sudanese as an "outgroup"' (Heraclides, 1987, p. 215). A southern unity grew up around hostility towards Khartoum rather than as a result of more lasting bonds. It was only during the 1960s, after a guerrilla war had started against the government, that a distinct black nationalism, based on the inequalities between the north and the south and the fears of assimilation by the north, began to emerge (Heraclides, ibid.).

The attitude of the northern rulers of the Sudan towards the south was that it was a 'cultural vacuum' waiting to be filled by the north (Wai, 1973, pp. 73–4). Token southerners were appointed to government posts, but real power was retained by the north, which sought to impose its rule, values and culture on the south. Between independence and the start of the Anyanya (which in the Madi language means the venom of the deadly Gaboon viper) guerrilla war in 1962, southern groups tried by constitutional means to improve their position. This was without any real success and hostility towards the north mounted. There was already a nucleus of southerners ready to fight the government in the groups of mutineers and deserters who had evaded capture after the 1955 mutiny. But despite the imposition of northern rule, the situation was bearable for many southerners in the early years of independence because of the relative disorgani-sation of the northern politicians. There was considerable conflict between the northern, Muslim parties in the first two years of independence. The main struggle was between the National Unionist Party of the Khatmiya sect and the Umma Party of the Ansar sect; the situation was later complicated when some members of the NUP split away to form the People's Democratic Party. The early governments were unstable and at one point Prime Minister Khalil of the Umma Party promised moves towards federation for the south – he went on to repudiate this offer in December 1957. During 1958, the government was in severe crisis as a result of demonstrations in the north, a row with Egypt over the Nile waters and the threat of guerrilla warfare in the south (as the former mutineers showed signs of military activity). Khalil was unable to form a strong government or to control the level of political conflict and on 17th November 1958, the army took over.

General Abboud became military ruler of the Sudan. He was intent on estab-lishing strong government and of exerting tighter control over the south. He launched a campaign of suppression and tried to impose Islam on the mainly Christian south; he was particularly opposed to the activities of Christian mis-sionaries in the south (Meredith, 1984, p. 272). His policies led to an exodus of southern Sudanese to neighbouring African states and desertions of some of the remaining southerners in the army (Morrison, 1976, pp. 16–17).

Under Abboud's oppression, the south grew more restive and there were increasing reports of clashes between the mutineers and army units seeking to wipe them out. The army took an increasingly harsh attitude towards civilians in the south, accusing them of sheltering rebels – on occasions whole villages were destroyed as a punishment for allegedly helping the mutineers. By late 1961, rumours were rife that a full-scale guerrilla war was about to be launched. By then, the government had abolished political parties and attempted to stop open political activity by southern leaders. The southern leaders, such as Joseph Oduhu, William Deng and Marko Rume fled into Zaire. In February 1962, they established the Sudan African Closed Districts National Union in Leopoldville. The union's aim was to gain total independence for the south. At first, SACDNU denied any links with the rebels still at large in the southern forests, though links developed between some of the union's leaders and the rebels.

The rebels had increased their strength during 1961 as a result of the release from prison of around 800 southerners implicated in the 1955 mutiny. Many of them moved into the forests to join the rebels, though they had no firearms and had to make do with machetes, spears and bows (O'Ballance, 1977, p. 57). As the rebel force grew, it was able to consider active resistance rather than just survival in the face of counter-insurgency sweeps by government forces. The number of guerrilla incidents increased during 1962 and in September 1963, the rebels announced the formation of the Land Freedom Army – though it soon became known as Anyanya. It established training camps along the southern border with Uganda and began to recruit among the southerners and among refugees in Uganda, Kenya, the Central African Republic and Zaire.

The guerrilla war was a very low level one to begin with, as the rebels were poorly armed. They concentrated on sabotage, while the government forces conducted a ruthless counter-insurgency campaign in which villages were destroyed and reprisals taken against civilians. But as the war gradually increased in intensity, Anyanya started attacking isolated police and army posts. The rebels became the focus of southern discontent and attempts were made by the SACDNU (the name was later shortened to Sudanese African National Union, SANU) leaders to gain control of Anyanya. This created divisions as the political leaders were not in agreement.

There was a half-hearted attempt at a political solution to the southern problem in 1964, after Abboud was overthrown and replaced by a civilian government – but this came to nothing despite the holding of a peace conference in Khartoum in March 1965. Following the conference, the war continued but SANU split in two. This reduced the effectiveness of Anyanya as political differences surfaced among the rebels. In July 1967, the Southern Sudanese Provisional Government was formed and for nearly two years it held sway over most of the rebels and became the dominant southern political movement. In March 1969, it fell apart and two rival groups – the Nile provisional Government and the Southern Sudan Liberation Movement competed for influence over the rebel forces.

At first the rebels relied for their arms on what they could capture from the government and for funds on the proceeds of ivory poaching. But as the fight continued, they sought external support. The main source of this support was Israel. It began to give low-level assistance in 1965 via the Obote government in Uganda. The Ugandans supported the rebels chiefly on ethnic grounds. There were kinship links and linguistic bonds between communities in southern Sudan and Uganda. Idi Amin, the Ugandan army commander and later military dictator, came from the Kakwa group, members of which could also be found in Sudan. Amin and his supporters and ethnic compatriots in the army became the main channel for Israeli aid to the rebels. The Israelis had already got a foothold in Uganda where they were training and supplying the Ugandan army. Having established themselves in Uganda, the Israelis sought to use it as a means of attacking the Arabs from the south (particularly after the Arab-Israeli war of June 1967). Sudan was a prime target for Israel because of its support for the Arab cause and because of the possibility that it could merge with Egypt. As Ade Adefuye has written, 'the Israelis therefore decided to back the southern Sudanese as a means of stabbing the Arabs in the back, prolonging the war in the Sudan and preventing any possibility of this merger with Egypt, or active support for it. This required the support of Uganda, which could be used as a base for military and material aid to the Southern Sudanese' (Adefuye, 1987, p. 61).

The Israeli aid, which increased dramatically after the 1967 war, gave Anyanya the opportunity to escalate the fighting considerably. It also helped Joseph Lagu (a former officer in the Sudanese army) to establish himself as a major southern leader. He set up an Anyanya government in Eastern Equatoria and became the major channel for Israeli support. His position as an 'effective leader able to speak for the bulk of the southern fighters was due in no small part to the flow of Israeli arms to him after the 1967 Middle East war' (Woodward, 1979, p. 175). Initially coming in from Uganda, as the war developed (and as the war in Eritrea grew in intensity as the Sudanese backed the Eritreans against the Ethiopian government), Ethiopia became another source of Israeli arms. On occasions, the Israelis carried out air drops of arms and other supplies to the rebels from Ethiopia and Uganda. The Ethiopian connection was cut after Numayri seized power in Sudan in 1969 and effected a rapprochement with Haile Selassie.

The Israelis not only supplied arms to the rebels, they also provided training for soldiers in Israel and sent officers and instructors to assist with training and organisation at Anyanya camps inside Sudan. The Sudanese government was aware of the Israeli role – though the government had direct military support from Egypt and benefited from arms supplies from Britain and the Soviet Union (and training from Soviet instructors in Sudan). A former Sudanese diplomat has said that the Khartoum government knew that about 200 Anyanya officers had been trained in Israel in 1969 and that Israeli instructors had trained at least two groups of rebels at camps inside southern Sudan (Beshir, 1975, pp. 91–2). It was also claimed, by a German mercenary who assisted Anyanya, that the Israelis had helped the rebels to lay mines in rivers used by government vessels (O'Ballance, 1977, pp. 126–8).

The Israelis continued their support to the end of the decade, but then came up against a serious problem when Obote decided to improve relations with Uganda following the overthrow of the Sudanese government in a military coup in May 1969 (which brought Colonel Ja'afar Numayri to power). Obote had taken an increasingly radical stance in foreign policy – one that was inconsistent with continued cooperation with Israel. He therefore called on the military assistance mission led by Colonel Bar-Lev to end its training programme for the Ugandan army and instructed Amin to curtail the clandestine links with Israel through which Anyanya received military aid. But Amin ignored the order and let the Israelis continue to have access to southern Sudan via Ugandan army bases in northern Uganda. Amin himself accompanied several groups of Israeli officers into southern Sudan to meet the rebels and deliver arms supplies (Adefuye, 1987, pp. 62–3). The Amin–Israel link not only enabled the southern rebels to continue the war, but also became an important factor in Amin's eventual overthrow of Obote. Both the Israelis and the southern Sudanese rebels wanted to see an end to Obote because of his turn against them. Their views coincided with growing opposition to Obote's policies and his autocratic style within the country and, particularly within the armed forces. Amin became one of the leaders of the opposition within the army and decided to strike during Obote's absence abroad in January 1971. He staged the coup and proclaimed himself head of state on 21st January. Many Ugandans, including former government minister Grace Stuart Ibingira, believe that the Israelis played a major liaison and planning role in the coup – arranging for Anyanya rebels in northern Uganda to link up with Kakwa elements within the Ugandan armed forces to stage the coup. Ibingira cites Colonel Baruch Bar-Lev, who led the Israeli military mission in Uganda as saying in 1976 that he had advised Amin on how to seize power (Ibingira, 1980, pp. 236–7). Some 500 Sudanese rebels assisted Amin to topple Obote (Adefuye, 1987, p. 64). After the coup, Amin received substantial Israeli help in reorganising the army to ensure Kakwa control and in integrating large numbers of Sudanese into the army.

Continued Israeli support for the rebels and the inability of the Numayri regime to crush the revolt entirely, though his control over the army enabled him to pursue the war in the south more vigorously and to put greater military pressure on Anyanya. Numayri's campaign was backed by Egypt and Egyptian pilots are said to have flown Soviet-supplied MiGs against both the rebels and Numayri's opponents within the Ansar sect (O'Ballance, 1977, pp. 107–8, 118–19). There were even reports that Soviet personnel took part in Numayri's operations (ibid., p. 118). The government offensive, combined with the offer of concessions to the southerners, led to the convening of the Addis Ababa talks on peace in 1972. Numayri agreed to give autonomy to the south and to an amnesty for those who had taken part in the rebellion. The Addis Ababa agreement ending the war was signed in the presence of Emperor Haile Selassie on 27th March 1972. The war in the south had ended (for the time being).

The south had not been Numayri's only problem after seizing power. The opposition of the powerful Ansar sect led to severe political conflict and an attempt to assassinate the new President during a visit to the Ansar sect's traditional base on Aba island in the Blue Nile. The attempt to kill him led to a military attack on the island, which destroyed the military power of the sect.

A more serious threat to Numayri emerged in July 1971, when a group of leftist army officers seized power. The coup took place on 19th July and was successful, at first. Numayri and several other members of the ruling Revolutionary Council were seized and a new Council led by Major Atta announced that it now constituted the government. But the participants in the coup were not united and their seizure of power led to demonstrations in Khartoum. Numayri loyalists in the army, supported by Egypt and Libya, took the opportunity to stage a counter-coup. The Libyan air force flew Sudanese units stationed along the Suez Canal (to support Egypt in the War of Attrition against Israel) back to Khartoum to oppose the new regime. By 22nd July, Numayri was back in control. He and the Egyptians blamed the coup on left-wing groups and the Sudanese Communist Party. It was therefore logical, given the Soviet Union's important role in training and arming the Sudanese armed forces and its strong links with the Communist Party, that it too came under suspicion. Numayri acted swiftly against the leftists, including some (such as Joseph Garang, the Minister for the South) who had served in his own government. Many were detained, some hanged. A number of suspected leftist leaders were handed over to Sudan by Libya. Numayri was obviously suspicious of the Soviet Union and although he officially announced that there was no evidence that Soviet military advisers had been involved, he said on 29th July 1971 that the 1,800 military personnel 'are on the verge of leaving the country because their mission has been completed'. He later said that there was no place for communism in the Sudan and that he would not accept the Soviets as colonisers (O'Ballance, 1977, pp. 110–13). The failed coup led to a swift decline in Sudanese–Soviet relations.

The Horn of Africa: the roots of a protracted war

For centuries the region of north-eastern Africa known as the Horn, encompassing Ethiopia, Somalia and Djibouti but also impinging politically and economically on Sudan and northern Kenya, has been fought over by the indigenous peoples. Conflict arose between competing factions within the Ethiopian (Abyssinian) empire, between the empire and communities it tried to absorb, between Muslim polities in the area of present-day Somalia and the empire and between rival clans and communities in Somalia. And while the conflicts have been generated within the region itself, they have often had a foreign input – whether from the Arab world to the north and across the Red Sea or from Europe.

In the 16th century, Muslim armies under Imam Ahmed Ibn Ibrahim al-Ghazi invaded highland Ethiopia from the Ogaden. The Emperor was defeated and his Muslim enemies conquered much of the Empire. Rather than accept defeat, the Emperor requested aid from the Portuguese, who were gaining an increasingly important position along the Indian Ocean littoral. The Portuguese dispatched a force of musketeers which helped the Emperor to regain control (Ottaway, 1982, p. 15).

While no direct parallel should be drawn between the Portuguese role and that later played by the USA and the Soviet Union, the incident was an indication that from the very start of European expansion into Africa, foreign military force was a factor in the military and political equation in the Horn. But until the late 19th century, the foreign role was limited. The region itself was uninviting and the European powers did not embark on their scramble for Africa until the closing two decades of the century. When that scramble started, the would-be colonisers found that they were up against a formidable foe in the Ethiopian Empire. After centuries of fighting for survival, the latter half of the 1900s saw a major expansion in Ethiopian military and political power and as a result expansion into and domination of surrounding communities. Under the Emperors Tewodros (1855–68), Yohannes II (1872–89) and Menelik II (1889–1913), the Empire almost doubled in size (Halliday and Molyneaux, 1981, p. 55; Schwab, 1985, p. 5). The dominance of the Amhara group was established firstly in the Shoa region and then further west and south, subjecting the Oromo peoples to imperial rule and establishing control over the Haud and Bale regions peopled by

Oromo and Somali communities. To the north, the areas inhabited by Tigrigna speakers were conquered, though imperial rule was not successfully established over Eritrea. Under Menelik II, Ethiopia took on its present-day shape and frontiers (Greenfield, 1965, p. 96). Further expansion was limited chiefly by the entry of the European colonial powers into the region.

The incentive for European expansion was not just the momentum built up by the scramble for Africa, but also the growing strategic and economic importance of the Red Sea following the opening of the Suez Canal in 1867. In 1869, the port of Assab on the coat of Eritrea was taken over by the Italians (the port was controlled by an Italian shipping company). In 1882, the Italian government took control of the port from the company and used it as a base from which to expand into the hinterland. Massawa was seized in 1885 and expansion continued into the 1890s. Although Menelik reached agreement with the Italians on a border between Eritrea and the Empire in 1889 (Selassie, 1980, pp. 1–2), the Italians attempted to invade Ethiopia in the following decade. The attempt ended with the Ethiopian victory at the battle of Adowa in 1896.

To the south and east, the French and British had occupied what is now Djibouti and northern Somalia, with the Italians taking the Somali coastal area running down to Kenya's northern border. With the exception of the Italian push into Ethiopia, the colonial powers were content to control coastal areas. This is one major reason why Ethiopia was able to retain its albeit fragile independence. Another is that the British were happy to see a united Ethiopia in place to prevent French and Italian expansion. In the late 19th and early 20th centuries, the British were the main foreign supporters of the Empire. From the mid-1900s through to the Italian invasion in 1935, the Ethiopians relied on foreign military support (chiefly in the form of arms and training) to maintain control over the peripheral areas of the empire (Clapham, 1986, p. 271).

Effectively, the political map of the Horn of Africa, still the subject of bloody conflict, was drawn up by the colonial powers. They created Eritrea, Somalia and Djibouti and fixed the limits of the Ethiopian Empire. The final acts in the colonial period were the Italian invasion and conquest of Ethiopia of 1935, the British–Ethiopian victory of 1941, which restored Emperor Haile Selassie to power, and the British administration of parts of the Ogaden (until 1955) and Eritrea (until 1952).

The end of the Second World War and the restoration of Haile Selassie to power were the prelude to great changes in the Horn. The Ethiopian Empire was back in business, but with the British controlling the Haud area of the Ogaden. The Italians retained their Somali possessions but had been forced out of Eritrea, which was under British rule pending a United Nations' decision on its future. The French and the British still had control of the rest of Somalia, but the latter were moving towards decolonisation.

The 1950s and the early 1960s saw the culmination of the process of change and decolonisation. In 1952, the future of Eritrea was decided and the British effectively handed it over to Ethiopia. This followed inconclusive investigations into the best course for Eritrea by UN commissions. The commissions somewhat half-heartedly consulted the Eritreans (though no referendum was held on the issue) on the question of their future status. Claiming historical rights and economic necessity (the latter on the grounds that without Eritrea's ports Ethiopia was effectively landlocked), Emperor Haile Selassie demanded that Eritrea be incorporated into Ethiopia. In this he was supported by a section of the Christian population of the Eritrean highlands (notably the landowners, who saw their control of arable land as being safest under imperial rule) but strongly opposed by mainly Muslim lowlanders, who wanted total independence. As Markakis has pointed out:

The common goal was to secure maximum access to the power of the state and the resources it commands. The Muslims saw independence as the most promising setting for the achievement of that goal, especially since any link with Ethiopia was for them a grievous political disability. Conversely, Christians believed that such a link guaranteed their political supremacy in Eritrea (Markakis, 1988, p. 52–3).

The split within Eritrea, combined with strong lobbying by Ethiopia, vacillation by Britain and other UN members and political support for Haile Selassie from the Americans, led to a very unsatisfactory decision to attach Eritrea to Ethiopia on a federal basis. This was supposed to give Eritrea internal self-government (based on a democratic, parliamentary system) but give Ethiopia control over foreign affairs, defence and taxation. But the constitutional arrangement was unworkable from the start. The Ethiopian Empire was a feudal monarchy. The Emperor could not have one province of the Empire enjoying democratic rights and effective control over their own internal government without risking threats to autocratic rule elsewhere. Haile Selassie intended to rule over Eritrea as he ruled over the rest of the Empire, as an absolute monarch. At the other end of the spectrum, the Muslims were determined to free Eritrea from the unwanted federation (which they rightly saw as just the first step towards total absorption into the Empire). In the middle, the majority of Christians harboured the vain hope that they could be part of the Empire but cling on to internal autonomy. In the end, they were all frustrated and remain so today.

The elections held were inconclusive and marked by Ethiopian interference. The Christian pro-federalists were the largest party but did not have a majority and so had to seek allies among the Muslim parties. An alliance was arranged and Eritrea embarked on a brief period of internal rule. It had a number of political parties, a free press and a trade union movement that had developed during the period of British rule. All this was an anathema to the Emperor and an obstacle to his wish to totally absorb Eritrea. He therefore set out to destroy the autonomy of Eritrea and its democratic institutions. Haile Selassie manipulated and intimidated political leaders and quickly replaced the relatively independent politicians heading the pro-unionist parties with puppets who would do his bidding. The press was soon brought into line with that in the rest of the Empire and gradually all independent institutions were destroyed. In 1956, Tigrigna and Arabic (the main languages of Eritrea) were replaced as the official languages by Amharic. The Muslims were totally alienated (many of them migrating to the Gulf and elsewhere in the Middle East), but, more importantly for the future, a lot of the poor and urban Christians (particulary workers, trades unionists and students) were pushed into opposition. Militant Christians, schoolchildren and students held demonstrations in Eritrea in 1957 against the dismantling of the federation – which was taking place regardless of UN guarantees. A general strike followed in 1958, during which a large number of people were killed when Ethiopian-controlled police opened fire on demonstrators in Asmara. In 1961, elections were held, but under strict Ethiopian control. There was no free exercise of the vote or free electioneering. The result of the election was a parliament controlled by the Emperor, though even then he had to use bribery, intimidation and detentions to compel it to dissolve the federation and endorse the annexation of Eritrea by Ethiopia in November 1962 (Firebrace and Holland, 1984, pp. 20–21; see also Selassie, 1980, pp. 51–3 and 62–3).

Eritrea was not the only conflict in the Horn generated by the spread of imperial rule. Oromo speakers make up one of the largest single language groups in Africa and have a population of some 15–20 million spread over Ethiopia, Somalia and Kenya. Many of them were swallowed up by Ethiopian imperial expansion under Menelik. In the 1880s and 1890s, the Oromo resisted Ethiopian expansion but were overwhelmed. Rebellions by Oromo speakers occurred within Ethiopia in 1928 and 1930, but they were crushed and resistance stifled by Ethiopia's foreign trained and armed security forces. But many of the Oromo never totally accepted Ethiopian (or as they see it, Amharic) rule and opposition groups re-emerged in the 1960s. A movement led by Tadesse Birru started agitating against the Emperor in 1965. In 1966, an extreme Oromo group killed many civilians when it planted a bomb in an Addis Ababa cinema. The following year, Birru's Oromo movement was banned and its leaders detained. Those who evaded detention went underground and formed the Oromo Liberation Front, which emerged openly as a guerrilla force in 1974 (Selassie, 1980, pp. 77–83).

Similarly, many of the Tigrigna-speaking people of the Tigre area of northern Ethiopia harboured a deep resentment of Amharic domination and of rule by a feudal emperor. They too had resisted Ethiopian rule in the late 19th century and had launched periodic revolts against imperial control – the most extensive being the Woyane revolt of 1943, which was put down by Haile Selassie utilising British air support. Tigre nationalism resurfaced as a strong nationalist movement in the early 1970s with the formation of the Tigre National Organisation. This was later succeeded by the guerrillia-based Tigre People's Liberation Front. The TPLF was not, as many have labelled it, a secessionist movement. Rather, as TPLF Central Committee member Yamane Kidane told the author in London in March 1989, the movement wanted an end to Amhar domination and the creation of a democratic Ethiopia in which all nationalities would have a role in government. This objective survived the overthrow of Haile Selassie.

If the Eritrean, Oromo and Tigrean conflicts could be termed as secessionist struggles or ethnically-based revolts against the imperial system, the other main cause of war and foreign intervention in the Horn, the territorial dispute between Ethiopia and Somalia, was very much an inter-state battle. It arose from disputed

Ethiopian control over the Haud and Bale regions of the Ogaden. These were areas brought under Ethiopian control during the period of imperial expansion. Menelik conquered the Harar emirate in the early 1980s and his control of the part of the Ogaden now claimed by Ethiopia was ratified in the Anglo-Ethiopian treaty of 1897 (it was later confirmed by the Anglo-Ethiopian agreement of 1942, following Haile Selassie's restoration). The rest of the Ethiopian–Somali border was set out in two treaties signed by the Emperor and the Italians in 1897 and 1908.

The Ethiopian conquest of the Ogaden brought Somali speakers and their traditional grazing lands under imperial control. No distinct Somali nation existed prior to the colonial period, but there was a distinctive Somali language and culture which bound together the numerous clans (the Ogaden region was named after the Somali clan of that name). The nomadic Somalis had tradition-ally traversed the Ogaden in search of pasture and had used wells in the area, including at Jijiga (where an Ethiopian garrison town was established after control was established) (Samatur, 1987, p. 182). Although Ethiopian rule was resented by the Somali clans, it impinged little on their lives and was not an important issue until decolonisation of the British and Italian Somali colonies drew near. It was only when nationhood and independence became a reality that a Somali state, rather than a loose 'nation' based on shared linguistic and cultural traditions, came into being and the desire for reunification of all Somali-inhabited regions became an important issue.

The desire for reunification had been partly fuelled by the British. They not only ruled northern Somalia but also controlled the Ogaden areas of Haud and Bale (part of Ethiopia but under British military rule after the defeat of the Italians) and the Northern Frontier District of Kenya, which had a largely Somali population. In the run up to decolonisation, the British toyed openly with the idea of joining all the Somali-inhabited areas together in a 'Greater Somalia'. This would mean refusing to hand Haud and Bale back to Ethiopia and detaching the NFD from Kenya. Both Haile Selassie and the Kenyan nationalists objected strongly to the scheme and it was quietly shelved, but not before it had excited considerable interest among the small Somali political elite.

The idea of a greater Somalia really came to the fore in the immediate aftermath of independence. Independence was granted in 1960 by both Britain and Italy. In a rather hasty and poorly-planned operation, the colonial rulers withdrew and the two portions of the country were joined together as a single state. While this was clearly the desire of most Somalis, it created a number of serious problems. Firstly, the location of the capital. There were two possible choices – Mogadishu in the formerly Italian south or Hargeisa in the formerly British north. Mogadishu won the day, to the anger and resentment of northern Somalis and the clans resident around Hargeisa. The town lost its previous importance as an economic and administrative centre. Furthermore, the political elite was divided into Italian and British educated groups, as was the army. A second problem was the lack of a major nationalist party or movement as had existed in a large number of African states prior to independence. As Lewis has pointed out: 'The Somalis have always constituted a nation, but political nationalism was absent largely because of the divisive forces within the nation; it was only after political partition that the way was opened towards the formation of a Somali nation-state' (Lewis, 1963, p. 147).

A longer period of preparation for unification and independence could have lessened the internal conflicts which followed independence. The conflicts were not just between the two halves of Somalia but also between the large number of competing clans. Political parties were formed around clan and local loyalties rather than political or national ones. This meant that the political system was fragmented and unstable. The first elections led to the formation of a weak government dependent on support from a wide array of parties and interest groups. In domestic terms they had conflicting aims and constituencies, but there was one issue that united the vast majority of them – the creation of a Greater Somalia. The national flag demonstrated the agreement on the pursuit of reunification of all areas claimed to be Somali – it consisted of a five pointed star, one point for each of British Somaliland, Italian Somaliland, French Somaliland (Djibouti), Ogaden and the Kenyan NFD. In the face of almost insurmountable internal divisions, irredentism became the cement that held together the Somali nation. In this way, Somalia, in Chris Clapham's view, has been very different from other African states whose 'boundaries have been as given and the national mission has been to construct some sense of identity among those peoples who chanced to find themselves within them. For the Somalis, the sense of nationhood has been taken as given and the national mission has been to expand the formal boundaries of the state to encompass all those peoples who already identified themselves as Somali' (Clapham, 1986, p. 255). And the expansion of the state boundaries was intended not just to include the restoration (as the Somalis saw it) of the Ogaden to Somalia, but also the NFD of Kenya. This of course laid the foundations for lasting conflict between Somalia and its neighbours and for extensive and persistent foreign intervention in the region.

Guerrilla warfare and inter-state conflict in the Horn

Ethiopia's ruthless and single-minded destruction of the federation with Eritrea had the obvious result of driving the Eritrean people (initially the Muslim population, but eventually the majority of the Christians too) into political and then armed struggle against the Empire. Muslim Eritreans started to organise politically to fight Ethiopia prior to the 1962 annexation. In 1958, Muslims in exile in the Arab world came together in Cairo to form the Eritrean Liberation Movement (ELM). It established cells inside Eritrea and tried to lay the groundwork for armed opposition to Ethiopian rule. But the movement had no clear programme and its attempts at organisation took place amid harsh repression of those who opposed the Emperor's policies. The movement was also opposed by other leading Eritrean Muslims in exile, notably in Cairo. They refused to join the ELM and Idris Mohammed Adam, a future leader of the

Eritrean Liberation Front (ELF), started a campaign of criticism of the ELM. The disarray among the Eritrean nationalists weakened the movement and made it easier for the Ethiopians to contain it.

The ELF itself was founded in 1960 following meetings in Cairo and Saudi Arabia. It drew greater support from the exiled Eritrean community in the Arab world and from the Arab states. It immediately began to compete with the ELM for influence over Eritrean nationalists. Both the ELM and the ELF claimed responsibility for the start of the armed struggle in Eritrea, even though it was started by a third group which had no direct contacts with the existing movements. The fighting started in the Barka region of Eritrea in 1961. It was initiated by Hamid Idris Awate, who has been described as a 'veteran outlaw' (Markakis, 1988, p. 55) and as a former NCO in the Sudanese army who took the initiative to form his own guerrilla group (Selassie, 1980, pp. 62–3).

But the ELF, even though it did not directly participate in Awate's action, was able to capitalise on the start of the fighting. It sent cadres to join Awate's men, whose numbers had increased as Eritreans deserted from the police and also from the Sudanese army. All the elements came together to form a guerrilla army under ELF command. The weapons from the struggle came from the deserters, from the Ethiopians and from supportive Arab states. Syria and Iraq were initially the most important sources of aid. Both supplied arms to the ELF and trained their guerrillas, whose numbers had reached the thousand mark by 1965. More importantly, as the southern rebellion in Sudan progressed in the late 1960s, the Sudanese government chose to give help and provide rear bases for the Eritreans to counteract the support given to the Anyanya rebels by the Ethiopians. Other Arab states such as Saudi Arabia and Kuwait gave financial help to the ELF, particularly after it became known that the Israelis were assisting the Ethiopian forces, notably by training units in counter-insurgency methods and by helping to establish commando units (Ottaway, 1982, p. 29).

But despite the receipt of aid and the growth in size of the guerrilla forces, the ELF did not make a major impact on Ethiopian control of Eritrea. One reason for this was that the ELF remained a predominantly Muslim organisation. Its members came mainly from the Western lowlands and its political outlook was strongly pro-Arab. The ELF leader, Idris Mohammed Adam, was outspokenly hostile towards the Eritrean Christians, blaming them for their support for union with Ethiopia. Because of the limited nature of the ELF membership, the front was unable to make any headway in establishing a presence in the populous and economically important highlands. The front's failures became a source of dissension within its ranks, notably in the late 1960s as increasing numbers of radical former students joined the organisation. Their Marxist leanings and desire for more militant and ideological policies led to growing factionalism. The factionalism increased as more support was gained from countries such as China and Cuba, which began supplying arms and training in 1966 and 1967, respectively. Cadres who were trained in China and Cuba saw the need for greater political education and direction and for the need to carry out extensive political groundwork before trying to establish guerrilla groups in new areas. They also opposed the sectarian and anti-Christian outlook of the leadership. The need to change this outlook was demonstrated in the Kassala guerrilla zone when a Muslim guerrilla leader accused Christian members of his unit of failing to carry out their duties. In the absence of the Christian zone commander, he executed 27 of them. On his return, the zone commander and other Christian members of the unit defected to the Ethiopians (Markakis, 1988, p. 58).

The conflict within the front came to a head in 1968, when ELF political commissars trained in China demanded the dissolution of the existing zonal system of command and the formation of a single command structure. After meetings with the exiled political leadership, changes were agreed and a central command was set up inside Eritrea. But this did not solve the problem of factionalism. Radical and conservative groups broke away from the ELF in late 1968, the former establishing the People's Liberation Forces (PLF) under Osman Saleh Sabbe. Christian cadres also broke away after another round of anti-Christian purges, in which as many as 300 Christian ELF members were tortured and shot (Markakis, 1988, p. 59). Some of the Christians joined Sabbe's PLF, while others set up their own small guerrilla group in the Asmara region.

The state of fragmentation reduced the effectiveness of the Eritreans and rendered useless the growing material aid from Cuba, China, Libya and other Arab states. The continuing supply of foreign aid, and notably the decision by Colonel Qadhafi of Libya to give extensive help to Sabbe, prompted Sabbe to announce the formation of the ELF–PLF in January 1972. Two years earlier, other factions from the ELF and from previously unaligned groups joined together to form the Eritrean People's Liberation Front (EPLF) – which had a strong Christian representation and an overtly pro-Marxist ideology. The EPLF received support from Sudan, the People's Democratic Republic of Yemen, China and Cuba (Selassie, 1980, p. 65). The formation of the ELF–PLF and the EPLF led to internecine fighting with the overall Eritrean nationalist movement, with the ELF almost ending its war against the Ethiopians in order to attack its fellow Eritreans.

But despite the relative impotence of the Eritrean movements as a result of the in-fighting, the existence of the different guerrilla groups served to tie down a large portion of the Ethiopian army and to increase the imperial regime's defence budget. The secessionist war in Eritrea was one factor in the military and civilian discontent which led to the 1974 revolution, though the revolution did not end the Eritrean war, in fact it led to an escalation of efforts on both sides to reach a military solution (see later chapters on the Horn of Africa after the revolution). The continuation of the war in the late 1960s and early 1970s necessitated ever greater Ethiopian reliance on foreign military help. The Ethiopians relied on the Americans (who in the 1950s had taken over from the British as the main providers of military hardware and training for the imperial army) to supply modern weapons and to train the officer corps and military technicians.

Another factor which served to reinforce Ethiopian military dependence on the USA was the ever present threat of Somali irredentism. Although at times the Ethiopians clearly exaggerated the threat in order to get more military aid, it was a very real threat.

Within a year of Somalia gaining independence its forces had launched attacks on Ethiopia in an attempt to press the case for the return of the Ogaden. The 1961 attacks were low-level and only resulted in skirmishes between Somali irregular forces and the Ethiopian garrison in the Ogaden. But in 1964, a short war took place along the Somali–Ethiopian border after another push into the Ogaden by the Somalis, this time using regular army units. The war which followed was short and sharp and resulted in very serious reverses for the Somalis. The Ethiopians were able to repel the attacking forces and to push into Somali territory. The commander of the Ethiopian third division (and later a short-lived leader of the post-revolutionary regime), General Aman Michael Andon, called on the Ethiopian government to let the army push on to Mogadishu (something which was within its powers). The request was refused and the conflict was brought to an end through Sudanese mediation (Ottaway, 1982, p. 24).

The military adventures by Somalia and the formation under Somali patronage of the Western Somali Liberation Front (WSLF) made concrete the rhetoric of the Somali government on the recovery of the 'lost' territories. Somali government statements and publications made it clear that despite the setbacks in the first two attempts to take back the Ogaden, the claims had not been dropped and that the Somali state would refuse to accept the colonial borders and, effectively, the OAU decision in 1964 that existing borders should be observed (Somali Ministry of Foreign Affairs, 1965). The Somalis also kept up the pressure for the return of the NFD from Kenya. This pressure took the form of attempts at insurrection in the NFD by ethnic Somalis armed and supported financially by Mogadishu and by the use of irregular forces, known by the Kenyans as shiftas, to undermine government control of the NFD (Castagno, 1964, p. 176). Although the campaign was a cause of serious concern to the Kenyans and forced them to maintain large garrisons of troops and paramilitary police in the NFD, the shifta problem never became a serious threat to the Kenyatta government and it was successfully contained. The revolt petered out when the Shermarke/Egal government launched its regional detente initiative.

But the Ogaden conflict was not destined to be dealt with so easily. The WSLF was used by the Somali government as a means of keeping alive the military side of the conflict with Ethiopia, though the WSLF was never totally under Somali control. The front recruited members in the Ogaden and among the Somalis who had left the area rather than stay under Ethiopian rule. In the mid to late 1960s, the WSLF launched a guerrilla campaign in the Ogaden, attacking isolated police and army posts and other government facilities. Low-level clashes occurred with the Ethiopian army. The area which was most problematic for the Ethiopians was Bale. There a Somali revolt had started in 1963 and been escalated the following year when Oromo groups in the area started their own revolt against the Ethiopians. The two revolts became linked and the Oromos cooperated closely with the WSLF (for a long time the WSLF was referred to as the Western Somali and Somali Abo Liberation Front, the Somali Abos being the Oromos). The Bale revolt continued for five years, with much of the region falling under rebel control. The rebellion fizzled out in 1970 following major Ethiopian offensives and the crackdown on the WSLF by the Somali military regime following the 1969 coup. In the wake of the coup, almost the whole WSLF leadership was imprisoned by the Barre regime (Halliday and Molyneaux, 1981, p. 76). The resulting disruption of the WSLF effort and the success of the Ethiopian campaign more or less ended the rebellion. The main Bale rebel leader, Waku Gutu (an Oromo) surrendered to the Ethiopians in 1970. The survivors of the Oromo rebel group later formed the Ethiopian National Liberation Front, a group whose aim was to unite Ethiopian minorities rather than to secede from Ethiopia. The WSLF was not destroyed by the regime's actions, but was rendered ineffective for some years, though scattered guerrilla groups survived in the Ogaden and the Somali government continued to press its claims to the area.

The Eritrean and Somali-Ethiopian conflicts became even more intensive and bloody after the 1974 revolution, but even before then they had led to an expansion of foreign military involvement in the region, which set the scene for the interventions which took place in 1977. The principal foreign actors in the drama were the United States and the Soviet Union. They took over from the former colonial powers as the chief backers of the contending forces (though the French did remain part of the equation by holding on to Djibouti and by stationing significant military forces there, which remained after independence and proved a deterrent to Somali ambitions as well as a vital part of the French strategic presence in Africa).

The United States' interest in the region developed in the 1950s as the Ethiopian dissatisfaction with the British became evident. The British had had the strongest foreign presence in Ethiopia for decades and was the chief supplier of arms and training for the armed forces. British forces spearheaded the liberation of the country from Italian occupation and then occupied Eritrea and Haud. It was British policy towards Haud and the brief flirtation with the idea of a Greater Somalia that began to turn the Emperor away from reliance on Britain. In 1951, Haile Selassie decided to dispense with the British military mission and to turn instead to the Americans; for a brief period the Norwegians and Swedes also helped to train the navy and air force, respectively (Clapham, 1986, p. 260). One factor in the growing US–Ethiopian relationship was US support for the Emperor's attempts to join Eritrea to the Empire. At the time of the UN decision on Eritrea's future, the US Secretary of State, John Foster Dulles, said: 'From the point of view of justice, the opinions of the Eritrean people must receive consideration. Nevertheless the strategic interest of the United States in the Red Sea basin and considerations of security and world peace make it necessary that the country has to be linked with our ally, Ethiopia' (cited by Firebrace and Holland, 1984, p. 19). Such bald selfishness and injustice was typical of US policy in Africa at that time and in the following thirty-five years.

The reason for US interest in the region was the communications centre built outside the Eritrean town of Asmara by the British. It had been vacated following the withdrawal of the British military mission and would provide an ideal communications link for the US armed forces and intelligence network given their growing global role. The US wanted the use of the base and in return was willing to support the Emperor's designs on Eritrea and build him a new army. An agreement for a twenty-five year lease for the base, which became known as the Kagnew base and which effectively became US territory for the period of the lease, was signed in 1953. The Ethiopians gained the income for the region from the presence of over 3,000 Americans who were resident at Kagnew (nearly 2,000 of them military personnel or civilian technicians), but more importantly got a commitment from the Americans to establish, equip and train three Ethiopian army divisions of 6,000 men each and to supply a Military Assistance Advisory Group (MAAG) to serve in Ethiopia.

The US military role increased in 1960 when the Ethiopians, fearing aggression from Somalia following its independence, called for an increase in the size of the army. At the time, the Ethiopian army, as was shown by its crushing victory in 1964, was much stronger and better trained than its Somali counterpart. The Americans would probably not have given increased aid had Kagnew not become a vital part of the global military base network and had not the Soviet Union extended trade credits worth $100m to Ethiopia the preceding year (Ottoway, 1982, p. 27). These factors influenced the Eisenhower administration into agreeing to create a fourth Ethiopian army division and to increase divisional strength to 10,000, giving Ethiopia an army of 40,000 men. A later congressional committee investigation of US aid to Ethiopia was told by an official who took part in the military aid programme that the decision to escalate military assistance was an effort to 'outbid the Soviets' (US Congress, 1970, p. 1917). Between 1953 and 1963, the USA gave Ethiopia military aid worth $73m.

The increase in the US role in Ethiopia was clearly an attempt to prevent the Soviet Union, which had just 'discovered' Africa, from gaining a foothold in Ethiopia and from endangering US use of Kagnew. But the US did not make any serious attempt to keep the Soviets out of Somalia. Immediately on independence, the Somali government sought to build a new army, and an army whose stated role was the recovery of the 'lost territories'. But the Somalis were too open about the possible use of force to recover the Ogaden, Djibouti and the NFD. This put Western governments, who were the first to be approached, off the idea of giving extensive military aid. The first Somali government approached Britain and Italy and then West Germany and the USA. They all refused requests for help in building an army whose size could only be justified by plans for aggressive action. The USA, West Germany and Italy made a combined offer to assist in the establishment of a force totalling 5,000–6,000 men at a cost of $10m. This was turned down by Somalia. Then, the Soviet Union put forward an offer to provide aid amounting to $30m and to equip and train a force of 10,000 men. At the same time, Somalia reached an accord with a number of Western governments on the training and equipping of the police force.

The Soviet offer led to the signing of a military assistance agreement in October 1960, which included the provision of MiG–15 aircraft and T–34 tanks. The offer was made without strings, although the Soviets did not openly support Somalia's irridentist amibitions. During the 1964 Somali–Ethiopian war, the Soviet government of Nikita Khrushchev offered to mediate (Patman, 1982, p. 46). The Soviet aid continued after the war, as did US aid to Ethiopia. By 1970, the Soviets had built an army of 12,000 men and supplied Somalia with 150 tanks. This gave it an edge in equipment, if not in men or the standard of training, over Ethiopia; although the Americans had sent Ethiopia F–5 fighter aircraft in 1966. The US decision was again an indication of the importance of Kagnew and the desire to outdo the Soviets (Lefebrve, 1987, p. 470).

The Soviet role in Somalia was important from a military point of view but had little effect on Somali political or economic developments. The country remained essentially pro-Western in foreign policy and utilised Soviet aid purely and simply to achieve a national aim – the recovery of the other Somali inhabited territories. The Somalis wanted a large army and the Soviet Union was the only state willing to provide it – 'the Soviets did not convince the Somalis to build a strong army. Rather the Somali government, having decided to build up its armed forces, shopped around until it found a foreign power willing to go along with its decision' (Ottaway, 1982, p. 39).

At the time of the coup in Somalia, the Soviet Union was important militarily but did not have great influence, even over the officer corps. The coup came about not, as some have suggested (Payton, 1980), at Soviet prompting or with Soviet support, but as a result of growing Somali dissatisfaction, both within and outside the army, with the Shermarke–Egal policy of regional detente, with the perception that the government had rigged the 1969 elections and with the increasingly chaotic political scene. The current Somali Ambassador to Britain, Ahmed Jama Abdullah, who was a senior provincial official during the elections and the coup, told the author in London in August 1989, that the people had become dissatisfied with the corruption and ineffectiveness of the government and the political system. He said that the existence of over sixty parties during the elections created chaos and ensured that the outcome would not be conducive to firm and well-directed government. He said that the military saw itself as the best placed national institution to rescue the country from its plight. To that one could add the fact that by pursuing regional detente and effectively dropping the claims to Somali territories, the Shermarke–Egal government had taken away the army's primary function.

The coup took place on 21st October 1969 following the assassination of President Shermarke. A Supreme Revolutionary Council took power under the leadership of Major–General Mohammed Siad Barre. Although receiving the effective support of the population in the wake of the coup, the armed forces had not carried out a popular uprising in the name of the people, let alone a revolution. Rather, as Marina Ottaway has identified, the coup must be seen against 'the background of a divided society suddenly deprived of the irridentist cause that had served as a unifying factor and of an army disproportionately large for the size of the country deprived of a raison d'etre' (Ottaway, 1982, p. 41).

The result of the coup was a reinstatement of irridentism, though also an effort to maintain good relations with neighbouring states. The Barre regime made it clear that it wanted to get the territories back, but it made no immediate threats of the use of military force to achieve this. In fact, it was under Barre that the WSLF leadership was imprisoned. But the coup did lead to the massive expansion of the armed forces and of Soviet–Somali relations. The two clearly went hand in hand. The Somalis could only get the military assistance it wanted from the Soviet Union, while for Moscow, Somalia offered a foothold in the Horn of Africa and a chance to influence political developments under the new regime. The latter was only possible because of the direction the Barre regime chose a year after the coup. As with the staging of the coup, there is no evidence that the Soviet Union had a role in pushing Barre towards the announcement that the regime would base its policies on 'scientific socialism'. The decision appears solely to have been a reaction to the lack of ideological direction under previous governments, the need to get increased Soviet economic and military aid and the poor chances of attracting Western aid, given the strong and growing US role in Ethiopia.

It was following adoption of Marxism–Leninism that the Soviet Union influenced Barre to form a socialist party, which Soviet party officials and theorists helped to establish and educate. And it was after the adoption of socialism that Barre requested a significant increase in Soviet aid. In the years after the coup, Soviet aid multiplied and the army more than doubled in size to 25,000, while large numbers of tanks and aircraft were provided. By the mid-1970s, the Soviet Union was giving at least ten times the level of military aid agreed under the 1963 treaty. Estimates put total Soviet aid in the 1970s at between $300m and $1bn. Over 2,500 Soviet military advisers went to Somali and 2,400 Somali soldiers and airmen were trained in the USSR (Patman, 1982, p. 47). The Somali army was equipped with 150 T–34 tanks, 100 T–54 tanks, and 300 MiG aircraft (from the old MiG–15s to modern MiG–21s). The army became one of the best equipped in Africa. In return, the Soviet Union was permitted to build naval and air reconnaissance facilities at Berbera. These enabled Moscow to compete with Washington in the Indian Ocean, where the Western powers had a much larger military presence. The Soviet Union was at the time expanding its naval presence around the world and its ability to project military power abroad. Berbera was a very useful facility for surveillance of US military activities in the Red Sea, the Gulf and the Indian Ocean and for increasing the reach of Soviet forces. The rationale behind the Soviet policy, which later involved the Soviet Union deeply in Angola and Ethiopia, was that support for progressive forces was in line with Soviet theories of revolutionary development in the Third World and with the Soviet desire to tilt the 'correlation of forces' in its favour in military, political and economic terms (for a fuller explanation of this concept see the chapter analysing the factors behind foreign powers' decision to intervene).

Needless to say, the increase in Soviet military aid to Somalia was balanced by greater US assistance to Ethiopia. In 1973, Haile Selassie visited Washington and asked for a massive $500m military aid programme. This was clearly out of all proportion to Ethiopia's needs or its ability to absorb military hardware. But the US administration did agree to a substantial increase in military deliveries and aid. In 1974, $12.5m worth of training was provided, $11m in credits were granted and Ethiopia purchased weapons worth a further $5m. Prior to the revolution, the USA agreed to provide even more aid in 1975 ($12.5m in training, $25m in credits and cash purchases of $20m – the deliveries and provision of aid went ahead despite the overthrow of Selassie).

The increasing Soviet and US role and the large forces available to Somalia and Ethiopia, not to mention the continuation of the Eritrean secessionist struggle, ensured that the conflict in the Horn would take on ever greater proportions, with an ever larger foreign role.

The Nigerian civil war: foreign arms, but at arm's length

The opening shots of the Nigerian civil war were fired on 6th July 1967 as the federal government forces attempted to forcibly end the secession from the federation of Biafra (eastern Nigeria). The decision to use military force followed the failure of the military government of General Gowon to pressurise the eastern region of the country to accept him as head of state and his government as the legitimate one. The Biafran leader, and one time Nigerian military governor of the east, General Ojukwu, engaged in months of negotiations in 1967 in order to safeguard what he saw as the very survival of the Ibo people of eastern Nigeria and to ensure that they had a voice in the running of Nigeria. When he deemed the negotiations a failure and with enormous popular backing from the Ibo people, on 30th May 1967 he declared Biafra an independent state.

The war was solely about the government of Nigeria and about the delicate balance of power between the country's regions and peoples. There was no quarrel with neighbouring states, no boundary dispute, no argument over natural resources between neighbouring states and no cross-border ethnic problem. The conflict was purely and simply over how a country with three very distinctive regions (the Muslim, Hausa–Fulani north, the Yoruba dominated west and the Ibo dominated east) should be governed. The system inherited from Britain was inherently unstable and the legacy of colonial rule was such to esnure that what little stability there was would be short-lived.

Britain had ruled Nigeria as two separate territories – the north was ruled indirectly through its emirs and other traditional, quasi-religious leaders, while the south was under the more direct rule of the colonial authorities. This led to two very real problems. The first was that the north became very remote from the south and its rulers remained accustomed to power and privilege, while the south experienced the full system of European colonial rule and developed strong, experienced nationalist parties. The second and closely related problem was that the north remained educationally and technologically backward. Lacking a large colonial presence and the infrastructure that accompanied it, the provision of education was poor and tradition remained strong. In the south (both the Yoruba areas in the west and the Ibo ones in the east), there was better provision of education and a faster pace of economic, technological, political and social development. Although regional and ethnic loyalties remained, the people were better educated, more modern in their outlook and better organised for business and politics.

The differences between the areas became obvious as independence approached. The Yoruba and Ibo led nationalist parties called for a speedy transition to independence and gained forms of democratic self-government years in advance of independence. The north was not in a hurry to achieve independence and did not gain the early experience of party and legislative politics. The north was wary of the modernised and politically more experienced south; scared that on independence, the northern traditions and structures would lose their sway over the north and that the country would be dominated by the more developed south. The southerners, on the other hand, feared that the numerically superior north (it made up half of the population) would be able to control a unitary political system more or less permanently.

The political system drawn up under British tutelage was designed to by-pass these problems by creating a federation of three regions, each of which would have a distinct regional government, and a federal government. The make-up of the federal government would be governed by an electoral system that ensured that no single region could dominate and that no matter how strong a party was regionally, it would have to become a national party or ally itself with parties from other regions in order to gain power.

On the face of it, this system had checks and balances to prevent domination. But it required goodwill, a willingness to cooperate and agreement on very basic issues like the populations of the regions and the orderly conduct of elections. But very early on, the system began to break down. The existing tensions between the regions increased rather than declined and the north–south split developed into a north–east or, to oversimplify the ethnic nature of Nigerian politics, a Hausa–Ibo conflict. The western region's parties were torn between those who favoured alliance with the north and those who wanted to team up with the east. The level of distrust and confrontation increased with the holding of a census in 1963. This claimed to show that the north had increased its population in relation to the southern regions, thereby affecting the electoral balance within the federation. The eastern, and some western, political leaders cried foul and demanded a recount. There then followed a serious constitutional crisis in the western region which resulted in the creation of a fourth region, the mid-western region. This did nothing to lessen the north–east competition for Yoruba allegiance; it also served to heighten the divisions within the Yoruba political community.

The divisions and distrust were such that all social and civil institutions (including the civil service, parastatal bodies, the education system, the police and the army as well as political parties) became totally politicised and the whole political and administrative system moved to the brink of total disintegration (Oyediran, 1979, p. 19). Regional and ethnic loyalties blotted out any idea of national ones. The stress on inter-regional conflict meant that appointments to federal bodies and regional institutions was made on political and ethnic rather than merit grounds – the same thing occurred in the police and the armed forces. In such a situation, corruption was inevitable. The growth of corruption and nepotism further fuelled the regional battle, as each region accused the other of tribalism, favouritism and corrupt practices. Any ideas there had been before and after independence of forging national unity were lost. As the political battle escalated any idea of common interests dissolved. As Muhammadu and Haruna have argued, there was 'a lack of nationally shared values . . . [and] it is for lack of such deep-seated values transcending ethnic boundaries that questions of principle invariably get befogged and become settled along ethnic lines' (Muhammadu and Haruna, 1979, p. 25).

It was hardly likely, then, that the elections held in 1964 would go smoothly and lead to a result universally acceptable. The arrangements for the elections, the actions of the northern-led federal government and the conduct of the campaign were so controversial that the main eastern political coalition (an alliance of the leading eastern party, the NCNC, with the western Action Group and a number of minority parties) boycotted the polling. There was then controversy over the results and accusations of vote rigging. The conflict over the elections was still intense when regional voting took place in the western region in 1965. The polls were, if anything, more chaotic, corrupt and controversial than the national elections. The elections were marred by violence and political killings. The central government seemed unwilling or unable to exert any control. Many analysts believe that the fighting during the western region elections was the final straw for the army officers who carried out the January 1967 coup (Luckham, 1970, p. 77).

Amid the increasing fragmentation, many young army officers, who saw themselves as part of a national institution, decided that the Augean stables of Nigerian politics had to be cleansed. Their answer was to carry out a military coup on 15th January 1967. In the course of the coup, the Prime Minister, Tafewa Balewa, two regional prime ministers (Ahmadu Bello from the north and Chief Akintola from the west) and several leading army officers were assassinated. The army seized power with an Ibo, Major–General Ironsi, in power. Ironsi effectively hijacked the young officers coup and prevented them from putting into effect their plans to destroy the old political system with its inherent instability and corruption. Even after Ironsi took over and arrested the coup leaders, there was still the possibility that the shock to the Nigerian system rendered by the coup could prove to be beneficial. But unfortunately, the coup came to be regarded as an Ibo coup against the north rather than as a blow against corruption. And it is not surprising that it came to be seen as such. The majority of those killed by the young officers were northerners – none of them were Ibos; while the majority of those who planned the coup and then those who took over from the coup leaders were Ibos.

After the coup, Ironsi appointed military governors to take over the regions and Lagos and appointed a new army high command. Unfortunately, he maintained ethnic tensions in doing so. Each of the military governors came from the major ethnic or regional group of the region which he commanded and nothing was done to alter the northern dominance within the high command (the new army chief of staff, General Gowon, was part of the northern political camp even though he was a Tiv from the central plateau region of Nigeria). As the head of the Nigerian army's artillery and later commander of the Biafran army has argued, both before and after the coup, most of the army units and installations were in northern hands and promotion remained a political operation rather than one based on military experience or competence (Madiebo, 1980, pp. 3–11). And in the aftermath of the coup, the politicisation of the army became a serious problem. This had always been a problem, while the army was more or less kept out of politics under the Civilian government, under the rule of the army 'the military and political problems had by the middle of 1966 become inextricable, the one from the other' (Luckham, 1971, p. 298).

The continuing tension and regional conflict came to a head in May 1966 when Ironsi, in a belated and hamfisted attempt to break out of the 'regional' mould of Nigerian politics, announced the dissolution of the regions and the suspension of the independence constitution. Combined with the suspicions that the coup could have been simply an Ibo plot for national domination, this action convinced many northerners that they would soon be ruled by the Ibos. The result was a horrific wave of tribal massacres of Ibos living in the north. No attempt was made by the northern-controlled police or army units to step in to stop the murder of thousands of Ibo families – men, women and children. Some Ibo army officers based in the north attempted to step in but were prevented from doing so by northern army officers and by the northerner officer who was military governor in the region (see Madiebo, 1980, for his account of the massacres in the north, from which he escaped only with the greatest luck).

As the crisis continued, Ironsi made a half-hearted attempt to reassert his authority. In the process of doing so, he was confronted by a northern military revolt. The northern officers killed Ironsi and a northern-dominated military government took over power on 29th July 1966, with General Gowon as head of state.

Given the continuing attacks on Ibos in the north and a mass exodus of Ibos back to their homeland, the situation was hardly a good one for the eastern region. Fearing that northern domination would now be extended and that the program against Ibos would continue, the Ibo military governor of the eastern region, General Ojukwu, refused to recognise Gowon's government. Not surprisingly Gowon tried to impose his rule and to force Ojukwu into accepting the north's fait accompli. But even Gowon had to admit that the legacy of distrust and violence was such that Nigeria was in mortal danger of disintegration. On 1st August he said on federal radio in Lagos that 'the basis for unity is not there' (Lagos home service, 1st August 1966). His answer was not to seek reconciliation but to press for a redivision of the country. The new military government announced the splitting of the country into twelve regions. Although the north was to be sub-divided along with the other three regions, the easterners saw it as a means of splitting the east and subjecting it to outside control. There was also the suspicion that as the oil industry in the east was becoming a major source of income, the northerners wanted to ensure federal (and in Ibo minds for federal read northern) control of the foreign earnings.

The army, like the political system before it, became increasingly polarised and any idea of cohesion was swept aside and when it 'was lost the nation was on the verge of disintegration' (Luckham, 1971, p. 298). And the talks between the military government and the east were unable to stop the process of disintegration. The result was the announcement of the eastern region's secession and the formation of the state of Biafra on 30th May and the start of the fighting on 6th July.

Although the war became the 'biggest, best-weaponed and bloodiest war in the whole history of black Africa' (Kirk-Green, 1971, vol 2, p. 462), it was a matter of small-scale offensives and skirmishes between lightly-armed troops to begin with. As the conflict escalated, it became a desperate fight by the poorly-armed Biafran army to resist the series of thrusts launched by the increasingly well-armed federal forces and to survive the ever-tightening blockade on land and at sea. It was clear almost from the beginning that Biafra had little chance of ultimate military victory given the disparity in size between the opposing armed forces and the decision of Britain and the Soviet Union to sell weapons, ammunition and other war material to the Nigerian federal government. All the Biafrans could hope to do was keep fighting long enough to wrest a political solution and concessions from General Gowon. But the poor showing of their army and the inevitability of military defeat meant that Gowon was under little pressure to concede anything to the Biafran leader, General Ojukwu. Contrary to many Western assessments, the Biafran army was not well led, though it was highly-motivated. The system of command, far from being well-developed (IISS Strategic Survey, 1969, p. 69; Porter, 1984, p. 91), was chaotic and far too dependent on the whims of Ojukwu (see Madiebo, 1980, for his account of the lack of a Biafran command structure and the constant interference in military decisions by Ojukwu's entourage).

At first Biafra kept going through the momentum of popular support for secession and through use of oil earnings which reached the region prior to the start of the war. The French were said to have sent £7m to Biafra in December 1966 (Muhammadu and Haruna, 1979, p. 34). But it soon became short of funds, weapons and ammunition. At the start of the war on arms embargo had been imposed by a number of European states and the USA. This affected Biafra more than the federal forces, as the latter had access to most of the existing arms and was able to buy more sophisticated weapons from Britain and the Soviet Union during the course of the war. The Biafrans had to rely on what they could capture and what could be purchased from international arms dealers. But in August 1968, France, which politically supported Biafra, reversed its embargo decision and started supplying arms to the Biafran forces. The decision to do so led to the provision of around 300 tons of weapons and ammunition in September and October 1968, an action which in the view of one commentator, prevented the imminent collapse of the Biafran state and 'helped to lengthen the period of the war by more than one year, a year within which the agony of malnutrition and starvation reached its peak among the civilian population in rebel areas' (Dudley, 1973, p. 207). France remained Biafra's main source of arms, although South Africa, Portugal and Israel are also thought to have sent small quantities to Ojukwu's army (Muhammadu and Haruna, 1979, p. 43). Ojukwu also sought to bolster his forces through the use of foreign mercenaries. It's not known exactly how many fought on the Biafran side, but it is clear that at times they played a role in leading Biafran special forces, notably in raids on Nigerian air bases. The mercenary leader in Biafra was called Steiner – and was believed to be the man who had helped the Anyanya rebels in Sudan. A number of British mercenaries served with the Biafran forces. However, the Biafran army commander, Alexander Madiebo, does not think that they added to Biafra's fighting capabilities. Rather, he feels that on occasions they weakened the forces and subjected the Biafran government to blackmail (Madiebo, 1980, p. 271).

The federal government did not suffer the same arms shortages that afflicted the Biafrans. They were able to purchase arms openly from Britain. The British say that they supplied only 15 per cent of Biafra's military needs, but critics of the British arms deliveries disagree. Suzanne Cronje says that the real figure could be as high as 45 per cent (Cronje, 1972, pp. 54–8 and 385–93). When the British refused to supply modern fighter and bomber aircraft and heavy artillery, the Gowon regime looked to the Soviet Union, which had expressed its willingness to give military assistance. The result was that the Soviet Union started supplying modern MiG fighters and then Ilyushin bombers. The fighters arrived during late 1967 and the bombers in 1968. The provision of the latter enabled the federal government to bomb the shrinking Biafran enclave (causing heavy civilian casualties).

The aircraft were a major boost to the Nigerian war effort, giving the federal government total control of the air. As Madiebo has pointed out, the Nigerian air attacks had a 'real effect on the course of the war'. He believed that Egyptian pilots were used to fly the Soviet planes (Madiebo, 1980, p. 189). There is no evidence to back up his contention; though Bruce Porter wrote that there had been reports of Egyptian mercenaries and East German pilots flying combat missions for the federal government (Porter, 1984, p. 106). The former Biafran army commander also believes that the Soviet supply of 122mm guns to Gowon had a major military impact – he said that 'when we reached the stage where the Nigerians had the guns and we had not, they simply overran our territory' (Madiebo, 1980, pp. 349 and 377).

The Soviet Union also assisted Nigeria economically during the war, agreeing to a $140m economic and technical assistance package in November 1968 – the deal may have included credits for arms purchases (Porter, 1984, p. 99). This was more than hinted at by the Soviet government newspaper *Izvestiya* when reporting the deal. It said that the Nigerian government had hard tasks ahead of it in building national unity and developing the economy, 'Soviet–Nigerian cooperation on a mutually beneficial basis is called upon to contribute to the successful fulfilment of these tasks. These are especially complex at the present time for Nigeria, it being in need of war material to defend its national unity and territorial integrity' (*Izvestiya*, 24th November 1968). Between the start of the war in 1967 and the Biafran surrender on 15th January 1970, the Soviet Union supplied six MiG–15s, thirty-six MiG–17s, two MiG–19s, four or five Sukhoi Su–7s, Ilyushin 28 bombers, an unknown number of armoured cars, 122mm howitzers and small arms and ammunition (Stevens, 1976, p. 185; Porter, 1984, p. 103; and SIPRI, 1975, p. 246). At least 170 Soviet and East European military advisers were sent to Nigeria to help in the integration of the weapons into the Nigerian armoury. Total Soviet arms supplies have been estimated at $15m in 1970 prices (McLane, 1974, p. 106); not huge but enough to have a strong influence on the course of the war, particularly the effective creation of a modern air force and the provision of heavy artillery. Some observers (notably Porter, 1984, pp. 104–5 and 111–12), have questioned the importance of Soviet supplies (given Britain's provision of fifty tanks, which were used to spearhead offensives, and naval craft which ensured the sea blockade and enabled the capture of Port Harcourt and Calabar), but the testimony of the Biafran army commander and the opinions of leading Nigerian analysts (see for example Ogunbadejo, 1976), suggest that the Soviet contribution to the war effort should not be underestimated.

The war ended in January 1970 with the surrender of the Biafran armed forces. The fighting and the blockade had cost over one million lives (mainly Biafran civilians who starved to death). Apart from the presence of some mercenaries on both sides, the fighting was carried out by Nigerians and Biafrans, there was no direct foreign intervention. Foreign arms supplies (or the lack of them) were crucial to the result of the war.

4 The war in Chad: France and Libya fight it out

It would be impossible here to provide a detailed and full account of the war in Chad, which has now been in progress for over twenty years. Instead, my analysis of the Chadian situation will concentrate on the roles of Libya and France, to a much lesser extent because of their much more limited role, the Soviet Union and Cuba. In Chad, one can see the open manifestation of Qadhafi's hegemonistic aims and the use of all possible means, from diplomatic ones to the overt use of armed force, to achieve his goals. One can also see the extent of African opposition to Qadhafi's policies and Libya's limited capacity to achieve its objectives.

Hostility between the peoples inhabiting the northern and southern regions of what is now Chad and interference from the area that is now Libya are centuries old. Prior to colonisation of the area by the French in the 19th and 20th centuries, the Muslim people of northern Chad frequently raided the south to seize slaves for sale on the Mediterranean littoral. The northerners also controlled the southern end of the trans-Sahara caravan routes, which dominated trade between North Africa and areas south of the desert. Much of this trade, particularly in the mid and late 19th century, was controlled by the Sanussi Order, which controlled Libya prior to the Italian conquest. The Sanussi came to exert much influence over northern Chad as far down as the northern end of Lake Chad. This influence was only ended by French colonisation of Equatorial Africa.

When Chad was granted independence by France in 1960, the non-Muslim southerners were placed in positions of power – politically and within the army and civil service – by the withdrawing colonial power. This was strongly resented by the northern Muslims, many of whom had fought the French for decades into the 20th century. The French, fearing a northern backlash against southern dominance, maintained significant forces in the Bourkou-Ennedi-Tibesti (BET) area of northern and eastern Chad until 1965. This greatly assisted President Tombalbaye, a Sara from the south of the country, in entrenching his power without undue opposition from the north. Using his mainly southern Chadian armed forces he made Chad into a one-party state and repressed harshly any manifestations of anti-government activity. Chadian Muslims were on the receiving end of this repression in 1965 when Muslim peasants in central Chad rose in revolt against heavy taxation and against the southern tax collectors. By 1967, most of the government officials had been forced out of the area. The tax revolt coincided with risings in the north following the withdrawal of the French forces. The Chadian troops who replaced the French in the BET area acted like an army of occupation and roused strong opposition from the chiefly nomadic tribes of northern Chad. Attempts to force the nomads to settle in permanent dwellings led to rioting in Bardai in the far north. After a southern soldier was killed in the disturbances, the government carried out mass arrests of perceived opponents in the north. In 1965, the Tebu Derde of Tibesti fled to Libya with 1,000 followers. In 1968, amid continuing repression and resistance in the north, the mainly Tebu Nomad Guards mutinied in Aouzou and attacked a garrison controlled by southern forces. The growing rebellion in the BET regions forced Tombalbaye to call for French military assistance. In return for limited military help, the French forced Tombalbaye to introduce Muslim ministers into his government for the first time since 1963. With French help, the BET rebels were driven out of many of the areas which they had controlled, although they were not defeated completely. Many of the rebels withdrew into desert areas or retreated into Libya, where they received a little aid from the regime of King Idris.

In 1971, most of the French troops were withdrawn and Tombalbaye again came under pressure from northern rebels and also from opponents in the south. Under Qadhafi, Libya had increased aid to the Front de Liberation Nationale (Frolinat), which had been formed by northern rebels on 22nd June 1966, although Libya's attitude to the movement was ambivalent. Libya supported it against the non-Muslim southerners but was keen to see a weak, destabilised Chad rather than a strong unified Chad, whether under southern or Frolinat control. One reason for this was Qadhafi's intention to seize control of the Aouzou Strip, which runs along the Libya-Chad border. Libya lays claim to ownership of the Strip, basing its claim on an unratified Franco–Italian treaty of 1935. Chad, which controlled the Strip when the country became independent in 1960, says that as the treaty was never ratified, the borders existing at the time of independence are the correct ones – it has received implicit backing on this from the OAU, which holds the borders established under colonial rule to be the legitimate ones.

Even at this early stage of the conflict, Frolinat was split into a large number of factions. Libya at first threw it support behind Abba Siddiq, who at one stage had been one of the few prominent Muslim politicians within Tombalbaye's Parti Progressiste Tchadien (PPT). Siddiq was willing to support Frolinat's armed struggle but based his policies on national reconciliation. This suited the Libyans who were wary of northern Chadian groups which favoured secessionism – something which would ensure that the groups would oppose Libyan control of Aouzou. The Libyan regime hoped to be able to help Siddiq build a unified liberation movement that would be willing to bow to Libyan demands over Aouzou. But Frolinat was split along political and ethnic lines – with the movement's First Liberation Army controlled mainly by Arabic groups from central Chad; the Second Liberation Army, which came to be known as the Armed Forces of the North (FAN), was controlled by the Tebu of the Tibesti mountains and the BET plains. Siddiq had the support of the First Army but not the Second. The Second Army or FAN was led by Goukouni Oueddei, the son of the Tebu Derde. Siddiq and the Libyans attempted to unify the Frolinat forces at a meeting at Sebha in Libya in August 1971. When this failed, the Libyans imprisoned Goukouni. He was released in late 1972, by which time FAN had come under the control of Hissein Habre, a member of the Anakaza clan of the Bourkou Tebu. Goukouni became second-in-command of FAN but was never able to cooperate with Habre.

Open Libyan support for Frolinat caused the Chadian government to protest strongly and to break off diplomatic relations in August 1971, accusing the Libyans quite accurately of seeking to subvert an internationally recognised government. Qadhafi responded by giving official recognition to Frolinat, in return for which Tombalbaye threatened to support exiled Libyan political groups opposed to Qadhafi. However, the Libyan wish to purchase modern Mirage combat aircraft from France led to reconciliation with Tombalbaye and a limited period of relative tranquillity in bilateral relations. This was in the period of Qadhafi's hostility towards the Soviet Union, something which limited the possible sources of sophisticated weaponry. Because of the danger of French-supplied arms being used against a pro-French regime, the Paris government demanded some form of reconciliation between Qadhafi and Tombalbaye before the aircraft deal could go ahead.

The two leaders met in Niamey, the capital of neighbouring Niger, and reached agreement on reconciliation. A joint communique signed on 12th April 1972 provided for a resumption of diplomatic relations, the withdrawal of the Frolinat leadership from Libya (they briefly moved their HQ to Algeria) and an end to Chadian military and other links with Israel (at this time Libya in concert with other Arab League states was conducting a campaign in sub-Saharan Africa to persuade states to cut all links with Israel – the campaign was successful and all but a few states cut links). A formal treaty was signed on 23rd December 1972, when Tombalbaye paid a state visit to Libya. Not for the last time, Qadhafi had sold out allies to whom he had pledged his support. Libya's lack of faith with Frolinat was not lost on some northern leaders, notably Hissein Habre, who had already harboured strong suspicions about Libya's motives in supporting the northern revolt against the Chadian government. Under the agreement with Tombalbaye, there was tacit Chadian recognition of Libyan interest in the Aouzou Strip and Libya used this to move its troops into the Strip in 1973. As its part of the bargain, Libya officially renounced its support for Frolinat and provided financial aid worth 23bn CFA francs to Chad. The cooperation between the two governments endured for three years. In March 1974, Qadhafi visited Ndjamena and there signed an agreement for the establishment of a joint investment bank.

The period of friendly relations ended on 13th April 1975 when a group of southern military officers overthrew Tombalbaye. He was succeeded by a military regime led by General Felix Malloum – a southern career officer who was steadfastly opposed to Libyan seizure of the Aouzou Strip, which he believed to be rightfully Chadian. The Libyans attempted to establish cooperative relations with Malloum with a view to settling the Aouzou issue without further conflict. The Libyan Foreign Secretary, Dr Turayki, visited the Chadian capital soon after the coup but was rebuffed over Aouzou. Malloum's assumption of power led to attempts by Hissein Habre and Siddiq to negotiate with the new regime, as they both opposed Libyan control of Aouzou.

Malloum's seizure of power coincided with growing differences between Hissein Habre and Goukouni Oueddei. Goukouni succeeded in having Habre expelled from FAN's council of war, and the latter split from FAN taking with him around 300 troops to set up a base in eastern Chad along the border with Sudan. But despite the split in the Muslim–northern forces, the war against southern control of the country, which persisted under Malloum, continued with increasing Libyan involvement. Libyan troops were still in control of Aouzou and were able to use the strip to assist the northern forces. It was Libyan control of the Aouzou that had been at the root of the Goukouni–Habre split, the latter being totally opposed to Libyan control of territory formerly Chadian and Goukouni being willing to put up with it in the interests of prosecuting the war against Malloum. But although Libya supported Goukouni, Qadhafi was also giving military assistance to the Volcan Army, which was the successor to the First Liberation Army. But Habre received no Libyan support and in June 1976 there was fighting between Libyan forces and Habre's units in northern Chad.

The Libyan aid supplied to Goukouni was sufficient to enable him to capture much of the BET region and to seize the northern town of Bardai, which then became his headquarters. Goukouni now became the effective leader of Frolinat and he united with the Volcan Army, now controlled by the pro-Libyan Ahmed Acyl, who had ousted Siddiq. Siddiq then resumed talks with Malloum and, through the mediation of President Bongo of Gabon, reached agreement with him on participation in the government. Unfortunately for Malloum, the agreement fell apart when Siddiq tried to get agreement on a purge of the armed forces. Malloum then looked to negotiations with Habre, who was ready to make an alliance with him to fight the Libyans. The alliance was forged in 1978 and the forces of the two leaders now turned their attentions to fighting the Libyan-backed groups. However, an offensive by Goukouni, the Volcan Army and Libyan troops in 1978 put the new alliance on the defensive. Malloum and Habre were forced to call on the French for military assistance – 1,000 combat troops and advisers – in order to stave off defeat. Although the northern forces were not immediately victorious, the Ndjamena government disintegrated and fighting broke out in the capital between Malloum's and Habre's forces. But all was not well in the northern–Libyan alliance and in late 1978 it was reported that the Libyans had imprisoned Goukouni temporarily after disagreement over the ultimate fate of the Aouzou Strip, for although Goukouni was willing to turn a blind-eye to Libyan control in return for military support, his final aim was to gain control over all Chadian territory including the strip.

Despite these factional problems, the northerners were victorious over the southerners, and in February 1979 Goukouni took Ndjamena. Following pressure from Nigeria and other African states, the new government and most of the factions involved in the conflict agreed to hold reconciliation talks in Nigeria. The Kano conference of March 1979 led to further talks and the eventual formation of a shaky ten-faction coalition with Goukouni as President, Lt–Colonel

Abdelkadir Kamougoue from the south as Vice-President and Hissein Habre as Defence Minister. Although at first the Libyans had seemed to want the Kano talks to fail and put pressure on Goukouni to refuse to cooperate, eventually the Libyans supported the unstable new government. Libya clearly was not interested in a final solution to the Chadian struggle that would result in a unified central government but was happy to see an unstable coalition in power that would be unlikely to last long and to challenge Libyan control of Aouzou. In late 1979, there were indications that Libya favoured a federal solution in Chad that would weaken central authority and create a Muslim entity in the north that could be effectively controlled by Libya. Goukouni was known to be opposed to this and soon after the Kano agreement, Libya shifted most of its aid to Acyl's Volcan Army. In April 1979, Goukouni demonstrated his growing opposition to Libya by accusing Qadhafi of invading areas of Chad south of the Aouzou Strip. But the disunited government in Ndjamena was unable to take effective action to stop Libyan incursions. Qadhafi justified his role in Chad by saying that Libya had intervened to 'help the people fight against the French troops, the same right as when we intervened in Uganda against Nyerere' (*ACR*, 1978–9, p. B67).

The creation of the coalition government did not stop the fighting and there were reports of massacres of southerners in northern Chad and northerners in southern Chad. A further attempt to achieve peace was made in April 1979 when the Nigerian government convened the second Kano conference. This was doomed from the start as both Goukouni and Habre refused to allow Libya to participate because of the occupation of Aouzou and opposed the presence of Acyl on the grounds that he was supported by Libya. The result of Kano II was hardly more stable than the first coalition, as it did not now include Kamougoue, who had been reconciled with the Libyans. The head of state of the new regime was Mohamed Shawa, with Goukouni as Minister of the Interior and Habre as Defence Minister.

The absence of Kamougoue from the government meant that he now assumed a position of total opposition and with Libyan support started a war in southern Chad in May. The following month factions loyal to the different members of the coalition started fighting in Ndjamena and Libyan-backed groups, including Acyl's Volcan Army, invaded northern Chad. Goukouni's forces fought and defeated the Libyan-backed invaders at Ounianga–Kebir, Gouro, Zouar and Faya Largeau. But this provided no solution as fighting started in earnest around Ndjamena between forces loyal to Habre and those loyal to Goukouni.

Yet another peace conference was arranged by Nigeria in August 1979 – this time with the participation of Libya and Libyan–backed factions. The conference ended with the signing of the Lagos accord on 12th August 1979. Under this agreement a 12 faction coalition was formed with Goukouni as President, Kamougoue as Vice-President and with the participation of Habre, Acyl, Siddiq and other smaller factions. To Habre's annoyance, Libyan occupation of Aouzou was not discussed at the conference. Something else not solved at Lagos was the continued presence in Chad of French troops, thought to number about 2,500. Libya and its allies wanted the French removed at once. As haggling started over this issue fighting broke out once more in Ndjamena. Under the Lagos accord peace was to be kept by a Pan-African force. The first members of this force, from Congo, arrived in January 1980. Unfortunately, they were able to do little to quell the factional fighting, as a result of which the government split in two. Two cabinets came into operation in Chad, one led by Habre and the other by Kamougoue. The situation was worsened by continued Libyan manoeuvring. At this time Libya's policy in Chad was described by the Libyan second-in-command, Major Jallud. He said that any solution in Chad that did not have the active support of Libya was bound to fail; and Libya clearly wanted to keep central authority Chad weak and to encourage sympathetic factions to disrupt any attempts to regain Aouzou. But Libya had a rival in 1979 and 1980 in Nigeria, which showed a strong, if temporary, desire to control events in Chad. In early 1980, Nigerian forces joined those of Congo, although Chadians said at the time that the Nigerians behaved like an army of occupation. But the arrival of the Nigerians, like the Congolese before them, did nothing to stem the fighting.

In November 1980, a peace conference was convened at Lome, Togo, but was totally unsuccessful in reconciling the competing groups. Habre attended the conference and used it to accuse Benin, which had by then sent its troops to Chad, of using its membership of the Pan-African peacekeeping force to further Libyan aims in the country. He warned the participants in the conference that he was unwilling to accept the growing Libyan military presence in Chad. Goukouni also attended the conference and used it to give the impression of wanting all foreign forces out of Chad while in fact he had reached agreement with Libya on joint action to take control of Ndjamena. He signed an OAU-drafted statement on the withdrawal of all foreign forces from the country just as a column of 4,000–5,000 Libyans was moving south to assist him in taking the capital.

By the time that Nigeria had convened yet another conference on Chad in December 1980, Ndjamena had fallen to Goukouni and the Libyans. The new conference was attended by a number of Chadian factions plus the presidents of Nigeria, Niger, Sudan, the Central African Republic, Cameroon, Togo, Benin, Congo and Sierra Leone. Qadhafi did not attend personally but instead sent his foreign ministers. Nigeria came under intense criticism at the conference from some of the Chadian groups and most of the other presidents for not condemning Libya's interference in Chad. The meeting, became very heated with the CAR, Cameroon, Niger, Sudan and Togo demanding the immediate withdrawal of all Libyan forces from Chad. They were supported by representatives of the governments of Senegal and Guinea. Nigeria, Sierra Leone, Benin and Congo sought to tone down the criticism of Libya. Goukouni Oueddei attended and came under attack from those suspicious of Libya for taking the position that he had the sovereign right to invite Libyan intervention in Chad without consulting other groups. A compromise solution was reached which avoided naming Libya but called for the withdrawal of all foreign troops.

But the conference was really a waste of time. In its immediate aftermath, Chad and Libya announced that they had formed a union and that the two countries would be merged. This was too much even for the more pro-Libyan participants in the last Lagos conference. On 14th January 1981, the presidents of Togo, Cote d'Ivoire, Niger, Benin, Sierra Leone, Nigeria, Guinea, CAR, Senegal, Congo, Ghana and Cameroon met in Lome and condemned the planned union unanimously, declaring it a violation of the accord on the future of Chad signed in Lagos in 1979. They called on Libya to withdraw its forces and once more decided to send a Pan-African peacekeeping force. The participants also called on Chad's neighbours to refuse to let their territories be used by Chadian dissident groups. Goukouni's position on the merger announcement, made by the Libyans, was unclear. Shortly before it was made public, Goukouni had told President Shagari of Nigeria that two of his senior military commanders had gone to Libya for consultations but had then disappeared. Goukouni had then gone to Libya, where he was told that the two commanders had been killed by dissidents. He had then been told that he must agree to a merger; because of the mysterious deaths of his commanders he said that he felt in no position to refuse.

Explaining his role in Chad, Qadhafi told the Arab People's Congress in Tripoli on 20th January 1981, that 'Libya intervened militarily in Chad in response to Frolinat, ending the war which had lasted many years and resolving the conflict in Chad in the interests of the friendly forces and the people's forces, which represented Frolinat which led the armed struggle for twenty years and defeated the racist and reactionary forces and imperialism backing them'. Qadhafi claimed that Habre had been fighting for succession, backed by Sadat and Numayri – both by then sworn enemies of Libya. He went on to say that 'the war in Chad was against the Jamahiriyah [Libya] . . . we have crossed the border in self-defence when an act of force was used to impose a pro-imperialist regime hostile to the Chadian people'. On the unity agreement, he said that there was an old, historical connection between the peoples of the two countries and that the borders were effectively open. He went on to say that eastern Chad was an Arab area and that a large section of the Chadian population was Arab and Muslim and that Arabic culture prevailed in the country. In a feeble attempt to allay the fears of African states opposed to his role in Chad, he said, 'we say to all those fearful minds in Sudan, Niger and other African countries that Libyan troops only intervened after urgent and recurrent appeals. The Libyans have no intention of sending their troops abroad or engaging in anything but defensive battles' (*ACR*, 1980–81, p. A41).

This position convinced no one, as even those willing to cooperate with Libya, such as Goukouni, realised that Libyan aims were based on the desire to control Aouzou and to exert hegemony over the rest of Chad. The union attempt was a watershed in Chad in that it convinced many neighbouring African countries that Libya was pursuing an expansionist policy that could later be turned against them. This served to increase sympathy and, in some cases support, for Hissein Habre – who was the most staunchly anti-Libyan of the Chadian leaders.

After Habre's split with Goukouni and Goukouni's use of the Libyans to defeat all the opposing factions, Habre once more withdrew with his armed forces to eastern Chad, where he received support from Sudan and, it is said, Egypt. While Libyan forces were in Chad in strength, Habre's ability to defeat Goukouni militarily was limited, but his forces were able to maintain control of eastern Chad and to prepare for an eventual offensive.

Politically, Habre's position was improving because of the outcry in the OAU over the proposed Libya–Chad union. The then OAU chairman, President Stevens of Sierra Leone, condemned the merger in 1981 and said the OAU had to ensure that Chadians were able to choose their own government. This was effectively an attack on the Goukouni-led Chadian Transitional Government of National Unity (GUNT) then in power in Ndjamena. On 15th January 1981, the OAU Standing Committee on Chad called on Libya to withdraw from Chad. Libya replied a month later with a statement accusing Stevens and the OAU Committee of 'unjustifiable interference in the affairs of Chad'. The statement, issued on 15th February 1981 by the Libyan government, said that 'the withdrawal of Libyan forces from Chad can only be requested by the party which had asked for them to come. The Libyan forces entered Chad in accordance with a treaty and in accordance with a request by the President of the people of Chad.'

But the OAU, notably President Stevens and Shehu Shagari of Nigeria, continued to work for a withdrawal of Libyan forces – but they were hampered by Goukouni's refusal to ask them to withdraw. At the annual summit of the OAU in Nairobi in June 1981, a resolution was passed calling for an African peacekeeping force to be sent to Chad. Under pressure from the vast majority of OAU members, Libya agreed to this. Foreign Minister Turayki, who represented Libya at the summit, said that this was in line with Libyan policy. This effectively forced Goukouni to agree to a withdrawal and on 29th October 1981 he issued a statement requesting the Libyans to leave. To everyone's surprise, Qadhafi complied immediately. Around 10,000 Libyans had been in Chad. They were pulled back to the Aouzou Strip, adding to the garrison of 4,000 stationed there. The OAU then proceeded to send another peacekeeping force to Chad.

Habre, by then backed by France and the USA, as well as a large number of African states, took advantage of the rapid Libyan withdrawal to launch a new offensive against Goukouni. He immediately captured large areas of eastern Chad and the town of Abeche. The Zairean, Nigerian, Togolese, Senegalese, Beninois and Guinean forces were neither equipped nor prepared to fight a war on Goukouni's behalf and so they played little role in stopping either his advance or the overall escalation of fighting. Goukouni's forces, having been reliant on the Libyans, were little prepared for a new round of fighting and, in addition, were outnumbered nearly two to one by Habre's men. As a result, Habre made rapid progress. The OAU forces, meanwhile, were increasingly impotent and in June 1982 the OAU Standing Committee on Chad decided to pull them out. Lacking external support and with increasing factionalism tearing his government apart, Goukouni was defeated by Habre, who seized control of Ndjamena in early 1982. Goukouni fled north and once more consented to ally himself with the Libyans. He set up his base at Bardai, in the far north, where the Libyans re-equipped his forces and assisted him in setting up an anti-government radio station, Radio

Bardai. Goukouni would have been hard pushed to retain strong Libyan support had not Ahmed Acyl of the Volcan Army been killed in an accident.

Having regained power and elicited support from France, the USA and Sudan, Habre moved to strengthen his position. He exploited factional differences in the south to isolate the pro-Goukouni forces led by Kamougoue, who fled the south and joined Goukouni in Bardai. By the autumn of 1982, most resistance in the south had been overcome and Habre controlled most of Chad, with the exception of the far north, which was under Goukouni's control. Goukouni, with Libyan support, was temporarily able to unify the anti-Habre factions and prepared to resume the fight. Western satellites revealed in November 1982 that Libyan forces were moving south from Aouzou to assist Goukouni against Habre. Around the same time Western intelligence reports disclosed that Qadhafi had greatly increased the purchase of arms from the USSR, which had previously been declining because of the Libyan debts to the USSR, estimated at between $2–4bn. The increased deliveries were believed to be an attempt by Qadhafi to offset the deliveries of arms to Habre from France, the USA and Egypt.

African opinion on Chad at this time was ambiguous. Many states remained intensely suspicious of Libya and wanted to ensure that Libya was not allowed to use its role in Chad to expand towards sub-Saharan Africa. Others supported Libya because of the increasing French and US presence in Chad, while others preferred to stay on the sidelines. Nigeria, the state best able to influence events in the region, was suspicious of Libya but was more openly hostile to the presence of French forces in neighbouring Chad.

The expected offensive by Goukouni and the Libyans started in early 1983. They advanced south rapidly, capturing Faya Largeau and posing a serious threat to Habre. The threat was increased by an outbreak of fighting in southern Chad, in which forces led by General Negue Djogo attacked government positions and gained control of part of the important cotton-growing districts. But it was the north that was the real problem. From its base at Bardai, the Libyan-backed opposition force advanced to capture Ounianga-Kebir in March and then Gouro. Habre's forces tried unsuccessfully to counter-attack and began to look increasingly vulnerable. Goukouni was receiving strong support from Libya and, according to Kamougoue in an interview in mid-1983, from Congo, Algeria and 'especially Benin' (*New African*, June 1983, pp. 33–4). When Faya Largeau was captured on 25th June, with Habre losing an estimated 700 men in the fighting, the situation began looking increasingly bleak for him. Goukouni now had control of about a third of Chad.

But help was at hand, in the form of French financial and military aid and the arrival of a detachment of Zairean commandos; Mobutu was by far the most active of the African leaders opposed to Libya's involvement in Chad. This enabled Habre to throw more troops into the fighting against the combined forces of Goukouni, pro-Libyan factions, the Libyans themselves and the forces of Qadhafi's Islamic Legion. Reports from Sudan said that Goukouni's successes had been largely due to Libyan combat support, notably the use of the Libyan air force against Habre's defensive positions. The size of the Libyan intervention pushed France into more active support for Habre – a result also of strong lobbying on Habre's behalf by Presidents Houphouet-Boigny of Cote d'Ivoire and Eyadema of Togo. The French launched Operation Manta, under which some 2,000 French paratroops were sent to Chad. The French intervention coincided with an unsuccessful attempt by President Sassou-Nguesso to start reconciliation talks. A meeting he convened of ten African heads of state in Brazzaville on 15th August 1983 failed to have any effect on the fighting.

The arrival of the French forces, backed by the dispatch of French aircraft to Central African Republic and Gabon to give air support to Habre, stemmed the advance of Habre's opponents. Prior to the arrival of the French, Goukouni had captured Habre's former headquarters at Abeche in eastern Chad and Oum Chalouba. Once the French arrived in force, Habre recaptured Oum Chalouba, which he used as a base from which to take back Faya Largeau. The Libyans reacted with savage bombing raids against both of the recaptured towns. The Libyans used napalm and phosphorous bombs and effectively destroyed the towns, forcing Habre to evacuate them. The French aircraft then came into action attacking Goukouni's forces and the Libyans in early September. Habre then launched counter-attacks, strengthened by $12m in military aid from the USA (given partly at the request of Senegal, Cote d'Ivoire and Zaire) and 2,700 combat troops from Zaire. Although Habre was able to recapture some areas taken by Goukouni, the French would not take part in a general offensive that could lead to direct fighting with Libyan forces, and the result was a stalemate. A long lull in the fighting followed, broken by periodic clashes and the shooting down of a French Jaguar combat plane over central Chad in January following an incursion by Libyan and GUNT forces in Habre-controlled areas. The aircraft was shot down by Libyan-supplied, and possibly Libyan-operated, SAM-7 missiles. The French retaliated by pushing the frontline a hundred kilometres north from its previous position, adding to the areas under Habre's control. Soon after the clashes, Libya and France reached a tacit agreement that their forces would not engage in direct conflict. This infuriated Habre, who wanted the French to assist him in pushing the Libyans out of Chad. He also had increasing problems with the Zairean troops, who refused to take orders from any but their own officers.

In early 1984, Nigeria once more tried to intervene to promote peace in Chad. The Libyan deputy leader, Major Jallud, was invited to Lagos where he held talks with Nigerian leadership on the future of Chad and the chances for a political settlement. At the end of the talks, a communique was issued stating that neither of the warring sides in Chad had the sole right to form the government. It also called for a peaceful solution to the conflict. The talks followed closely on a visit to Nigeria by the French External relations Minister, Claude Cheysson, who called on Nigeria to assist France in finding an end to the Chadian dispute. The French and Nigerian sides agreed on the need for both French and Libyan forces to be withdrawn from Chad and for an effective international peacekeeping force to take their place. Cheysson also held talks on Chad in Ndjamena, Tripoli and Addis Ababa (*New African*, April 1984, p. 34).

Although nothing immediate resulted from the contacts, the stalemate in Chad remained unchanged and Franco-Libyan contacts continued. They resulted in a meeting in September 1984 between President Mitterrand and Colonel Qadhafi at which an agreement was signed on mutual withdrawal of forces from Chad. The French stuck to the agreement and pulled their forces out by 11th November 1984, but the Libyans violated the accord and their troops remained in northern Chad.

Soon after the French withdrawal, Habre accused the Libyans of strengthening their forces and of increasing the presence in Chad of the Islamic Legion, rather than withdrawing its forces. Against Habre's wishes, the Zaireans withdrew their soldiers from Chad, leaving Habre to face the combined GUNT and Libyan units. However, Habre did have effective political support within the OAU which ensured that he was recognised by the organisation as the legitimate President of Chad, even though the OAU continued to search for a political solution that would lead to reconciliation between Habre and Goukouni. During late 1984 and 1985, the OAU continued to search for solutions to Chad's problems without any degree of success. The chief obstacles were Libya's determination to retain the Aouzou Strip, Libya's willingness to shift its support for the Chadian factions at a moment's notice, Libya's clear intention of having a veto over any regime (such as Habre's) that is considered to be hostile and the evident personal and political hostility between Habre and Goukouni. Attempts were made to bring the opposing factions together in Mali and Congo, but there was always a last minute hitch.

Habre gained the most from the lull in the fighting, consolidating his position in the centre and south of Chad and rebuilding some of the shattered economic and administrative infrastructure. Goukouni and the GUNT fared less well. The coalition that Goukouni headed began to fall apart with some groups rejoining Habre and others just competing for Libya's favours. Goukouni only retained his position through Libyan support and through the presence in northern Chad of some 6,000–7,000 Libyan troops and members of the Islamic Legion.

In February 1986, the GUNT forces attempted to raid inside Habre's lines (south of the 16th parallel) and met with a swift and bloody rebuff. The GUNT forces had once again been supported by the Libyans, but had been no match for the increasingly well-organised Chadian army. Habre asked for the French to back him and once more French combat troops flew into Ndjamena, although they were not deployed in areas where they were likely to be involved in heavy fighting. The situation worsened when on 18th February a Libyan Tupolev bombed raided Ndjamena airport. The GUNT tried to advance again in early March but was once more beaten back.

Part of the reason for the poor performance of the GUNT forces was the internal struggle within Goukouni's coalition. The main protagonists were pro-Goukouni groups and those supporting Acheikh Bin Oumar – the successor to Acyl as head of the Volcan Army and its political wing the Revolutionary Democratic Council (CDR). Although Acheikh, like Acyl before him, was pro-Libyan, at one stage he was imprisoned by Qadhafi for trying to oppose

Goukouni. Acheikh was only released after agreeing to a formula for greater unity within GUNT worked out by representatives of all the different factions at a meeting in Cotonou, Benin, in late 1985. This agreement did little to unify the anti-Habre forces, partly because of Libya's habit of shifting its support from one faction to another according to short-term expediency.

Whatever the situation was within GUNT, it retained sufficient Libyan support to pose a continuing threat to Habre. In an interview in early 1985, the Chadian Foreign Minister, Gouara Lassou, said that Libya still wanted to make Chad its colony and was using Chadian factions to get its way. Many of the factions, he believed, did not want to help Libya but were effectively its prisoners: 'Those Chadians who are in Libya are used by Qadhafi; he employs them. They are not free any more to leave Libya. If they were in government in Ndjamena, Libya would find some other means of fostering conflict in Chad.' The Minister expressed the belief that as long as there was not a stronger power in the area, Libya would continue its attempts at expansion – 'Qadhafi wants to dominate not only Chad, but the whole of sub-Saharan Africa' (*Africa Now*, February 1985, p. 21).

At this time it was abundantly clear that the Libyan forces had not withdrawn from Chad and were still there in force, backed up by the Islamic Legion. Qadhafi strenuously denied the existence of the Legion, but Chad's Information Minister, Mahamat Soumaila, said that his government had actually captured members of the Legion, who were made prisoners of war. He said that the prisoners included men from Sudan, Benin and Senegal. They had admitted being part of the Legion and had revealed that the force was 5,000 strong and was used to supplement the Libyan regular forces.

Throughout 1985 and early 1986 efforts were made to bring the warring factions together. The then chairman of the OAU, President Diouf of Senegal, was particularly active in trying to weld together an OAU reconciliation plan. At one stage, a reconciliation plan was signed by the Habre government and factions of the GUNT after a meeting in Gabon. However, the factions were not strong enough to force the plan on the rest of the GUNT and the agreement did little other than exacerbate the growing differences between members of the GUNT.

With the failure of the peace efforts and the growing restlessness of the GUNT factions, it was clear that further outbreaks of violence, either between different GUNT factions or between Habre and the GUNT–Libyan forces were likely. By mid to late 1985, it was believed that the Libyans had reinforced their deployments in Aouzou and in northern Chad and had over 7,000 regular troops in northern Chad backed by 300 tanks, sixty aircraft and members of the Islamic Legion – the Libyan force greatly outnumbered the GUNT troops who numbered only a few thousand and were poorly armed. But sections of the GUNT were beginning to chafe at Libyan control of their struggle against Habre. In September 1985, the Ndjamena government reported that dissident GUNT forces under a senior officer of the pro-GUNT Armed Forces of Chad (FAT) had attacked Libyan positions at Faya Largeau, leaving several hundred dead. It was clearly in Habre's interests to spread reports of fighting between the Libyans and their proteges, however independent observers also reported fighting within the anti-Habre alliance. Habre's Information Minister said that the fighting was an indication of the 'ever increasing explosive relations' between the 'slave-dealer regime of Tripoli' and the Chadian rebels (Ndjamena home service, 7th September 1985). Habre's government said that the Libyans had established their headquarters in Chad at Ouadi Doum, 400 kilometres south-east of the Aouzou Strip. where they had constructed an airfield large enough to receive the huge Ilyushin-76 supply aircraft sold to the Libyans by the Soviet Union. The Ndjamena government said that the airfield was used as a staging post for arms and ammunition dropped by plane to pro-Libyan forces operating against Chad along its southern borders with the Central African Republic and Cameroon. In one of its few attacks on the USSR, the government said that Soviet and East German technicians were assisting the Libyans in their operations against Habre. There is no firm evident that the Soviet Union actively assisted the Libyan forces inside Chad, but the hundreds of Soviet and eastern bloc advisers and technicians working with the Libyan armed forces and helping them maintain Soviet-supplied weapons and equipment will have given invaluable assistance to the Libyans in their support for the troops inside.

The level of hostility between Habre and the Libyans showed no sign of subsiding, despite the peace efforts. In mid-September 1985, Ndjamena radio, run by the Habre government, stated in no uncertain terms its view of the Libyan role in Chad:

As we can see what is at stake is very important and the megalomaniac Libyan thinks that one day he will have the opportunity to invade Chad and carry out his crusade against the freedom of the African peoples and even the entire world, with the assistance of his money. Therefore the struggle of the Chad people is far from being just a struggle for survival. By facing Qadhafi's aggressive army, Chadians are accomplishing a continental duty. They are preventing Tripoli's terrorist from taking a path to sow death and affliction wherever he wants, first in Chad's neighbouring countries and later on the entire African continent. The stateless people who support this policy of the destruction of Chad are only puppets whom Qadhafi is manipulating at will with his petro-dinars (Ndjamena home service, 11th September 1985).

Reports of clashes between GUNT factions and the Libyans continued into 1986. It was clear that the stalemate, in which the Libyans were happy to maintain control of Aouzou and northern Chad while Habre was unable to extend his control north of the 16th parallel, was not to the liking of the GUNT factions. As a result some of them had turned against their Libyan patrons and against their own leaders. In southern Chad, the stalemate had led to a reconciliation between pro-GUNT forces operating there and the Ndjamena government. This further weakened the position of Goukouni and the Libyans. In the summer and autumn of 1986, the GUNT finally came apart at the seams with serious differences leading to a factional struggle between Goukouni and Acheikh Bin Oumar. The Libyans decided to abandon Goukouni and shifted their support to Acheikh. Goukouni was seized by the Libyans and put under house arrest. In October, there were reports that Goukouni had attempted to break out of his incarceration and had been seriously wounded during clashes between his personal bodyguards and Libyan troops. When news of this clash leaked out, Goukouni's faction of the Chadian forces, known as the Popular Armed Forces (FAP), attacked the Libyans attached to their units and other Libyan positions at Bardai and in the Tibesti area. Initially, FAP was successful in taking control of some areas held by the Libyans, but in December the Libyans and the factions still loyal to them struck back and were reportedly intent on wiping FAP out as a military political force. But the Libyans did not find this an easy task as Goukouni's forces were intensely loyal to him and were fighting in their home area.

Not surprisingly, Habre took advantage of the fighting between his opponents to launch attacks against Libyan and GUNT positions in the Tibesti. He proclaimed that Goukouni's forces were now on the side of 'Chadian patriots' and he persuaded the French air force to drop supplies to isolated FAP units. Early in 1987, Habre's forces captured the most southerly Libyan base at Fada, in the Ennedi region, and he was able to get the French to give his forces a minimal level of air support, though this did include a major raid against the Libyan airfield at Ouadi Doum. The Libyans tried to counter-attack but were defeated by Habre's forces at Kalait. Goukouni, probably as a result of Libyan coercion, attempted to get his forces to stop the fighting by appealing from Tripoli for all fighting to end, but this had no effect and fierce clashes continued between FAP and the Libyan-controlled forces and between Habre's units and the Libyans. Libyan soldiers captured by the government during the fighting were paraded in Ndjamena and Habre took maximum propaganda advantage of his successes against the Libyans.

For once, the Libyans seemed to be in serious trouble in Chad. They lost Bardai and Zouar to FAP and Fada to the government and were on the defensive elsewhere in northern and eastern Chad. In early 1987, African observers believed that the Libyans had lost around 1,000 men in the new round of fighting.

It was this less favourable position that prompted Libya to take a more cooperative view of peace efforts in 1987. Through its friends in Congo, which continued to support Libya over Chad, Libya approached the OAU to call for mediation. Although the OAU continued its attempts to arrange a peace conference, many African states – notably Nigeria, Senegal, Zaire and Egypt – were suspicious of Libya's sudden interest in peace. It was suspected that Libya's intentions were not sincere and that it would take part in peace talks only while its forces were on the defensive.

Meanwhile, under Libyan pressure, a new GUNT leadership was formed minus Goukouni. Acheikh became President of GUNT. Goukouni resisted the move but was able to do little as for the early months of 1987 he remained effectively under house arrest in Libya and was unable to speak openly either to his supporters or to the international media.

The Chadian government remained on the offensive, both militarily and politically. In January 1987, it launched a strong attack on the Soviet Union, accusing it of turning a blind eye to Libya's 'annexationist' policies in Chad and of allowing its advisers in Libya to assist the Libyan forces in northern Chad. Ndjamena radio said that Soviet advisers and technicians were based in the Aouzou Strip and had at times been present at the Libyan air base at Ouadi Doum inside northern Chad. The USSR made no direct answer to these claims but its radio programmes beamed to Africa in French and English attacked the Habre government for using French military support and for allowing the French and the Americans to intervene in Africa via the Chadian conflict. However, the Soviets did not condemn Libyan actions in Chad nor did they directly support them in their statements on Chad. In fact, apart from limited technical and logistical help to the Libyan forces, they did turn a blind eye to what was going on. The only real advantage sought by the USSR from the conflict was the opportunity to criticise US and French intervention in Chad.

As the propaganda war raged, the fighting continued in northern Chad. In early January, Ndjamena radio broadcast government military communiques reporting the defeat of Libyan-backed counter-attacks against Zouar and Fada. The Chadians said that 784 Libyan soldiers had been killed in the fighting, eighty-six T-55 tanks had been destroyed and thirteen captured and a number of SAM-7 anti-aircraft missile systems had been captured. Although some of the Libyan losses might have been exaggerated, it is clear that the Chadians had inflicted a major defeat on Libya. Libya made no open comment on its setbacks but instead chose to slam the Ndjamena government for relying on French and US military supplies and French air support. Tripoli radio accused Habre of allowing France and the USA 'to escalate their flagrant military interference in Chad'. The radio said that 'all these events and lines and threads stem entirely from the heart of the NATO plot, which is determined to strike at the Libyan Arab revolution' (Tripoli home service, 6th January 1987). The Libyan posture was somewhat disingenuous, for although it is true that Washington and Paris were keen to strike at Libya and undermine Qadhafi, the Chadian crisis had its own particular origins and dynamics and was not part of a Western plot to undermine Libya.

Despite his obvious military successes, Habre was still interested in peace and in the first week of January received the OAU Secretary-General, Ide Oumarou, to discuss the possibility of talks with Libya and the Chadian factions. Oumarou also had discussions in Libya, but as usual they were to no avail and the fighting continued.

Habre's position grew stronger politically in early 1987 when southern forces under Colonel Kotiga, which had for years conducted a guerrilla war in the south, agreed to join the government side. At the same time, Kamougoue was dismissed from the GUNT leadership by Acheikh, with Libyan backing, and he too effected a reconciliation with Habre and later in the year was included in Habre's cabinet. Habre's military position was strengthened by the integration into his Chadian National Armed Forces (FANT) of pro-Goukouni sections of GUNT's National Liberation Army (ANL). A senior Goukouni aide, Adoum Yacoub, also joined forces with the Ndjamena government. He called on all ANL forces formerly loyal to Goukouni to fight alongside the FANT forces. Habre also had the support of French troops – though they played little part in the fighting – sent out as part of Operation Sparrowhawk, aimed at supporting Habre against the Libyans.

Qadhafi was fiercely critical of renewed French support for Habre. In a speech to preachers of his Islamic Call organisation on 12th January 1987, Qadhafi said that the cause of the 'revolution' in Chad was the attempt to impose Christianity on Muslims. The Libyan leader tried to get round the problem of Habre's adherence to Islam by saying that he was an agent of the Israelis and the imperialists – he had sought the aid of Christians and Jews in his fight against Muslims and so was their tool, Qadhafi said. Justifying his continued fight against Habre, he said 'he has gone over to the ranks of the Christians, the crusaders, the ranks of the enemies of Islam and he must therefore be fought against. Fighting him is a jihad' (Tripoli home service, 12th January 1987). This position once again showed Qadhafi's use of Islam as a political tool. The Libyans had been prepared to abandon the Muslim northerners in Chad in favour of an agreement with the Christian Tombalbaye, but were now using Islam as a weapon against Habre. That the speech was made to Islamic Call preachers, many of whom had been working in West Africa, demonstrates the use made of the large Muslim population of the region in Qadhafi's strategies. Unfortunately for him, many West African Muslims saw Habre's victories as a great success for Africa against Arab invaders rather than as a defeat for Islam. In interviews with individual West Africans during the author's research trip to West Africa, he was told repeatedly that Habre's successes against Qadhafi had been welcomed by Africans and seen as the first major victories by black Africans against foreign invaders.

But Qadhafi is either unaware of this strand of thinking or is unconcerned about the opposition his policies arouse in ordinary Africans. He retains an untarnished belief that Africans will eventually see that Qadhafi's policies and his anti-imperialism are correct policies to follow, even if they involve Libyan aggression against African states in the name of anti-imperialism. In his speech to the Islamic Call preachers, Qadhafi made strong threats against West African states that he said were helping the French in Chad. He said that the French wanted the Muslims of Chad to kill one another until they wipe each other out – 'this is the reason for France's presence in Chad. Therefore we must speed up the destruction of Habre, its agent, and its bases in Chad, Central Africa and Cameroon. France also has a big naval base in Senegal and in Cote d'Ivoire, Sierra Leone, Gambia; all these areas, including Togo, have crusader bases against Islam.' He called on the preachers to return to West Africa to fight against the 'crusader' presence. Qadhafi made a point of telling those preachers going to Nigeria that they should seek to influence the Nigerian government and people of the need to adopt a firm stand against French and American involvement in Chad. He said that the Western arms going to Chad threatened Nigeria.

But few governments came out in direct support of the Libyans. President Mobutu of Zaire, a long-time opponent of Qadhafi, made a point of visiting Chad in mid-January to express his strong support for Habre. At a joint press conference in Ndjamena, Mobutu said that Zaire would not hesitate if its assistance was needed by Chad in defending its sovereignty. Habre used the press conference to reaffirm his determination to push the Libyans out of Chadian territory. He said that the Chadian people 'will be obliged to continue

the war with determination until they liberate the whole of their national territory
... Not a single inch of our territory can be left under foreign occupation'
(Ndjamena home service, 15th January 1987). The President stressed that he
meant the Aouzou Strip as well as Libyan occupied areas of northern Chad. At
a separate press conference two days later, Habre stressed that he was willing to
settle the conflict peacefully, but only if Libya withdrew from all Chadian territory.

The new GUNT leadership attempted in January to restart the peace process
with the assistance of Algeria and Congo, both of which support Libya and the
GUNT and are critical of the French role in the conflict. But Acheikh's position
as GUNT head remained ambiguous because of Goukouni's imprisonment by
the Libyans and the suspicion that Acheikh had been imposed on the GUNT by
Libya. A Libyan envoy sent by Qadhafi to brief Jerry Rawlings of Ghana on the
Chadian situation told journalists in Accra that Goukouni was not under arrest,
'he is free to move around and could even return to his home village in Chad to
be a chief if he wished to, but he cannot return as a political leader as the political
situation has changed' (Accra home service, 19th January 1987). Although on the
whole Ghana supports Libya, the Rawlings government has some doubts over
Chad and while critical of French and US intervention does not support Libyan
military intervention either (Interview with Ghanaian Foreign Secretary). And it
is statements such as that by the Libyan envoy that increase African suspicions
about Libyan intentions. Many governments sympathetic to GUNT and towards
Libya were unsettled by the removal of Goukouni and by Libyan statements that
his political career was over. They believed that it was up to Goukouni's
supporters and the Chadian people to decide whether or not he still had a
political role to play, it was not Libya's prerogative (unattributable interviews in
Burkina Faso, Cote d'Ivoire and Ghana in November 1987).

As 1987 progressed, so did Habre's offensive in northern Chad. In late
January FANT forces succeeded in gaining control of the areas previously
controlled by Libya around Zouar. They then attacked Libyan positions in the
Tibesti mountains and defeated Libyan counter-attacks against Zouar. In
February, the Libyans were defeated at Oueita, north of Fada, and retaliated with
heavy air raids against Fada and Zouar. Soon after, Libyan television reported on
the fighting north of Zouar and Fada claiming victory for GUNT forces and
omitting to mention the Libyan role in the fighting. However, the Libyans were
unable to give precise details of the areas in which the fighting took place or the
casualties suffered by Habre's forces, instead they concentrated on criticising
Habre for utilising French aid and for accepting arms supplies from Egypt.
Libya's sole military initiative at this stage was to start bombing Chadian and
French positions south of the 16th parallel.

Libyan opposition forces based abroad reported in mid-1987 that the Libyans
had suffered serious losses during the continued fighting and that the Libyan
defeats had angered the Soviet Union, as large quantities of sophisticated Soviet
arms had been abandoned by the Libyans. The National Front for the Salvation
of Libya (NFSL) said that the USSR had refused Libyan requests for replace-
ments for the weapons destroyed or lost in Chad. The Soviet Union had also

reportedly used the opportunity of Libyan setbacks to demand faster repayment of the massive debts Libya owed Moscow for arms supplies. The same source backed Chadian claims that Libya had stationed several thousand troops in Sudan's Darfur province for possible action in eastern Chad in the event of further successes for Habre (NFSL newsletter, no. 57, May/June 1987).

Fighting continued throughout the February to July period with further advances made by the government forces. Their big success came in August when they pushed into the Aouzou Strip. On 8th August, the Chadian government announced that FANT forces had gained control of Aouzou and freed the area 'after fourteen years of illegal occupation' (Ndjamena home service, 8th August 1987). Habre's Information Secretary, Togoi Hamadi Moumine, said that Chad would now be able to exploit the Strip's mineral resources, including uranium. FANT also claimed the capture of Bardai. Libya was forced to admit the Chadian attack on Aouzou and on 9th August, Tripoli radio said that 'the forces of the agent Habre, with the help of the imperialist forces, have attacked the Aouzou region inside SPLAJ [Libyan] territory'. Libya complained to the UN Security Council and the OAU about the attack, but to little avail. At first Libya was unable to recapture Aouzou and had to content itself with bombing Faya Largeau and other Chadian towns.

August also saw political successes for Habre in the form of the installation of a new government team including both Kamougoue and Negue Djogo, both former opponents now reconciled with Habre.

Libya could only react to the military and political setbacks by accusing imperialist forces – France and the USA, in particular – of using Chad as a springboard for aggression against Libya. On the military front, Libya could still only respond by using its air superiority to carry out bombing raids against military installations and towns in northern Chad.

On 19th August, the Chadian government released details of the fighting for Aouzou and produced fifteen Libyan officers captured in the Strip. At a press conference attended by Western journalists they admitted that they had been defeated by the Chadian forces and that they had been trained at bases inside Libya by Soviet advisers. But in late August, the Libyans launched heavy counter-attacks against the Chadian positions in Aouzou. The Libyans immediately claimed total victory while Habre said that the attacks had been driven off. In fact, the attacks were partially successful and areas of the Strip were again taken under Libyan control. During heavy fighting, the Chadians reported shooting down two MiG-23 aircraft and a combat helicopter. The Libyans for their part claimed to have killed 600 FANT soldiers and captured large quantities of French and US-supplied weapons. The Libyan armed forces general command claimed to be in complete control of the Strip. A FANT High Command communique released on 28th August admitted that some territory had been lost to Libya but denied that control over the entire area had been lost. On 30th August, the commander of the Libyan armed forces, Colonel Abu Bakr Yunis Jabir, visited the village of Aouzou along with a group of foreign journalists to demonstrate Libyan control. Habre said that the Libyans had only succeeded in gaining control of an undefended post in Aouzou and had not beaten his forces.

Whatever the military position in Aouzou, the Chadians won an important propaganda victory when on 4th and 5th September 1987 they carried out an audacious raid on a Libyan military base at Ma'tan al-Sarah well inside Libyan territory. The Libyans were said to have lost 1,713 troops in the fighting there and to have had tens of tanks and aircraft destroyed and large quantities of Soviet-supplied equipment captured. The Chadian attack received worldwide attention and was a serious blow to Qadhafi's prestige. At first the Libyans ignored that the attack had taken place but several days later tried to make it into a propaganda show to demonstrate 'imperialist' attempts to destroy the Libyan revolution.

Political manoeuvring accompanied the fighting. In early February, Goukouni Oueddei issued a statement in Libya disclosing that the confrontation between FAP units and the Libyans had been the result of a misunderstanding and that Libya remained the ally of the Chadian people. There was, however, considerable speculation that the statement had been issued under duress and that Goukouni remained a prisoner. To avoid further problems resulting from the uncertainty surrounding Goukouni, in mid-February he was allowed to travel to Algeria (a supporter of the Libyan position in Chad), where he attempted to regain some political role in Chad and to set himself up as a possible intermediary between Habre and the Libyan-backed GUNT. But Habre was suspicious that Goukouni was once more being used as a tool by the Libyans and did not respond enthusiastically to Goukouni's apparent release. Qadhafi tried to clear away suspicions about his opposition to Goukouni when he gave an interview to the French paper *Le Monde* in February. He said that Goukouni was still an ally and a friend and remained the leader of the Tibesti area of Chad. The Libyan leader repeated that Aouzou was Libyan territory and that Habre was trying to seize it on behalf of the USA and France as part of a massive plot against Libya. Qadhafi's deputy, Major Jallud, said on 11th February that Libya and Chad had been on the verge of a settlement until the French intervened and escalated the conflict. He said that Libya wanted to find an 'African solution' to the war in Chad but that the first condition for a solution was the withdrawal of French forces from Chad (Tripoli television, 9th February).

In February, the then OAU chairman, President Sassou-Nguesso of Congo, tried to start another peace initiative, but his stress on the problems caused by the French presence in Chad and his known friendship with the Libyans meant that Habre did not take his efforts seriously. An attempt was also made by the Sadiq al-Mahdi government in Sudan to mediate between Tripoli and Ndjamena, but Mahdi's rapprochement with Qadhafi and the suspected presence of Libyan troops in western Sudan undercut the Sudanese claim of impartiality. Qadhafi did little to encourage those searching for a peaceful solution. Tripoli television reported on 14th February that the Libyan leader had told a French magazine that he believed that the Habre regime was one installed by the French and Americans in order to destabilise Libya – such a position hardly held out much hope that Habre would agree to negotiations with Qadhafi or that the latter was willing to negotiate seriously with the Chadian President. In interviews with the British *Sunday Times* and the American *New York Times* in mid-April, Qadhafi kept up his attacks on Habre and refused to give details of the military position in northern Chad and Aouzou, saying that there had been no major battles in Chad because the terrain meant that there were no fixed positions over which to fight.

In May, an OAU ad hoc committee on Chad, headed by President Bongo of Gabon, made an attempt to get peace talks going and to start discussions on the dispute over ownership of Aouzou. The OAU efforts were supplemented by those of President Sankara of Burkina Faso, who paid several visits to Libya after the OAU summit at the end of July to try to arrange negotiations. Sankara was a friend of the Libyans but was said to have great respect for Habre following the Chadian victories against Libyan forces in northern Chad, in the Aouzou Strip and at the Sarah base (interviews with Western diplomats in Abidjan, Cote d'Ivoire, in early November 1987). The main issue on Sankara's agenda was the Aouzou dispute.

Following the OAU summit, Habre was in a good position politically. At the summit he had been elected as one of the vice-chairmen of the OAU, thereby emphasising the fact that he was recognised as the legitimate President of Chad. At the summit, the OAU heads of state appealed to Chad and Libya to avoid further bloodshed and to cooperate with the ad hoc committee. One blow to the peace process was the decision of President Bongo to resign as head of the OAU ad hoc committee. He did not go into detail about his reasons, but reliable diplomatic sources said that he felt that Libya was unwilling to cooperate with his committee or to adopt a sincere attitude towards negotiations.

Amid the negotiations, President Mitterrand of France visited Chad for talks with Habre. This elicited an explosion of Libyan rhetoric about the war against the imperialists on Libya's southern borders. During Mitterrand's visit, Qadhafi claimed that it was proof that France was using Chad for aggression against Libya. He added that the Libyan people had no intention of fighting the Chadian people but were only defending themselves against imperialist aggression launched from Chadian territory. Buoyed up on a wave of rhetoric, the Libyan leader continued his propaganda attacks on Habre and France throughout August and September – at a time when there was an extended lull in the fighting. In a speech on 17th September, the Libyan leader said that the war between Chad and Libya had now ended 'following the ejection of the mercenaries from Aouzou . . . the Great Jamahiriyah has completely closed its borders with Chad, thus leaving Chad to the Chadians' (Jana, 17th September 1987). The Ndjamena government reacted with scorn to Qadhafi's statement that the war was over. It said that Libya was still massing thousands of troops in Sudan's Darfur province ready for an attack on Libya and was continuing overflights of Chadian territory by Libyan combat aircraft. Ndjamena radio said on 17th September that the conflict with Libya had not changed 'one iota' and Libya remained intent on annexing Chad. The radio emphasised that the war would only be over when all

Libyan troops were evacuated from Chadian territory. Qadhafi, it said, was only saying the war was over because of the increasing international support for Chad. Throughout the latter part of 1987, Chad repeated its warnings that Libya was building up its forces in Sudan ready for a new invasion of Chad. It also claimed that Libya was training over 1,000 Lebanese from political and military factions in Lebanon for use against Chad. This was hotly denied by the Libyans, although they did not deny that they were providing military training for some Lebanese groups. Chad also condemned continued Sudanese and Algerian political support for Libyan policies towards Chad. In late September, Chad's suspicions of Arab support for Libyan annexation of Aouzou were heightened when a meeting of the Arab League expressed full support for Libyan measures to defend its territorial integrity – this was interpreted by both the Libyans and Habre as Arab League support for Qadhafi's claim to the Aouzou Strip.

Towards the end of 1987, the new OAU chairman, President Kaunda, and a number of other African leaders attempted to arrange talks between Chad and Libya over Aouzou. At first the talks failed to take place as the Libyans did not turn up at the scheduled time. When the talks were rearranged at Libya's request, President Habre accused Kaunda of making concessions to Libya. In October, he accused Burkina Faso of 'playing Libya's game' by trying to reconcile the different factions of GUNT. Habre accused a number of countries, including Ghana, Sudan, Burkina Faso and Uganda of assisting Qadhafi in his aggressive policies towards Chad.

Generally, the military situation was quiet at the end of 1987, though in late November, the FANT High Command said that its forces had clashed with units of the Islamic Legion which it claimed had infiltrated into eastern Chad from Sudan's Darfur province. The Chadians said that the Legion had been defeated but it issued a strong warning to Sudan to stop the Libyans from using its territory for aggression. Libya denied the report of the clash, saying that the forces involved were not Libyan but members of the Chadian Hadjarai ethnic group loyal to former Foreign Minister Idris Miskine.

During the closing months of 1987 and January 1988, Qadhafi made a series of speeches in which he reaffirmed Libya's claim to the Aouzou Strip and its opposition to the French role in Chad, which he described as a 'French colony'. He said that all Libyans should be prepared to defend Aouzou, which was part of Libya and of the Arab world. He said aggression against Aouzou was aggression against the Arabs as a nation. Qadhafi gave no indication that he was interested in peace and seemed fairly content with the military stalemate – given the defeats his forces suffered in 1987.

Habre for his part was keen to confirm that Chad was still at war with Libya and that he was not prepared to cede Aouzou or any other Chadian territory to Libya. He said that he was interested in peace and was prepared to cooperate with the OAU in finding a peaceful settlement but that 'our Libyan enemy' has no interest in peace (Ndjamena home service, 10th January 1988).

Overall, the Chad conflict was in a position of stalemate with no prospects of either a peaceful or a military solution. Libya had shown no desire for a settlement and both Qadhafi and Habre were intent on pressing their claims to Aouzou. Most African states viewed the Chad conflict as a running sore that could infect the rest of the continent, but were unable to find a workable solution. With the exception of the states closely linked with Libya – Congo, Ghana, Burkina Faso, Algeria, Sudan and Benin – most African states were opposed to the Libyan role in Chad and feared that Chad could be used by Libya to expand its presence and influence further into Africa. They were heartened by Habre's victories, which they saw as an indication that opposition to Qadhafi was not futile.

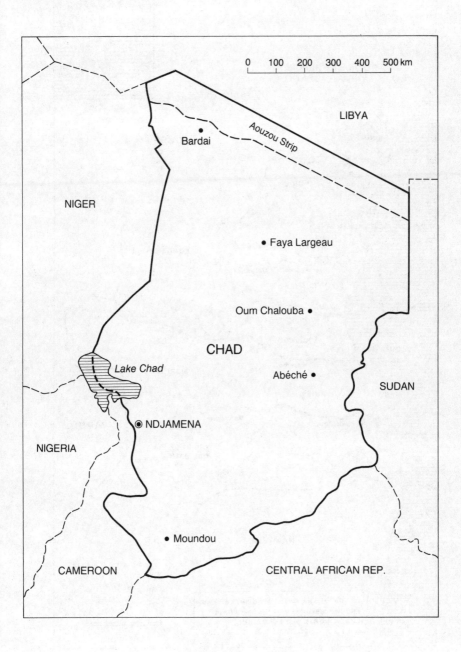

Map 3 Chad

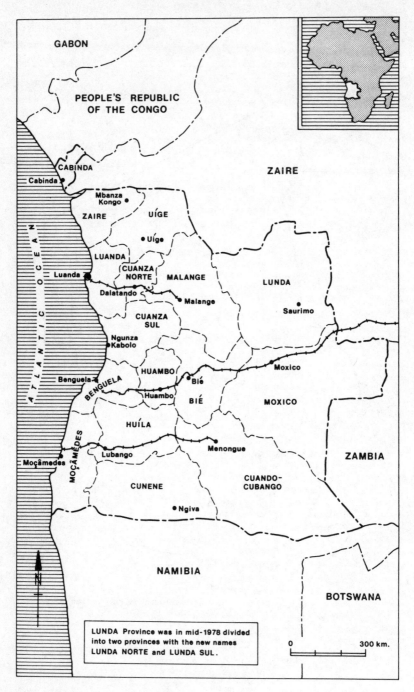

Map 4 Angola
Source: Keith Somerville, *Angola: Politics, Economics and Society*, London, Pinter Publishers, 1986.

5 Colonial and imperial collapse fans flames of fire

The year 1974 was a turning point in the contemporary political and military history of Africa. It saw not only the Portuguese revolution with the consequent decision to dismantle the last remaining colonial empire in Africa, but also the end of the Ethiopian Empire, following the fall of Haile Selassie. These two events led to the independence of Angola, Cape Verde, Guinea Bissau, Mozambique and Sao Tome e Principe and to the evolution of a hardline Marxist–Leninist military regime in Ethiopia. In Angola, the progress towards independence was synonymous with progress towards civil war. In other parts of southern Africa, the end of the Portuguese empire enabled liberation movements to step up their struggles for majority rule, freedom from South African occupation and the destruction of the apartheid system. In Ethiopia, the change of regime led not to a settlement of the Eritrean war and the dispute with Somalia but a stepping up of the secessionist struggle in the north, a decline into open war between Ethiopia and Somalia and the flaring up of regional conflicts within Ethiopia.

Elsewhere in Africa in the early and mid-1970s, the Spanish withdrawal from its Saharan territory led to the start of a liberation war by the Polisario Front against the Moroccans and Mauritanians, who took over the former colony; and in Uganda, the struggle of Ugandan exile movements against Idi Amin ended with a short, sharp war in 1979 with foreign forces fighting to maintain Amin in power.

The Portuguese revolution: one war ends and another begins

On 25th April 1974, a military coup by young Portuguese army officers brought to an end four decades of fascism in Portugal and prepared the way for the independence of the country's African possessions. The coup itself was a product not just of social, economic and political conditions in Portugal but also of the discontent within the armed forces over their role in Africa. Fighting had been in progress for over twenty years – the Angolan armed struggle began in 1961, that of Mozambique in 1964 and of Guinea Bissau in 1963. The wars had drained the economy and the military. Far from being won, the conflicts were being lost. To many of the hundreds of thousands of Portuguese who were fighting or had fought in the colonial wars, decolonisation was the only answer if the wars could not be won. Portugal had always been the poorest and most backward of the European powers which grabbed huge chunks of Africa for their own. This perhaps explains both its unwillingness to give up the territories and its poor military performance.

But whatever the reasons, by 1974 the armed forces had had enough. They had virtually lost control of all but the capital of Guinea Bissau, were unable to recapture Frelimo's large liberated areas and were even too weak or inefficient to make headway against the divided and faction-ridden movements in Angola. After effecting the April coup and sparking off a social and political revolution, the Armed Forces Movement pushed for an end to the African wars. Troops in Guinea Bissau reportedly told their commanders in August 1974 that 'If you don't now make a firm peace, or if you try to stop the peaceful withdrawal of our forces, then I and all my men will declare ourselves prisoners of the PAIGC' (cited by Davidson Slova and Wilkinson 1976, p. 19). The feelings were much the same in Angola and Mozambique. The result was a decision by the Armed Forces Movement, which had seized power for itself in July 1974, to negotiate timetables for independence in each of the colonies (including Cape Verde and Sao Tome e Principe).

Because its struggle had been more advanced and as a result it had a more developed political and administrative system in its liberated areas, Guinea Bissau was the first to achieve statehood, on 10th September 1974. Mozambique had a lengthier transition to independence, but a Frelimo government took over power from the Portuguese on 25th June 1975; Sao Tome and also Cape Verde followed suit in mid-1975. Angola created problems though.

Unlike the other countries, Angola had three movements competing for power and claiming to represent the Angolan people. The strongest and most obviously national movement was the MPLA. It was a socialist liberation front (though with a strongly Marxist leadership nucleus) based originally on the Luanda area and the mestico (mixed race) and Mbundu peoples. Its area of guerrilla struggle had been in the far east of Angola along the border with Zambia and in the Dembos forest north-east of Luanda (see Somerville, 1986, pp. 21–45; and Marcum, 1978). The FNLA, based solely on the Bakongo people of northern Angola and southern Zaire, had been fighting in the north and had based itself in Zaire, where President Mobutu (related by marriage to FNLA President Holden Roberto) was willing to give it strong support to achieve power. UNITA, made up mainly of Ovimbundu people of the central plateau and south-east of Angola, was the smallest of the groups and had been formed when the former FNLA Foreign Secretary, Jonas Savimbi, broke away from Roberto, accusing him of tribalism. UNITA was based in the centre and south-east but was not militarily active, except on occasions to attack the Benguela railway and units from the MPLA. The MPLA accused UNITA of cooperating with and receiving arms from the Portuguese.

The three movements had a history of hostility and none of them was in a position to take power single-handedly when the Portuguese revolution took place. The MPLA was the best placed numerically and militarily to press its case, but was undergoing a major factional struggle in the early 1970s – a struggle which came to an end after the April 1974 coup, with a large faction led by the eastern Angola guerrilla commander, Daniel Chipenda, leaving the MPLA and allying itself with the FNLA.

The Portuguese made vain attempts to bring the movements together to form a coalition government but failed. The Alvor agreement of 15th January 1975, which formed a transitional government representing the three movements, lasted a matter of weeks before fighting broke out; and the later Nakuru agreement, made under the auspices of the OAU, lasted only a few days before clashes between the groups destroyed it. The efforts to achieve a peaceful solution by the Portuguese were not helped by clandestine meetings arranged by a rightist Portuguese general and sometime leader of the post-coup regime, Antonio Ribeiro de Spinola, to put together an anti-MPLA coalition of the FNLA, Chipenda's faction and, at a later stage, UNITA, with Zairean and South African backing. The idea was to create a coalition that was strong enough militarily and politically to destroy the MPLA's chances of taking or even sharing power. The inevitable consequence of the split between the Angolan movements and of growing external interference was civil war with extensive foreign military intervention.

In Guinea Bissau, Cape Verde, Mozambique and Sao Tome, the transition from colonial rule to independence was smoother in the short term, with the dominant liberation movements taking over the levers of power from the departing Portuguese. Although Guinea Bissau was to suffer internal factionalism and eventually a military coup, independence brought an end to war and created relative stability – the same can be said of Cape Verde and Sao Tome. But Mozambique was situated in the volatile and rapidly changing southern African region. It had white supremacist Rhodesia and apartheid South Africa as immediate neighbours – they were undergoing their own political and, increasingly, military conflicts. Having enjoyed close relations with the liberation movements fighting in Rhodesia and South Africa and being guided by a party adhering to the ideals of Marxism and African solidarity, it was obvious that the end to the liberation war in Mozambique would not necessarily mean an end to conflict and bloodshed.

The shockwaves emanating from the Portuguese revolution not only toppled the colonial regimes in the Portuguese territories in Africa, but also shook the white supremacist regime of Ian Smith in Rhodesia and the apartheid regime in South Africa. Firstly, the independence of Mozambique was a blow to the links that had grown up between Pretoria, Salisbury and Lisbon which included intelligence and even military cooperation against the African nationalist movements. Secondly, Mozambique's independence opened up Rhodesia's north-eastern and eastern borders to guerrilla infiltration and did the same for north-eastern South Africa. Thirdly, Angola's impending statehood would open Namibia's northern border to attack by guerrillas of the South West African People's Organisation (SWAPO). Fourthly, and perhaps most importantly, there was the psychological impact of the collapse of the Portuguese, the mass exodus of the Portuguese settlers from Angola and Mozambique, the independence under black, socialist rule of neighbouring states and the growing links of solidarity between the independent states of southern Africa and the liberation movements.

Zimbabwe: regional and international involvement

Rhodesia (or Zimbabwe as it later became) was the most seriously affected by the independence of Mozambique. With the exception of the southern border with South Africa, the country was now surrounded by independent African states committed to political support (and in some cases military aid) to the nationalist movements – the Zimbabwe People's African Union (ZAPU), the Zimbabwe African National Union (ZANU) and, later and more briefly, the Front for the Liberation of Zimbabwe (Frolizi). Guerrillas from ZAPU and ZANU units had been active, though not successfully so, since 1964. They had tried small-scale infiltrations from Zambia and carried out attacks on farms and isolated outposts. The most spectacular attacks, and most spectacular failures, had been at Sinoia on 28th April 1966 – when a group of twenty-one guerrillas of ZANU's Zimbabwe National Liberation Army (ZANLA) penetrated into Rhodesia from Zambia and reached the town of Sinoia, where they were intercepted and attacked by the Rhodesian security forces; seven of the guerrillas were killed and the infiltration attempt ended – and in the Wankie area of south-western Zimbabwe in July 1967, when a combined force of about seventy guerrillas of ZAPU's Zipra (Zimbabwe People's Revolutionary Army) and South African ANC crossed into Rhodesia to set up a base in the region of the Wankie Game reserve; a series of clashes took place in August and September in which thirty-one guerrillas were reported to have been killed and a similar number captured, leading to the destruction of the unit. Militarily the clashes were failures for the liberation movements, though they did prove that guerrillas could get into the country and that they would stand and fight against the Rhodesian security forces. Furthermore, the movements (at least, ZANU for certain) learnt the lesson that large-scale infiltrations without prior political groundwork in the target area would not work. The ZANU leadership in exile now started to seriously rethink the guerrilla strategy. As Mayor Urimbo, ZANU Political Commissar during the war and later a member of the ZANU Political Bureau, said: 'We thought that it was easy to just go and get a gun and go and fight in Zimbabwe . . . . It was realised that the people had to be mobilised if we were to conduct a successful struggle' (cited by Martin and Johnson, 1981, p. 11). Urimbo and William Ndangana, the ZANLA Chief of Operations, told the author in Harare in 1982 that the early guerrilla attacks had failed because they relied totally on the idea of armed struggle divorced from political work. The defeats and the effective failure of ZANU and ZAPU to establish guerrilla groups inside the country between 1964 and 1968, they said, led to a more gradualist approach concentrating on politicisation of both guerrillas and the populations of target areas prior to the infiltration attempts. Urimbo, Ndangana and George

Rutanhire (a guerrilla and political commissar with ZANLA and later Deputy Minister of Youth and Sport) all give much of the credit for the development of more politically-orientated tactics and for the eventually successful attempts to mobilise the local population before launching guerrilla actions to the advice and training given by the Chinese instructors who aided ZANU. After the training of initial groups of ZANU guerrillas in China in 1964, 1965 and 1966 (including Ndangana and the ZANLA commander Josiah Tongogara), the trained cadres carried out their own training programmes in camps in Tanzania. But in 1969, as ZANU sought to develop and perfect its more political strategy, eight Chinese instructors were sent to the ZANLA camp at Itumbi in Tanzania (Martin and Johnson, 1981, p. 12; this was confirmed by Urimbo, Ndangana and by ZANLA's Chief of Training, Mark Dube, in conversation with the author in April 1982). The instructors taught not only military skills but also Maoist political mobilisation techniques. Urimbo believes that the lessons taught by the Chinese were crucial and that ZANU 'saw the Chinese ideology as the most effective when organizing the people' (interview with author).

In addition to the military and political training, the Chinese also supplied ZANU with arms (mainly rifles, submachine guns, ammunition, mines and explosives). Some military material was also received from North Korea, Romania and Yugoslavia. By the end of the liberation war in 1979, North Korea was supplying heavy weapons, including mobile artillery, to ZANU. By then, Bulgaria and Cuba had also been persuaded (chiefly by Mugabe, Tanzania's President, Julius Nyerere, and Mozambique's President, Samora Machel) to send some arms and to give training and other forms of assistance (financial, educational and medical).

The ZANU strategy which developed from the lessons of Sinoia and from the Chinese teachings was to spend a protracted period preparing the peasants for the arrival of the guerrillas by giving them political education and by mobilising them against the Rhodesian regime. They needed little encouragement to hate the white government but extensive education in the aims of the liberation struggle, the benefits to be gained and the methods by which the war would be fought.

ZANU's main problem was infiltration. It could get some guerrillas in via Zambia, but the Zambian government had poor relations with ZANU and favoured Joshua Nkomo's ZAPU. The opportunity to break out of this situation came in the early 1970s, when the Frelimo forces in Mozambique succeeded in establishing liberated zones in Tete, bordering north-eastern Zimbabwe. The ZANU leadership in Lusaka (notably the late Herbert Chitepo) asked Frelimo for permission to use its liberated areas to send guerrillas into Zimbabwe. The requests were put in 1969 and 1970 at meetings between ZANU and Frelimo military commanders. At first Frelimo was unhappy about helping ZANU. This arose as a result of Frelimo's longstanding ties with ZAPU. The two movements, along with the ANC of South Africa, the MPLA in Angola, SWAPO, the PAIGC and the Comoros movement Molinaco, were part of a loose alliance of liberation movements which had come together at a Soviet-backed conference in Khartoum of African liberation movements. The movements present became known, by the Soviets and their allies, as the 'authentics'. They were the only ones recognised and supported by the Soviet Union within their given territories. The movements gave each other mutual support (such as the joint ANC–ZAPU infiltration) and cooperated politically and diplomatically. Under this loose arrangement, Frelimo felt that it should first offer access to Zimbabwe via its liberated zones to ZAPU. Frelimo was also suspicious of ZANU because it had split away from ZAPU and was constantly denounced by the latter group's leaders.

Frelimo's initial reluctance to help ZANU broke down after it offered ZAPU the chance to use routes into Zimbabwe via Tete. ZAPU was unable to take up the offer because its military wing was not as strong or as politically conscious as ZANLA and was in no position to launch a new phase of the struggle. Unwilling to pass up the chance to strike a blow against the Rhodesian regime (which along with South Africa was assisting the Portuguese military forces in Mozambique), Frelimo decided to give ZANLA the chance to prove itself. In November 1969, Machel told ZANLA leaders Noel Mukono, Josiah Tongogara and William Ndangana that their request was under serious consideration. In May 1970, Chitepo and Tongogara met Machel in Lusaka and agreement was reached on infiltration through Tete – one thing that may have helped ZANU was the support it received from Tanzania and China, both of whom still enjoyed very close ties with Frelimo, despite its good relations with the Soviet Union. Machel agreed that in the first instance, four ZANLA guerrillas would enter Tete and work with Frelimo to acquire the necessary guerrilla experience (Tongogara, cited by Martin and Johnson, 1981, p. 18).

Urimbo led the four guerrillas who joined up with Frelimo in 1970. He sees the move into north-eastern Zimbabwe via Tete as the opening of the crucial phase of the guerrilla war, the one that eventually forced Smith to the negotiating table – even though it took until 1979 (interview with author). Prior to the move into Tete, Urimbo and ten other ZANLA guerrillas had conducted reconnaissance missions along the Zambezi valley in the north-east. Once with Frelimo, the ZANLA guerrillas saw in practice the techniques of political mobilisation and of preparing for military struggle by setting up arms caches and safe routes for retreats and for further infiltration of cadres. The lessons gained here convinced Urimbo and other guerrillas of the value of the Chinese advice, though it did lead to arguments with Cuban-trained guerrillas who wanted immediate military action followed by political work (along the lines of Castro's guerrilla operations in Cuba in the 1950s). But the Frelimo–Chinese advice came out on top in the end. But there was still a delay before Frelimo would agree to full-scale infiltration by ZANU, it still felt that ZAPU should be given a chance.

The delay led to splits and problems with ZANU itself, particularly over moves towards unity with ZAPU, supported by some members of the ZANU leadership in exile. There were similar splits within ZAPU and the unity moves did not lead to any effective cooperation. But the emerging divisions within ZANU were later to have serious consequences, notably the Nhari revolt in December 1974 (which was brought about by differences over guerrilla strategies, leadership and the need for heavy weapons, which Nhari thought could be obtained from the Soviet Union).

However, in September 1971, ZANLA guerrillas were allowed by Frelimo to cross into Zimbabwe from Tete. From then onwards, this became the most important route for guerrilla infiltration and to supply the guerrillas. Following Mozambique's independence in 1975, the country became the rear base for ZANLA, enabling it to step up the struggle and spread it to other areas of the country. The new phase of the struggle was launched, somewhat prematurely because of heavy security force activity in the north-east, in December 1972 with an attack on the Altena farm. Other attacks followed and the guerrilla struggle escalated, despite setbacks such as the Nhari revolt (which led to in-fighting within ZANLA) and the assassination of Herbert Chitepo in Lusaka in 1975.

ZANU continued to receive Chinese support and assistance with training and small arms, but as the war progressed, the movement needed more sophisticated and heavier weapons. Approaches were made to the Soviet Union through diplomats in Tanzania and Mozambique and through Nyerere's and Machel's direct contacts with the Soviet leadership. But the efforts were to no avail. The USSR stuck rigidly to its alliance with ZAPU, even though the latter was in a weak position militarily and carried out relatively few combat operations. Witness Mangwende, the current Zimbabwean Information Minister and former Foreign Minister, told the author in 1982 that Soviet officials and ministers rebuffed rudely ZANU requests for arms and that 'ZANU never got even a single penny from the Soviet Union' let alone arms and artillery. The only Soviet-made arms that got through to ZANU came from Cuba, Ethiopia and Mozambique.

Despite its earlier alliance with ZAPU, Frelimo fully supported ZANU throughout the mid and late 1970s, even though this led to Rhodesian raids into Mozambique and the creation by the Rhodesian Central Intelligence Organisation (CIO) of the Mozambique National Resistance Movement (MNR). The MNR was created by the Rhodesians by recruiting former Portuguese troops who had fought in Mozambique (many of them Mozambicans, but some of them expatriate Portuguese) and former Frelimo members who had been purged or had deserted from Frelimo's forces. The Rhodesians formed the organisation in the wake of the April 1974 coup in Portugal and finally sent its members into Mozambique in mid-1976 when Mozambique imposed economic sanctions on Rhodesia. An anti-Frelimo radio station was also set up by the Rhodesians (Hanlon, 1984, pp. 220–21).

The MNR was used initially to collect information on ZANLA bases and infiltration and to disrupt the local economies in areas housing ZANLA guerrillas. It later progressed to sabotage, terrorist attacks and outright banditry and indiscriminate killing (author's unattributable discussions with European aid workers based in Mozambique in February 1987). The MNR had their base at Umtali (now called Mutare) in eastern Zimbabwe. The Rhodesian air force supplied MNR units inside Mozambique and Rhodesian troops directly assisted the rebel forces. By the end of the Zimbabwean liberation war, MNR units were active in Manica and Sofala provinces and had bases at Gorongoza, Inyanga and

Chisumbanje. They no longer limited their attacks to ZANLA related targets, but had launched an externally-backed attempt to destroy the Mozambican economy, sabotage regional transport links and to undermine the Frelimo government. When Zimbabwe became independent in April 1980, the MNR offices in Zimbabwe, the bases and the radio station were all moved to South Africa.

The Rhodesians also carried out their own raids into Mozambique, attacking refugee camps, suspected ZANLA bases and also the economic infrastructure in the border areas. The aim was to disrupt ZANLA operations and to try to force Frelimo into dropping support for ZANLA. The most serious attack took place on 9th August 1976 when Rhodesian units attacked a refugee camp at Nyadzonia in Mozambique. Over 1,000 Zimbabwean refugees were killed or wounded in the attack, carried out by regular troops and special units such as the Selous Scouts.

But the attacks on Mozambique and the full-scale counter-insurgency war waged by the Rhodesian forces failed to stem the tide of ZANLA operations. The guerrillas spread their area of activity from the north-east down the eastern side of Zimbabwe and into the south-east. The only areas not greatly affected by ZANLA activity were the south-west and western side of the country. Those areas were either scenes of ZAPU operations or were free of guerrillas.

The main bar to ZANLA's further escalation of the war was the lack of heavy weaponry, such as the portable recoilless rifles which the Soviet Union supplied to the PAIGC in Guinea Bissau and which proved invaluable in changing the nature of the war from guerrilla actions to larger scale attacks. Nevertheless, the scale and success of ZANLA's war were decisive in forcing the Smith regime to the negotiating table. The widespread presence of ZANLA guerrillas and ZANU political cadres in northern, eastern and south-eastern Zimbabwe ensured that ZANU swept the board in those areas in the pre-independence elections.

Even though ZAPU had a large guerrilla army and a secure base in Zambia, it never launched guerrilla campaigns on the scale of ZANLA's. Although it too had learnt lessons from the failed attacks of the late 1960s, it did not adopt the same type of political mobilisation strategy as ZANU. Rather, it relied heavily on military aid and advice from the Soviet Union, Cuba and Eastern Europe. Large numbers of guerrillas were trained in the socialist countries. More importantly, ZAPU's allies, particularly the Soviet Union, provided substantial quantities of weapons, including artillery, armoured vehicles and even old MiG aircraft.

After the independence of Angola, large military training camps were set up there for ZAPU and an even larger army was created. Although guerrillas were trained and sent into northern and western Zimbabwe, a large portion of the ZAPU army was trained in tactics closer to conventional warfare and kept in readiness in large camps in Zambia. Attempts were made in 1972, in 1975 after the abortive southern African detente exercise (see Martin and Johnson, 1981, pp. 115–90 and Meredith, 1980, pp. 145–96, for further details of the detente exercise) and then in the closing years of the struggle to join the two guerrilla armies. At one stage a Joint Military Command was formed by the military leaders of ZANU and ZAPU and then, in January 1976, a joint military unit known as the Zimbabwe People's Army (Zipa) launched operations into Zimbabwe. This was the first major guerrilla campaign following the lull during the detente period. Zipa was backed by the frontline states and, because of the involvement of ZAPU, received Soviet arms destined originally for Zipra forces. The army was commanded by Rex Nhongo of ZANLA with ZAPU's Alfred 'Nikita' Mangena as the second-in-command. The uniting of sections of the guerrilla armies, albeit temporarily, was complemented by the formation of the Patriotic Front by ZANU and ZAPU. But the unity measures never really bore much fruit and Zipa proved a highly unsuccessful combat unit – partly because its two constituent parts had received very different political and military training.

Zipa effectively fell apart towards the end of 1976. The fighting was again left to ZANLA and Zipra, with the former playing the major role. Zipra cadres continued to receive extensive weapons supplies from the Soviet bloc and some analysts believed that ZAPU's intention was to wait for ZANLA to wear down the Rhodesian forces and then launch a conventional style push across the Zambian border using the armoured vehicles and heavy weapons sent by the USSR. The existence of large military and refugee camps in Zambia led to them becoming targets for Rhodesian commando and air raids. Two particularly large raids were carried out in October 1978 on camps near Lusaka – over 200 cadres and refugees were killed during the attacks. The attacks and the presence of large numbers of heavily armed Zipra soldiers in Zambia made the Kaunda government extremely nervous. Restrictions were placed on the activities of Zipra personnel and the Zambians became loth to permit large-scale infiltrations across the Zambian border into Zimbabwe, according to a ZAPU cadre interviewed by the author in 1982 (unattributable interview with former ZAPU cadre who received military training in Moscow). At one stage, Zambia stopped the supply of heavy weapons to Zipra by the Soviet Union as they were being stockpiled at camps in Zambia rather than being sent into Zimbabwe with guerrillas. During 1979, when the supply of weapons resumed, around $60m worth of Soviet arms were delivered to ZAPU, including SAM-7 surface-to-air missiles, 120mm artillery, armoured vehicles, recoilless rifles and lighter weapons (*ACR*, 1981–2, p. B863). By the time of Zimbabwe's independence, ZAPU forces had also received MiG fighters and T-34 tanks, though these were never used in combat – in 1981 and 1982, during the escalation of domestic conflict between the ZANU government and ZAPU, the Mugabe government refused to allow ZAPU to bring the aircraft and tanks into Zimbabwe from the old ZAPU camps in Zambia, fearing that they could be used against the government (Somerville, 1984, p. 207).

At no stage during the liberation war did non-African forces fight alongside the guerrillas. The military trainers from China stayed in the ZANLA camps in Tanzania, while Cuban and Soviet instructors were only present at the camps in Angola. In the closing months of the war, several hundred Mozambican troops had joined ZANLA forces inside Zimbabwe – this was both to keep an eye on MNR bases in Zimbabwe and to watch the movements of Rhodesian forces in order to prepare for Rhodesian strikes into Mozambique (Martin and Johnson,

1981, pp. 317–18). The presence of the troops, at the most 500 regular soldiers, strengthened the ZANLA presence and gave the Mozambican forces much-needed battle experience. The other foreign forces in Zimbabwe were several thousand (the lowest estimate is 2,000) South African paramilitary police and special units. They had entered the war after the abortive ZAPU–ANC campaign in the Wankie area. The South Africans played a direct role in the fighting and only withdrew just before independence in April 1980. An unknown number of British and American mercenaries served with Rhodesian units – including the Rhodesian Light Infantry, the Selous Scouts and the Greys Scouts. Among the Americans were a number of Vietnam veterans (information supplied in unattributable correspondence with an American Vietnam veteran who served with the Rhodesian Light Infantry in the last two years of the war).

The war very nearly became more internationalised in April 1979 in the run up to the installation of the puppet Muzorewa government. The Cubans and Mozambicans, in consultation with ZANU and ZAPU suggested establishing closer political unity within the loose Patriotic Front alliance and then creating a liberated zone in one of the areas controlled by nationalist guerrillas. In the liberated zone, the Patriotic Front leaders would declare an independent government prior to Muzorewa's assumption of the post of Prime Minister. The zone would be protected by a Mozambican mechanised battalion with artillery and anti-aircraft support (Martin and Johnson, 1980, pp. 305–8). That the Cubans were involved in the planning of the operation suggested that their troops could be used to strengthen the zone. But the plan, which would undoubtedly have led to a major war with South African and Cuban involvement, was aborted when ZAPU leader Joshua Nkomo turned it down. He probably did so because the operation would have been launched from Mozambique into one of the guerrilla zones secured by ZANLA forces. ZANU's leadership had gone along with the plan while it had frontline states' support but were relieved when it was dropped, 'for they were convinced that they were gradually winning the war and internationalisation of the conflict at that point, particularly the involvement of the Soviets, could have perverted the outcome' (Martin and Johnson, 1980, p. 308).

Angola: civil war and superpower competition

If suspicion and distrust on both sides of the nationalist movement in Zimbabwe prevented internationalisation of the Zimbabwean struggle, it was the hostility of the three different nationalist groups within Angola that led directly to civil war and heavy foreign military involvement.

The run up to independence had been comparatively smooth in the other former Portuguese colonies, but in Angola it was beset by division and bloodshed. The attempts of the OAU and at times the Portuguese to bring the MPLA, FNLA and UNITA together in coalition government were doomed to failure because of the different ideologies, power bases and foreign supporters of each of the movements. Throughout the struggle they had been in competition. In the early 1960s, Holden Roberto's FNLA forces had sought out and killed MPLA cadres attempting to infiltrate Angola across the Zairean border. Fighting had continued sporadically between guerrillas of the two groups right up to 1974, while UNITA forces had frequently launched attacks against the MPLA in eastern and south-eastern Angola.

It was hardly surprising that there was no goodwill or willingness to cooperate on a long-term basis. This hostility was magnified by the attitudes of the movements' foreign supporters. The FNLA was supported by Zaire, which was determined to prevent the formation of an MPLA government in Luanda and was willing to commit its military forces to ensure this. Roberto's movement was also backed by the USA and China. Washington did not want to see the MPLA, a socialist movement with a history of good relations with the Soviet Union and Cuba, installed in power in a politically sensitive region; while China was increasingly hostile to any groups supported by the Soviet Union, the rationale behind its African policies in the mid to late 1970s had become total opposition to the role being played by the Soviet Union in Africa. Although the South Africans had supported the Portuguese during the colonial war, once it was clear that Angola would become independent, Pretoria wanted to stop the MPLA (with its open commitment to supporting SWAPO and the ANC) from forming a government in Angola. It was ironic that Zambia, so often a champion of liberation in southern Africa, lined up alongside South Africa over Angola. It did not want a pro-Marxist government in Angola and in control of the Benguela railway, a vital route for Zambian trade. Opposing this line up of forces were the Soviet Union, the states of Eastern Europe and Cuba. Despite a break of two years in the early 1970s at the times of the Neto-Chipenda split in the MPLA, they had consistently supported the MPLA and were the main source of arms and military training. They were loth to see a socialist movement prevented from gaining power by right-wing movements backed by South Africa and the West.

This array of competing forces led to the most extensive war in Africa since the end of the Nigerian conflict and the most serious example of foreign military intervention since the end of the colonial era.

The foreign military build-up in Angola started within a month of the April 1974 revolution. In May, 125 Chinese military instructors and 450 tons of Chinese weapons had arrived in FNLA camps in southern Zaire (Somerville, 1986, p. 41). The advisers and arms had been asked for prior to the April coup. At that time the FNLA request received the backing of frontline states like Tanzania. They believed that the split within the MPLA was reducing its ability to fight the Portuguese and so the FNLA and UNITA should be encouraged to escalate the struggle and be helped to do so. A Tanzanian journalist and former government official told the author in 1985 that he had met Jonas Savimbi, leader of UNITA, in Dar es Salaam in 1974 during a visit to Tanzania during which the Tanzanians agreed to ask the Chinese to supply UNITA with arms. The journalist told me that Tanzania later became convinced that Savimbi had no intention of fighting the Portuguese and instead wanted arms to build up his movement to oppose the MPLA (unattributable interview).

The arrival of the Chinese assistance for the FNLA was soon complemented by CIA funding of the FNLA and covert US military assistance to Holden Roberto, according to the former CIA operative John Stockwell who played a leading role in the clandestine US operation to assist the FNLA and to obstruct the MPLA (Stockwell, 1978, pp. 67 and 258). With support from China, the USA, Romania and Zaire, Roberto sought to establish a military force that would give him the upper hand in any military struggle for control of Angola. Utilising substantial US financial help, he also sought to improve his political position in Angola by buying up Luanda's leading newspaper, *A Provincia de Angola* and one of the capital's television stations (Bridgland, 1986, p. 119).

The ink was hardly dry on the Alvor agreement of 15th January 1975, when Roberto began to make his military moves to ensure his dominant position. With the open support of the Zaireans, Roberto moved significant military forces into northern Angola – in the early months of 1975 the FNLA forces were joined by 1,500 Zairean regular troops and Zairean armoured cars. The FNLA started to move against the MPLA in February 1975. The latter movement had particularly strong support in Luanda, something which was a serious obstacle to Roberto seizing power. Within a month of Alvor, FNLA forces supported by those of Daniel Chipenda attempted to expel the MPLA from the capital. At first there were only skirmishes, but in March the FNLA launched extensive attacks on MPLA units around Luanda, destroyed a training camp at Caxito and sent 500 troops into the slums of Luanda to wipe out the MPLA stronghold there (Somerville, 1986, pp. 42–3; Bridgland, 1986, p. 119). In fighting between the MPLA on one side and the FNLA–Chipenda forces on the other, an estimated 5,000 people were killed in Luanda between February and June 1975 (*Financial Times*, 14th June 1975). As the fighting continued in the capital, the FNLA–Zairean incursion into the north became a full-scale invasion. Concerted efforts were made to push the MPLA out of northern Angola.

The influx of Chinese and Western aid to the FNLA and the invasion of northern Angola led to a resumption of Soviet aid to the MPLA. The first deliveries of Soviet arms, sent via the People's Republic of Congo, arrived in the closing months of 1974, though the quantities were quite small. In March and April 1975, arms supplies increased, with an escalation in the size and sophistication of the weapons. The Cubans were also helping the MPLA, though not on the scale that they were to do so later in the year. April 1975 also saw the entry of the South Africans into the war. The South Africans had troops based along the Angola–Namibia border and at the Ruacana power station inside Angola (ostensibly to protect South African technicians there). The Johannesburg *Star* newspaper reported on 12th April, that South African units had clashed with MPLA forces in a cross-border clash. The following month, Daniel Chipenda visited Windhoek for talks with South Africa military and political leaders on aid for the FNLA–Chipenda forces – his meeting was followed by ones between Roberto, Savimbi and the South Africans. In April, President Kaunda of Zambia visited Washington and urged the US government to give military and financial assistance to UNITA and the FNLA (Bridgland, 1986, p. 120).

Soon after the clashes with South Africa in the south, the MPLA forces there became involved in skirmishes with UNITA. The fighting escalated after May 1975, when Savimbi chose to ally himself with the FNLA against the MPLA. Fighting had also spread to the oil-rich Cabinda enclave in the north. There the Zairean and French-supported Front for the Liberation of the Cabinda Enclave (FLEC) and the FNLA were involved, quite separately, in fighting with MPLA units. According to former CIA agent Philip Agee (in Ray *et al*:, 1980, p. 5), the French intelligence services provided military support for FLEC from Francophone Africa states and also helped the CIA to recruit Western mercenaries to fight for the FNLA.

During the escalation of the fighting, various African heads of state tried to avert a civil war and to arrange ceasefire and peace talks. The Nakuru talks in June produced an agreement, but it lasted for barely three days, and the Congolese and Senegalese governments attempted to get the MPLA and UNITA to merge – this again was unsuccessful as UNITA declined to join up with the MPLA (Bridgland, 1986, p. 123).

The conciliation attempts failed and the fighting became more intense. By the end of July, the FNLA had been forced out of Luanda and the small UNITA force in the capital had been withdrawn. But the MPLA was in no position to celebrate. A combined FNLA–Zairean force was making rapid headway in northern Angola and the South Africans were intervening more heavily on UNITA's side in the south, while the Soviet Union was stepping up its arms supplies. The Soviet government newspaper *Izvestiya* said on 16th July that the Nakuru agreement was now null and void and that a civil war was under way with the West utilising the FNLA to try to destroy the MPLA. The Cubans were also becoming more closely involved. In May 1975, the MPLA leader, Agostinho Neto, had met Cuban Politburo member Flavio Bravo in Brazzaville and asked him for more help in training and arming MPLA forces. The Cubans agreed to send advisers to MPLA training camps inside Angola. It is hard to pinpoint the exact timing of the arrival of the Cuban military instructors, some observers say they were in the camps in June 1975 (Klinghoffer, 1980, pp. 110–11), others say August (Marcum, 1979, p. 191) and some as late as October (Wolfers and Bergerol, 1982, p. 29). There is also disagreement over the numbers of advisers sent, but the most reliable account, by Gabriel Garcia Marquez, the Colombian writer and friend of Fidel Castro, is that 480 advisers were dispatched to Angola (Marquez, 1977).

By the time of the Cuban arrival, the internationalisation of the conflict was well under way, with the Zaireans and South Africans using their troops to support the FNLA and UNITA inside Angolan territory and the USA supplying aid amounting to $40m to the FNLA and UNITA (Stockwell, 1978, p. 258). The South Africans had stepped up their presence in southern Angola in June and July and by mid-August had over 1,000 regular troops based at Ruacana and Caleque in southern Angola. In September, South African troops captured the town of N'Giva and gave direct combat help to UNITA forces fighting the

MPLA. The main South African invasion took place on 23rd October, when a South African armoured column joined up with UNITA to carry out a concerted drive towards the north. UNITA tried to keep up the fiction that the offensive launched in October was carried out solely by its own troops. On 26th October, it announced the capture of the town of Sa Bandeira, omitting to mention that the attack on the town was led by the South Africans. The armoured column then moved on the port of Lobito. Savimbi claimed that he had a force of 5,000 men and fifty-five armoured cars in his attack column (Bridgland, 1986, pp. 129–30). In fact, the force was primarily a South African one.

By the beginning of November, the MPLA was in a desperate position. The South African–UNITA column was heading for Luanda from the south, while the FNLA–Zairean forces were nearing the town from the north. The latter force had captured Caxito on 17th September following Mobutu's decision to reinforce the FNLA–Zairean units (who already had Portuguese and Western mercenaries serving with them) with the seventh and fourth Zairean commando battalions (Stockwell, 1978, p. 163). At the same time, Zairean forces joined FLEC in Cabinda in a bid to sever the enclave from Angola before the projected independence date of 11th November.

Although right-wing commentators have said that over one thousand Cuban combat troops had been sent to Angola in October (Robert Moss in the *Sunday Telegraph*, 30th October 1977), there is no evidence of Cubans other than the 480 instructors being present in the country prior to 7th November, when at the request of the MPLA an airlift of Cuban troops began. The advisers had been involved in the fighting though, as they had been present at MPLA training camps near Benguela that were attacked on 3rd November by the South Africans during their advance. By independence day, there were an estimated 2,800 Cuban troops serving with the MPLA (Somerville, 1986, p. 45).

The presence of the Cubans and the massive influx of Soviet arms – particularly the Stalin Organs (122mm multiple rocket launchers) – enabled the MPLA to turn back the FNLA–Zairean advance and then to repel the South African–UNITA forces. The FNLA was smashed by the MPLA using 122mm rockets and then pushed completely out of northern Angola, along with the Zaireans and the CIA-funded Western mercenaries (a number of British and American mercenaries being captured, tried and then executed or imprisoned by the MPLA government). The South Africans and UNITA were harder to dislodge, but by January 1976, there were 10,000–12,000 Cubans fighting alongside the MPLA, armed with an estimated $200m worth of Soviet arms. According to Klinghoffer, the Soviets sent $30m worth of arms between March and July 1975, $80m between August and mid-November, $90m between the end of November and January 1976, the escalation in supplies coming at the point when the MPLA was in the greatest danger and as the first Cubans arrived (Klinghoffer, 1980, pp. 27–8). The arms supplied by the USSR, along with instructors and technicians, included MiG-21s, T-34 and T-35 tanks, armoured personnel carriers, SAM-7 missiles and 12mm multiple rocket launchers. A number of Soviet warships were stationed off the coast during the heaviest phase of the fighting, though it is unclear whether they played any direct role in helping the MPLA–Cuban forces. The South Africans were eventually forced out of the south in March 1976. They had suffered an ignominious defeat. In a statement to the South African parliament at the end of January 1976, Defence Minister P.W. Botha admitted the retreat and said that forty-three South Africans had been killed in the fighting (probably an under-estimate, as the South Africans sought to play down the extent of their setback). As the South Africans retreated back into Namibia, they systematically destroyed the infrastructure of Angola as they went. Economic facilities and transport installations were demolished and fifty major road bridges in the south of the country were blasted by the SADF. The Angolan government estimated the damage at $6.7bn (Angolan Government, 1983).

UNITA's bid to seize power effectively ended with the South African withdrawal. On 14th March, the retreat of the South Africans and the advance by the Cuban–MPLA column, forced it to abandon its last major stronghold at Gago Coutinho. Savimbi had to abandon the town despite support from twenty French mercenaries (jointly funded by the CIA and the French secret service) and supplies of anti-tank missiles from a US stockpile in Kinshasa (Bridgland, 1986, p. 198). The remains of the UNITA army abandoned attempts to hold towns and moved into the bush along the Namibian and Zambian borders. The movement, bereft of its foreign military support though not South African arms and other supplies, was unable to directly confront the government and Cuban units, though it was able to keep small guerrilla units inside southern Angola. These carried out small-scale guerrilla raids and sabotage attacks. They received military and medical supplies and financial aid from the South Africans, and it is thought that Chinese aid to UNITA, started on a small scale just before the civil war, continued for a year or two after Angola's independence, though this was denied by the Chinese. In the north, the FNLA launched sporadic guerrilla attacks across the border from Zaire for a couple of years, until Angolan counter-insurgency offensives and Zaire's decision to end support for the movement effectively ended the FNLA's existence as a credible movement.

The victory over UNITA, the FNLA, Zaire and South Africa led to the consolidation of MPLA control over most of the country (only small pockets in the south remained in UNITA's hands). The new government's security was ensured by the presence of around 15,000 Cuban combat troops and the continuing shipments of substantial quantities of modern Soviet weapons. In the wake of independence, several hundred Soviet military advisers arrived in Angola to establish a training team to help build a national army from the MPLA's guerrilla force. Some Cuban and Soviet advisers also helped train ANC, SWAPO and ZAPU guerrillas in camps in Angola. Angola's support for these liberation movements and the MPLA's increasing emphasis on Marxism–Leninism ensured the hostility of the South Africans and the suspicion of neighbouring conservative states, such as Zaire. The United States of America, whose interventionist but rather half-hearted stance on Angola had failed miserably, refused to come to terms with the MPLA victory and denied recognition of the MPLA government, using the presence of Cuban troops in the country as a pretext. US policy was to develop, under Ronald Reagan and his African affairs chief Chester Crocker, into direct opposition to the MPLA through military, financial and diplomatic aid to UNITA and, for a number of years, tacit support for South Africa's war of destabilisation in southern Africa.

The scattered groups of UNITA guerrillas launched a campaign of sabotage (backed and often openly assisted by the SADF) in southern and central Angola, wreaking havoc with the local agricultural economy and depriving the country as a whole of staple foods. UNITA guerrilla leaders openly admitted killing peasants who went out to work the fields in Bie province in order to disrupt food supplies (Bridgland, 1986, p. 239). Transport routes, notably the Benguela railway, became prime targets. The strategy achieved UNITA's aims of weakening the government and preventing the MPLA from launching its political and economic programmes in parts of the country, and Pretoria's objective of destabilising the country and disrupting a vital part of the southern African transport network. By 1979, the Benguela railway had virtually ceased to operate.

But the South African withdrawal did not limit the SADF to backing UNITA. Between March and August 1976, seventeen raids were mounted into Angola by the South African army and over the remaining years of the decade, raiding into Angola became a regular occupation for South African soldiers based in northern Namibia. SADF personnel took part in UNITA attacks in southern and central provinces – one soldier being captured by the Angolan army during a sweep against UNITA in Cuando Cubango in August 1976. They attacked Angolan army outposts, laid mines inside Angola, carried out sabotage attacks and attacked refugee camps housing people who had fled from South African-controlled Namibia – the largest raid against the camps took place against the Kassinga refugee camp on 4th May 1977, in which 612 men, women and children were killed. During 1977, one South African raid took the SADF 200 kilometres into Cuando Cubango province in the south.

As well as having to fight UNITA and the South Africans, the MPLA also had to cope with its own internal dissensions. Always vulnerable to factional strife, the party suffered a serious blow in May 1977, when Nito Alves, a former Central Committee member and Minister of the Interior, carried out a coup attempt supported by small sections of the party and armed forces. The coup failed but the Finance Minister and a number of senior party leaders were killed in the fighting. Cuban troops played a role in supporting the government and suppressing the coup (Somerville, Winter 1984, p. 299). There were Western reports at the time of the coup of Soviet complicity in the coup attempt, but these were without firm evidence and were based almost totally on Alves's attendance at the Soviet Communist Party Congress in 1976 and his praise for the Soviet Union afterwards (Klinghoffer, 1980, p. 131). Far from supporting the coup, the USSR remained a firm backer of the Neto government.

For a period, though, in the late 1970s and early 1980s, the Angolan army achieved a string of successes against UNITA. The army gained strength as it grew into a better trained, armed and more experienced force. UNITA was limited to small-scale raids and a settled presence only in areas along the border with Namibia where South Africa could offer direct military assistance and logistical support. This situation was to change in the early 1980s, following the adoption of a more aggressive policy by Pretoria, with the backing of the Reagan administration.

Zaire: foreign intervention in the Shaba conflicts

The end of the civil war in the 1960s and President Mobutu's establishment of a ruthless, autocratic regime led to a period of relative political stability for Zaire. Although the government was unable to root out all opposition and small groups of rebels remained active in mountainous and heavily forested areas of the south and east of the country. Most of the rebels were Lumumba loyalists. One group though, the Katangan gendarmerie which had been loyal to Tshombe, had fled into northern Angola in the wake of the civil war and the crushing of the Katangan secession. They remained a more or less cohesive force in Angola into the mid-1970s. During the Angolan civil war, Zairean links with the FNLA automatically put the Katangans on the side of the MPLA, which made no attempt to disband or disarm the group. During the FNLA–Zairean offensive in 1975, the Katangans were said to have fought alongside the MPLA in defence of Luanda. At the end of the war, President Neto of Angola is believed to have allowed members of the Congolese National Liberation Front (FNLC) to have facilities in Angola and to contact Zairean exiles in northern Angola (*ACR*, 1977–8, pp. B592–3). Relations between the FNLC and the Katangans may well have developed during this period.

In March 1977, during a period of increasing tension between Angola and Zaire, due mainly to the maintenance of Zairean support for the FNLA, the Katangans and other refugees in northern Angola crossed into Zaire's Shaba province and occupied a number of towns in Western Shaba. The exiles and former gendarmes reached to within twenty-five miles of the major mining centre at Kolwezi. Initially, the Zairean army was totally unable to cope with the incursion. President Mobutu accused Angola, Cuba and the Soviet Union of having masterminded the attack and some Western commentators said that Cuban and Soviet personnel were involved in the attack, though eyewitnesses in Shaba said that no Cubans or Soviets were involved, an account backed by US intelligence reports at the time; though the Soviet Union was clearly sympathetic to the FNLC. On 16th April 1977, the Soviet Communist Party paper *Pravda* referred favourably to the 'Congo National Liberation Front which is leading the rising in the south of Zaire' – the paper had earlier rejected 'fabrications' about Soviet involvement in the incursion.

When the incursion started, the FNLC claimed responsibility. Mobutu feared a more general uprising and requested help from his allies in Europe, America and Africa. The result was that a major Western-backed rescue mission was organised. On 7th April, 1,500 Moroccan troops were flown to Zaire by French Transall military transport aircraft along with sixty-five French military advisers.

The French advisers and Moroccans played a major role in the defence of Kolwezi and the organisation of the counter-offensive that cleared the area of rebels. US military, logistical and financial aid was also provided to the Mobutu government, while the Belgians sent an unknown number of advisers to assist in a retraining programme for the shaken and clearly ineffective Zairean army. The French logistical and support role was vital for the success of the operation. The French were keen to support Mobutu and by doing so increase influence in a strategic region. Furthermore, there was strong pressure from conservative African states such as Senegal and Cote d'Ivoire for the French to come to the aid of a fellow conservative leader (*ACR* 1977–8, p. B594). President Giscard d'Estaing defended the French action on the grounds that the aid to Zaire had been of a limited nature and because France had committed itself to 'combat the subversion of friendly African countries' (*Le Monde*, 24th April 1977). Although there was clear cooperation between the Western powers over Shaba, D'Estaing denied that French aid had been provided after consultation with the Carter administration in Washington – he was keen to project the action as a purely French one. This was both for home consumption and in order to persuade Zaire and other African states that it was France, first and foremost, which could be relied upon among the Western powers to come to Africa's assistance.

The first Shaba crisis caused a serious deterioration in Zairean–Angolan relations, which had been poor to start with. The situation worsened in late 1977 and early 1978. In May, the FNLC and the remnants of the Katangans launched another invasion from across the Angolan border and from the Zambian border region of Mwinilunga. It started on 11th May and again the Zairean army was totally unable to stem the advance by the rebel force of 4,000. One reason for the Zairean army's bad performance was the purge that had taken place after the first debacle, another was that the FNLC fighters had started infiltrating into Zaire in small groups well before the main attack was launched. Many were in place in Shab on 11th May and were able to organise themselves to attack and push back Zairean forces. Fighting raged for several days, during which time FNLC units reached Kolwezi. Once more the Zaireans seemed unable to cope with the attack and the units in Shaba dissolved into a rabble which spent more time killing civilians and looting than fighting the rebels. A number of massacres took place in Kolwezi during the fighting, some carried out by the rebels and some by the army. At least forty-four European civilians were killed in Kolwezi during the fighting in the town; some of them as a result of being used as human shields by the Zairean troops.

The threat of total anarchy in the important copper-mining area and the threat to the lives of 600 Europeans there (not to mention the likelihood that Mobutu could lose Shaba completely), led to another Western-sponsored rescue mission. On this occasion French and Belgian combat troops played a direct role in the fighting. On 19th May, 400 paratroops of the French Foreign Legion were dropped into Kolwezi and 1,000 Belgian troops were sent to the Kamina air base in southern Zaire to assist in what French and Belgian spokesmen said was a 'limited operation' to rescue the threatened Europeans. In fact, it was very clearly a counter-offensive to smash the rebels and restore Zairean government control. The French troops engaged the rebels in several clashes in and around Kolwezi, killing an estimated 300 rebels before regaining control of the town. The rebels retreated, killing forty European hostages as they fled. Thousands of Zaireans died during the fighting – at least 2,000 in Kolwezi itself – along with 250 Europeans. By the end of the fighting, a total of 600 French Foreign Legion personnel, 100 paratroops and three companies of regular soldiers from other units were involved in the fighting (Chipman, 1985, p. 13). A total of 1,750 Belgians were also fighting on behalf of the Zaireans. The operation to fly in the French and Belgian forces had been directed by the USA, using aircraft from the US Military Airlift Command and utilising French air bases in Dakar and Libreville to refuel the troop carriers (Mangold, 1979).

Again the primary reason for the Western and particularly the French, military intervention was to protect Mobutu and ensure Western access to a mineral-rich region. The French had huge investments in Zairean mining and purchased over a third of their copper from the Shaba mines. As George Moose has argued, the French saw their task in Shaba II 'as not only the immediate securing of the expatriate community's safety but also the reestablishment of order in Shaba that would permit the continued functioning of the mining sector and end the threat the invasion had posed to the very existence of the Zairean government' (Moose, 1985, p. 71). The Americans had had similar objectives in launching their logistical programme to support the French and Belgians.

Once the immediate threat to the Zairean government had been quashed and a semblance of order restored, the French and Belgians made it abundantly clear that while they, along with the Americans, were prepared to help rebuild the Zairean army and to supply weapons and financial aid, they had no intention of maintaining a permanent armed presence in Shaba. To fill the security vacuum that this would create in Shaba, the French used the 1978 Franco–African summit in May 1978 to put together a joint African force (financed and given logistical support by Paris, Brussels and Washington) to replace the French and Belgian troops. The 1,500 strong force consisted of Moroccan, Togolese, Senegalese, Ivorian and Gabonese troops. The initiative shored up the regime in Zaire but did nothing to solve its basic problems of political instability and economic chaos.

In the wake of the crisis, President Carter issued sweeping and totally unfounded accusations of Soviet and Cuban involvement in the invasion. He said that he knew that 'the Cubans have played a key role in training and equipping the Katangans'. On 30th May, he repeated the accusations, adding in the Soviet Union for good measure, at a NATO summit in Washington. Carter's account was contradicted by the Belgian Foreign Minister when he visited Angola in September 1978. He said that there was no evidence of foreign participation in the Zairean rebels actions (*ACR* 1978–9, p. B578).

The only positive development to emerge from the two Shaba conflicts was reconciliation, though not warm or cooperative relations, between Angola and Zaire. On 10th June 1978, President Neto promised to disarm any FNLC elements left in Angola, while Mobutu agreed to disarm and end support for the FNLA, FLEC and UNITA. After mediation by the Portuguese and Congolese governments, President Neto visited Kinshasa from 19th–21st August to cement the new chapter in relations.

French military intervention: a continuing story

The military involvement of the French government in Zaire and its covert aid to FLEC, the FNLA and UNITA were far from the only French adventures in Africa during the 1970s. Not only did France continue to maintain significant military forces in Africa and to enjoy the use of army, naval and air bases around the continent, but it used its presence to interfere brazenly in the domestic affairs of African states – either to give direct security assistance to unstable regimes or, on occasions to topple leaders no longer acceptable to the government in Paris. French military involvement and the use of armed force against perceived opponents in Africa was not limited to the use of the French armed forces. There is strong evidence to show that French mercenaries were also employed by the Giscard d'Estaing government to further its objectives on the continent – notably in the Comoros and Benin.

The activist and interventionist policy of the French government came in for heavy criticism from many African leaders (mainly from non-Francophone or from radical Francophone countries) in the last four years of the decade. France was seen by many African states as a greater threat to the security and stability of the continent than the Soviet Union or Cuba. At the Khartoum summit of the Organisation of African Unity in late July 1978, France came under very heavy attack for the role it had played in Zaire, Benin and Sao Tome (the latter two being threatened by mercenary led coups for which France was held largely to blame in Africa). President Giscard d'Estaing's calls for a pan-African military force (backed by France and other Western powers) was denounced by President Nyerere of Tanzania as 'the height of arrogance'. He went on to say that 'it is quite obvious, moreover, that those who seek to initiate such a force are not interested in the freedom of Africa. They are interested in the domination of Africa'. Nyerere said that Africa was threatened more by the West than by the Soviet Union and China and that the continent rejected 'the right of West European countries to dominate Africa'. Resolutions of the summit and of the earlier OAU Council of Ministers meeting in Tripoli denounced foreign military intervention in Africa and the use of mercenaries to overthrow or threaten governments.

But the French still had their supporters within the OAU. Senegal, Cote d'Ivoire, Togo, Gabon and, obviously, Zaire, all gave backing to the French involvement in Africa and to its policy of military support for friendly states. President Houphouet-Boigny of Cote d'Ivoire summed up the feelings of this group when he said that 'I believe that Europeans have understood the absolute necessity to see to it that our development takes place in an atmosphere of absolute security.'

The idea of a pan-African force, apart from the isolated case of the joint force sent to Chad by the OAU and the Western-backed one in Zaire, did not take off. Most African leaders opposed the idea of a permanent or ad hoc force put together with the backing of any external powers. They saw the idea as a means for countries like France to get African states to do their dirty work on the continent or to protect outside interests on the continent. Far from ensuring security, the idea was seen as a destabilising one that would render Africa ever more vulnerable to foreign influence and pressure.

But regardless of the failure of the initiative, the French continued to play an activist role in Africa until the end of Giscard d'Estaing's presidency. One of the main areas of involvement was Chad (see chapter on Chad), but French forces also played an active and interventionist role in Mauritania, the Western Sahara, Niger, Djibouti and the Central Africa Republic, French mercenaries, generally thought to have been acting on behalf of the French government, also intervened, with varying degrees of success in the Comoros, Benin and Sao Tome e Principe.

Apart from direct military intervention, the French armed forces maintained a strong presence in Africa (particularly West and Central Africa) and bolstered a number of conservative regimes there in the process. At the end of the 1970s, the French had troops stationed in six African states and advisers in seventeen. This represented a reduction in the numbers of troops stationed in the region but an increase in the spread of the advisers. The troops were still stationed in Djibouti (3,500 plus aircraft and naval craft), Gabon (between 200 and 400 plus an air force unit), Cote d'Ivoire (400), Senegal (1,200) and Cameroon (number unknown but under 100) and the Central African Republic (1,100). The advisers were scattered around the same and other former French territories plus Burundi, Rwanda and Zaire (the latter hosting 128 advisers). The French had base facilities in Djibouti, Gabon, Cote d'Ivoire and Senegal. They may have enjoyed the use of facilities in Cameroon and Togo, too (Luckham, 1982, p. 57; and *ACR* 1978–9 and 1979–80).

Some of the instances of French intervention in the affairs of host states or the dispatch of forces to help close allies were in answer to requests from the governments of those states – notably the use of a small detachment of about 270 French troops in Niger in 1973 to help the head of state, President Hamani Diori, to maintain power at a time of severe drought and internal unrest. Diori feared a military coup and used French military support to stave it off. The French were keen to help maintain stability in Niger because of concern of the government in Paris of continued access to uranium deposits in northern Niger. The French also wanted to give a clear message to Libya not to interfere in Niger. But French help did not save Diori from the consequences of economic mismanagement and internal discontent – he was overthrown by the army in 1974. But the new head of state, Seyni Kountche, remained close to France, even though he asked the French to withdraw their troops. But in 1976, Kountche renewed the Franco–Nigerian Defence Cooperation Agreement and in 1977 there were said to be around a hundred French military advisers in Niger (*ACR* 1977–8, p. B723). Although by the end of the decade there were no French forces stationed in

Niger (there had been 200–300 in 1970), there were still several score of military advisers. The French remained Niger's major source of military equipment and training and there was implicit in the relationship a French guarantee of assistance in the case of external aggression.

The fear of external aggression was a real one for Niger. It shared a common border with Libya, which from the early years of Colonel Qadhafi's rule showed every intention of interfering in the affairs of its African neighbours and of using subversion and military force where necessary to achieve Libya's objectives. An uneasy relationship developed in the mid-1970s, with an improvement in 1978 during a visit to Niamey by Qadhafi. Kountche later visited Tripoli, where he turned down a Libyan proposal to acquire a major financial stake in Niger's uranium industry. But Libya's increased military involvement in Chad led to worries in Niger about Libya's ultimate intentions. This served to keep Niger close to France, particularly in the military sphere.

In the Horn of Africa, France continued to rule the small enclave of Djibouti until 1977. The Republic of Djibouti came into being on 27th June 1977. However, its size, its small population and its geographical location (sandwiched between Ethiopia and Somalia) ensured that it remained heavily dependent on France for its security. Thus security was threatened by rivalry between the Afar and Issa nationalities within the state and by Somali irredentism. Shortly before independence, the French military forces in Djibouti carried out operations Lovada and Saphir against small groups of Somali guerrillas operating in Djibouti. It was the French presence and the fear of an open conflict with France that largely prevented Somalia from pressing its claims that Djibouti should be part of Somalia through the use of military force. At the time of independence, there were 4,300 French troops based in Djibouti (two infantry regiments, naval patrol units and air force personnel manning a squadron of twelve Mirage combat aircraft), this had been reduced to 3,500 by 1980. The French retained the use of airfields and dock facilities in Djibouti. The independence accords reached with France included a military protocol allowing France to station up to 4,500 troops in Djibouti. It also included a provision allowing French military intervention at Djibouti's request 'if the Republic of Djibouti was the victim of aggression and in the case of legitimate defence' (*Marche Tropicaux*, 1st July 1977). French military aid was provided to Djibouti; in 1978 it totalled 57m French francs (*ACR* 1978–9, p. B207). Although by the beginning of the 1980s, France had withdrawn some of its troops, it had upgraded the weapons of the remaining garrison – which was equipped with AMX tanks, 150mm artillery pieces, helicopters, Mirages and transport planes.

France maintained a high profile in Francophone West Africa, with troops based in Cote d'Ivoire, Gabon and Senegal. Frequent military exercises were held by the French in cooperation with the armies of the host states. In 1981, for example, 1,500 French soldiers and 1,800 members of the Ivorian forces held an exercise at Touba, close to the border with Guinea. At the time, relations between France and Cote d'Ivoire, on the one hand, and Guinea on the other were far from good. The holding of a major exercise close to the border was a clear message to President Sekou Toure of Guinea that France was ready to support Cote d'Ivoire if it was called upon to do so. The exercises were held under the 1961 defence agreement. It was hardly a coincidence that the exercises followed closely on the Libyan military intervention in Chad in support of Goukouni Oueddei.

France's relations with Gabon mirrored those with Cote d'Ivoire, though there was some strain in the late 1970s, when rumours started circulating that the French were building a major air base there. President Omar Bongo strongly denied the rumours and said that the construction of a large airfield was under way, but that it was to be used by the Gabon armed forces as a base for a squadron of Mirages being purchased from France. But the Gabon government did not deny that 500 French troops were stationed near Libreville (including 400 marines) or that regular joint military exercises were held by the armed forces of the two countries.

After Djibouti, Senegal hosts the largest French force in Africa (around 1,100 troops plus aircraft and naval vessels). The bases in Senegal have been used to conduct operations in the Western Sahara and Mauritania (see below) and as a staging post for the interventions in Zaire and Chad. The Senegalese government sees the relationship with France as the backbone of its foreign and security policies. Joint military exercises and war games are held regularly; and, as with the exercises in Cote d'Ivoire, are used to convey messages to potential or perceived aggressors. In 1979, extensive war games were held in the tense Cassamance region of Senegal (the area containing the most serious internal opposition to the government and one in which Libya has frequently been accused by the Senegalese of interfering in order to subvert the government). The French forces taking part included 400 marines, two companies of paratroops, combat helicopter units, Jaguar fighter-bombers and air transport units (Luckham, 1982, p. 55).

Perhaps the most serious example of French military intervention in Africa in the 1970s took place in the Central Africa Empire, which as a result of the coup involving French forces once more became the Central African Republic. The coup, carried out by French troops based in CAR with the assistance of units flown in for that purpose, removed Emperor Bokassa. He had ruled the CAR since overthrowing President David Dacko on 31st December 1965. Bokassa had received extensive support from France after taking power and was seen as one of France's closest allies on the continent, despite his openly repressive regime and his appalling human rights record. On 4th December 1977, Bokassa had himself crowned as Emperor of Central Africa in a ludicrous ceremony paid for largely by the French. France was a vital economic and military support for Bokassa, regularly paying his budget deficit and training and equipping his armed forces. Over 1,000 French troops were stationed in the country and under a defence agreement signed in August 1978, a French military base had been set up at Bouar. Although under the defence agreement between the two countries they could only be used for defence against external aggression, in January 1979, French officers and NCOs are said to have led a Zairean commando unit in brutally repressing demonstrations in Bangui by schoolchildren and students. The students were protesting against having to wear uniforms bearing Bokassa's name and effigy. Unable to cope with the scale of the riots, Bokassa called for external help. About 200–300 Zairean commandos were sent to the CAR in late January. They suppressed the demonstrations with extreme ruthlessness, killing many of the students – some reports said 12 died, others said over 100 were killed (*ACR* 1978–9, p. B519). But reports in a leading publication on Africa said that in the repression that followed the protests as many as 1,000 opponents of the government were killed (*West Africa*, 5th February 1979).

Despite this close relationship with France, Bokassa also cultivated good ties with Libya and in the late 1970s was drawing closer to Qadhafi. He was perhaps aware that his brutal rule was beginning to become a severe embarrassment for the French. It was during a visit to Libya on 20th September 1979 that the French intervened to overthrow Bokassa. Bokassa was said to be in Libya seeking military assistance in return for allowing Libya to use military bases in the CAR – one at Ndele near the country's northern border with Chad and the other being the French Bouar base. From Libya's point of view, the use of the bases would be a huge strategic asset in the war in Chad and a springboard for possible military adventures further south. In addition, Bokassa was a Muslim and could be a useful ally in the Muslim world. Qadhafi is said to have admitted that he was willing to cultivate relations with dictators such as Idi Amin and Bokassa because they were Muslims and because at times they adopted foreign policies in tune with Libya's. The Libyan leader agreed that their internal policies might be repressive but said that 'I dislike even more the interference [in African affairs] of France and Tanzania' (Blundy and Lycett, 1986, p. 185).

Prior to his overthrow, Bokassa had become too tainted with charges of personal involvement in atrocities for even the French to maintain open support for him. He was accused of taking part in the beating to death of schoolchildren who had protested against him. The French withdrew their military assistance for his regime (prompting the trip to Libya) and established relations with the former president, David Dacko, and with other opposition figures. When Bokassa flew to Libya, the French decided to act. They launched Operation Barracuda, which involved the dispatch of French commando units to Bangui to install David Dacko as President. Dacko immediately restored the country's republican status and its previously close ties with France. French troops used to overthrow Bokassa remained in the country (amid severe criticism of the whole operation in France itself) and the base at Bouar was reactivated. In January 1981, the French force in CAR was reinforced with 500 marines and four Jaguar aircraft following the announcement of the union between Libya and Chad.

Dacko broke off all relations with Libya after the coup, accusing it of subversion and of supporting two of Dacko's opponents, Idi Lala and Ange Patasse. Libya only regained a foothold in CAR when Dacko was overthrown by General Kolingba on 1st September 1981. Dacko's political demise followed months of domestic unrest and the suppression of opposition groups. Once again the French may have had a role in the ending of Dacko's rule, as they were close to the army and were becoming impatient with the President's inefficiency and intolerance of all opposition (though this was something they were willing to put up with in other, more stable states). One reason for the change in French policy towards Dacko was the defeat of Giscard d'Estaing in the May 1981 elections and his replacement by Francois Mitterrand. Mitterrand had severely criticised French policy in CAR, saying that d'Estaing had not rescued the country, as he claimed, by getting rid of Bokassa, he had just substituted 'corrupt men for corrupt men' (*Africa Confidential*, 15th October 1981). But Mitterrand did not withdraw completely from the CAR's affairs, as troops stayed in the country (which was a vital rear base for French involvement in Chad) and France continued to give vital budgetary and other financial support.

If French involvement in the CAR was overt, that in the events in the Comoros in 1978 was clandestine in the extreme. In May 1978, a coup took place in the Comoros in which a force of mercenaries (mainly former French paratroops) led by Bob Denard overthrew the Marxist government of Ali Solih and put in power Ahmed Abdallah (who himself had been ousted by Solih in 1975). Abdallah was pro-French and acquiesced in French retention of the Comoros island of Mayotte, the site of a French naval base. The coup was clearly a conservative one and one that greatly improved the French position in the region. French complicity, if not planning and funding, of the coup was suspected (ACR 1978–9, p. B190). Immediately after the coup, a hundred Tanzanian troops which had been stationed on the islands to support Solih were withdrawn. They were replaced by French mercenaries and by French military advisers. In November 1978, Abdallah visited Paris to sign treaties confirming the closeness of political and military relations. A defence agreement was included which allowed for 'mutual assistance' in cases of external aggression. The French also undertook to train and equip the Comoran armed forces (*Marche Tropicaux*, 17th November 1978). The French showed no willingness to give up Mayotte and continued to station over 2,000 men there and to use the base as a vital part of its naval presence in the Indian Ocean. The French presence on Mayotte and its military activities in the Indian Ocean were denounced by the OAU Council of Ministers meeting in Tripoli in 1978 as 'flagrant aggression against the independent states of Africa'. Abdallah consented to the French presence though at OAU meetings he made weak and ineffectual calls for the return of the island to the Comoros.

A less successful mercenary attack was made against the pro-Marxist government of Mathieu Kerekou in Benin. On 16th January 1977, a mercenary force led by Denard (going under the alias of Gilbert Bourgeaud) arrived in Cotonou by air and launched an invasion attempt. The mercenary group, was made up of former French soldiers, a few Africans and about a hundred Beninois. They attacked installations between the airport and capital city but were unable to make real headway and fled after three hours of shooting. Eight people were killed during the coup attempt. A UN enquiry blamed Morocco and Gabon (for whom Denard was working – he was also employed by the French secret services) for staging the coup attempt (Allen, 1989, p. 39).

Western Sahara: the desert war

A guerrilla war has been in progress in the Sahara for the past seventeen years. It is being fought between the Polisario Front (a liberation movement representing the peoples of the Western Sahara) and the Moroccan government (which claims sovereignty over the same area). Conflict over the region has been going on, with periodic lulls, since 1956, when the Moroccans first put forward a serious claim to the area of the Western Sahara then controlled by Spain. At times the struggle has taken on a distinctly international aspect with France, Mauritania and Algeria becoming directly involved in the fighting and the USA, Libya and Cuba playing supporting roles. The conflict has also had a serious effect on the continental politics of Africa by disrupting a series of OAU summits.

Although the Moroccans, Mauritanians and Saharawis (a collective name for the ethnic groups inhabiting the Western Sahara region, including parts of southern Morocco and northern Mauritania) all lay claim to the Western Sahara and all refer to historical justifications for their respective claims, prior to Spanish and French colonisation of the region, there was no Saharawi state, no established Moroccan control or Mauritanian control over the region. It was inhabited by a number of nomadic peoples whose loyalties were to family, clan and tribe. Certainly, the nomadic peoples saw themselves as distinct from the more settled Berber peoples to the north and from the black Africans to the south, but there was no real sense of nation, rather a shared way of life and culture (Hodges, 1983, p. 149). Like with many colonised peoples, the effects of rule by a single colonial power did much to create a sense of unity, even if it was a rather negative unity based on common opposition to something rather than the sharing of common objectives and values.

When Morocco became independent in 1956, the Moroccan nationalists, notably the Istiqlal party, laid claim to areas to the south of the country which were still under Spanish rule. Although Spain recognised Morocco, it refused to hand over the territories of southern Morocco which it still controlled. It also denied that Morocco had any legitimate claim to the Spanish Sahara. The Moroccan nationalists had a strong claim to the Spanish ruled part of Morocco but a more dubious one to the Sahara. The Istiqlal and other Moroccan nationalists also laid claim, with little justification other than territorial expansionism, to the French colony of Mauritania.

Within weeks of the independence of Morocco, the nationalists started a war of liberation in southern Morocco. With the assistance of the people of the region, and many Saharawis who were excited by Morocco's achievement of independence, had formed the Army of Liberation. This movement sought to continue the low-level guerrilla struggle started by Moroccan nationalists in Spanish Morocco in 1954. During 1956, hundreds of guerrillas joined the Army of Liberation and large numbers of Saharawis of the Reguibat and other ethnic groups trekked north across the desert to take part. Some Saharawis also launched attacks in the Tindouf area of Algeria – a region controlled by the

French but also claimed by Morocco – and in northern Mauritania. The latter attacks threatened French mining interests around the settlement of Zouerate. In 1957, the Army of Liberation made a concerted attempt to seize the Ifni region, the most important part of Spanish Morocco. The offensive largely succeeded and the Spanish forces withdrew to an area along the narrow coastal belt. But the success there was not translated into gains in the rest of the Sahara region. The guerrilla attacks in the Spanish Sahara, Algeria and Mauritania angered the French, who drew up a plan for a joint counter-offensive with the Spanish. Codenamed Ouragan, this took place in February 1958. Although it left Ifni in Moroccan hands, it effectively destroyed the Army of Liberation in all its other operational zones. Many of the Saharawi guerrillas slipped away into the desert, but the liberation forces were smashed and no more serious nationalist activity took place in the Sahara or surrounding areas for over a decade. Morocco's only gain from the brief war (one which the Moroccan government was careful to keep a safe distance from by not directly involving Moroccan regular forces) was Spain's recognition of Moroccan sovereignty over Tarfaya (Thompson and Adloff, 1980, p. 111).

But this setback did not push the Moroccans into dropping their claims to the Spanish Sahara or Mauritania. The claims to the former became stronger after mining operations started at the Bou Craa phosphate deposits in Spanish Sahara. At around the same time as the guerrillas campaign, the leaders of the Mauritanian nationalist movement indicated their interest in the Spanish Sahara. The future Mauritanian President, Mokhtar Ould Daddah, said in 1957, 'I cannot help evoking the innumerable ties which unite us; we bear the same names, we speak the same language, we conserve the same noble traditions, we honour the same religious leaders, graze our herds on the same pastures, give water to them at the same wells. In a word we are referring to that same desert civilisation of which we are so proud. So I invite our brothers of the Spanish Sahara to dream of this great economic and spiritual Mauritania.' Given Morocco's claims to Mauritania, Daddah also appealed to the Saharawis to end their support for the Moroccan-led Army of Liberation (cited by Hodges, 1983, p. 100). Daddah was right in recognising cultural, ethnic and religious similarities between the people of Mauritania (at least the originally nomadic and Arabic-speaking peoples of northern Mauritania who formed the political elite) and the communities in the Sahara, but his main reason for advancing the claim seems to have been to create a buffer of some sort between Mauritania, still then under French rule, and Morocco.

But the people of the Sahara were not greatly interested in unity with Mauritania or with Morocco. Those who had fought with the Army of Liberation had done so more because of the enthusiasm for revolt against colonial rule engendered by the period of decolonisation and because of their own warlike heritage (desert raiding had been a way of life for many of the Saharawi people before and even during colonial rule) than because of any attachment to the ideals or aims of the Moroccan nationalists. The defeat of the Army of Liberation led to a scattering of its Saharawi members and some disillusionment with the manner of Moroccan leadership. The people of the Spanish Sahara did not have any great nationalist yearnings at this time and political life (partly because the indigenous peoples were excluded from the administration of the territory for a long time) was more or less non-existent. It was to be a decade or more until any significant Saharawi nationalist stirrings occurred.

The 1960s were a period of conflict in the north-west African region. Even after Mauritania's independence in 1960, the Moroccans maintained their claim to the country – even though this was rebuffed by the OAU following its formation. Morocco also claimed the Tindouf region of Algeria, which contained major ore deposits of commercial value. The Moroccan government claimed that one of the Algerian nationalist leaders, Ferhat Abbas, had recognised Morocco's rights over Tindouf as part of an agreement which brought about Moroccan recognition of the Algerian liberation movement during the liberation war against France. The government of independent Algeria asked Morocco for time to establish itself in power before considering the Moroccan demand for the return of Tindouf. Unwilling to wait for negotiations, the Moroccans launched incursions into Algeria in July and September 1963 and then a major invasion in October. At first, Algerian counter-attacks were successful, but then the Moroccans continued their advance to within a few miles of Tindouf. OAU mediation brought the fighting to an end before it became more serious – Cuba had sent several hundred combat troops to Algeria to assist the revolutionary government there in the event of a full-scale invasion. An agreement on demilitarisation and future joint exploitation of the Tindouf area was signed in February 1964, but never seriously implemented by either side.

The Morocco–Algeria conflict led to a period of poor relations. Algeria opposed Morocco's designs on both Mauritania and the Sahara; one reason being that a larger, economically stronger Morocco would be in a better position to attempt another invasion of Tindouf. In 1966, Algeria openly supported Mauritania in its opposition to Morocco's irredentist claims and also made it clear that it would prefer Mauritanian control of the Sahara rather than see Morocco gain more territory.

It was only in 1969 that King Hassan of Morocco and President Houari Boumedienne of Algeria patched up their differences. At a meeting in January, the Alegerian leader offered Morocco an agreement on joint exploitation of certain of the Tindouf deposits and they both adopted a more conciliatory approach to their border dispute and towards regional developments, such as the Sahara and Mauritania. This was followed by Hassan issuing a personal invitation to President Daddah of Mauritania to attend the Islamic Summit in Rabat in September 1969. There he formally dropped Morocco's claims to Mauritania and agreed on the opening of diplomatic relations. Ambassadors were exchanged on 2nd February 1970 (Rabat home service in Arabic 2nd February 1970). The warmer relations established between the three states led to agreement on future policy towards the Spanish Sahara. All three agreed to put ever greater pressure on Spain to withdraw and to support the Saharawis in opposing Spanish rule. Relations improved further following tripartite talks at the Rabat summit of the OAU in June 1972. According to Mauritanian accounts of the meeting, Algeria agreed to recognise Mauritanian and Moroccan claims to the Sahara, and therefore to effective partition of the territory following the withdrawal of the Spanish. However, publicly Morocco, Mauritania and Algeria all supported the UN resolution passed in December 1966 by the General Assembly calling for a referendum in the Sahara on the future of the territory – a move opposed by Spain. The call for a referendum was backed by the OAU Council of Ministers in 1969 – a position to which the OAU has adhered ever since. In 1973 and early 1974, Mauritania and Algeria continued to campaign forcefully for a referendum; Morocco called weakly for one, its original support for the idea having been tactical in order to put greater pressure on Spain to withdraw.

But the international and regional efforts had little effect at first. This was due partly to Spanish intransigence and partly to the seeming acquiescence to Spanish rule. But in the late 1960s, things began to change in the Sahara. There was a gradual but nonetheless important growth in nationalist feelings, particularly among the small educated elite. In the closing years of the decade, the more modern Saharawis came to hear of the UN debates on the Sahara, of the existence of valuable mineral deposits at Bou Craa and of the growing Algerian–Mauritania–Moroccan cooperation to get rid of the Spanish. As Tony Hodges has pointed out, many Saharawis had access to radios, the medium by which scattered and nomadic peoples could best keep in touch with domestic and regional political developments (Hodges, 1983, p. 152). As they learned more about moves to end Spanish rule, Saharawis became more determined that they should have a say in the future of their country. In 1966, a well-educated Saharawi, Mohammed Sidi Ibrahim Basiri, founded a Saharawi newspaper in Morocco. A year later he returned to the Sahara and began to espouse nationalist views and to attempt to organise his countrymen. He founded a movement known as the Organisation for the Liberation of Saguia el-Hamra and Oued ed-Dahab – it was better known as the Muslim Party or Harakat Tahrir. The movement became popular among urbanised, educated young Saharawis. Its only major political action was to present demands for greater freedom to the Spanish colonial authorities. But in June 1970, its members tried to organise a counter-demonstration on the day that the Spanish had planned an official gathering to support continued Spanish rule. The demonstration took place in El Ayoun on 17th June 1970. It was crushed ruthlessly by the Spanish and at least twelve people were killed. This proved to be a turning point in Saharawi nationalism (Hodges, 1983, p. 155; and Thompson and Adloff, 1980, p. 128). The killings caused bitterness and a growing distrust of Spain. Nationalist-inclined Saharawis began to look to leaders like Basiri and to the external supporters of the anti-Spanish cause for support.

In response to growing Saharawi nationalism, the Spanish authorities set up a territorial council known as the yemaa (also rendered as djemaa). Some moderate Saharawi nationalists, including traditional leaders of the important Reguibat community, took part. Other nationalists looked for Mauritanian or Moroccan support and a number of groups, such as PUNS and MOREHOB (the Resistance

Movement of the Blue Men) sprang up but then faded away. The latter group was Moroccan-backed but only lasted a year, ceasing to be a credible movement in mid-1973.

The major result of the El Ayoun incident was the formation of the Polisario Front. It emerged from a group of educated Saharawis led by El-Ouali Mustapha Sayed – a member of the Reguibat. He formed a loose nationalist group while studying in Rabat. Between 1971 and 1972, the group became increasingly radical and began to favour independence as an alternative to Spanish, Moroccan or Mauritanian rule. In 1972, El-Ouali toured areas of southern Morocco, Mauritania and the Spanish Sahara seeking support from fellow Saharawis. In the same year, he started looking for foreign assistance to enable him to start an armed struggle against the Spanish. His movement approached Libya, Mauritania, Algeria and Iraq. At first only the first two were interested. One commentator believes that Colonel Qadhafi pledged Libyan support for the embryonic liberation movement as early as February 1972 and promised arms supplies (St John in Lemarchand, 1988, p. 130). Tony Hodges cites El-Ouali as saying that 'we came to Libya barefoot and left armed' (Hodges, 1983, p. 162). Qadhafi himself later admitted in a letter to King Hassan that he had given arms to Polisario very early on; he said that 'the Libyan Arab Republic fulfilled its Arab national duty by furnishing arms to the front and setting up an office for it in Tripoli' (*Jeune Afrique*, 9th April 1976).

At first Polisario, which was officially launched as a movement at a secret congress near the Western Sahara–Mauritania border on 10th May 1973, was not strongly anti-Moroccan, but harassment of its members by Morocco in 1972 and 1973 led to a determination not to submit to Moroccan control. The founding congress of the movement was followed ten days later by an armed attack on a Spanish unit in Saguia el-Hamra. Over the next two years, utilising Libyan arms, growing Algerian support and growing Spanish weariness with the cost and effort of policing the Sahara, Polisario escalated its hit-and-run attacks against Spanish garrisons and installations. Prior to 1975, Mauritania allowed Polisario to operate from its territory – though Algeria did not. At its second congress in August 1974, Polisario came out in favour of total independence.

By the time of the second congress, it was clear that a confrontation between Polisario and Morocco was inevitable. King Hassan had become alarmed by signs from Spain that it was considering some form of autonomy for the Sahara and was favourable towards direct talks with Polisario. The Spanish government was also prepared to cooperate with the UN, or so it said, over a referendum. To combat this threat to Morocco's claims, in July 1974, Hassan started a campaign of denunciation of Spanish attempts to set up what he described as a 'puppet state [in] the southern part of our country' (cited by Hodges, 1983, p. 174). The king also called on Moroccans to rally round to prevent the Sahara from falling into the wrong hands.

Following the Polisario congress in August 1974, the front sent a message to Hassan warning him not to attempt to expand into the Sahara. But by then, Hassan had started work on new military garrisons along the border with the

Sahara and had commissioned the building of a road to link Tan-Tan with the border. A month after the Polisario warning, Hassan submitted Morocco's claim to the Western Sahara to the International Court of Justice. He did not inform Algeria or Mauritania of his decision – something which went a long way towards destroying the cooperation built up after 1972. Mauritania issued a counter claim at the ICJ. In December 1974, the UN General Assembly supported the moves to have the Saharan issue decided by the Court. In reaction to this move, Spain suspended plans to hold the referendum, pending a Court ruling. On 16th October 1975, the Court ruled that neither Morocco nor Mauritania had any historical justification for their claims. It put greater emphasis on the right of the inhabitants to self-determination than to the two countries' claims.

The ICJ decision gave new heart to Polisario, which was already in a strong position, having successfully eluded Spanish counter-insurgency sweeps and having started clandestine contacts with Spain over the issue of Saharan independence. By early 1975, Spain had withdrawn most of its forces to the coastal belt, leaving the interior to Polisario and the front's forces had been strengthened by desertions of Saharawis from the Spanish territorial forces. Polisario had also begun to fight the Mauritanian armed forces, notably after Spain's abandonment of La Guera.

The ICJ rejection of the Moroccan claim was turned by Hassan into some kind of victory – or that's the way he tried to present it to the Moroccan people. He followed the announcement of the ICJ ruling with his own appeal for a 'Green March' by the Moroccan people into the Western Sahara. This was to be a peaceful march by unarmed civilians. The objective was to pressurise Spain into relinquishing control of the territory. Hassan called for 350,000 volunteers. In the end, he got nearly 500,000. They were assembled in camps along the border in November 1975. Anxious to avoid a confrontation, Spain opened talks with Morocco and Mauritania. Hassan turned up the pressure by starting the March and crossing into the Sahara. As a result, Spain signed an agreement with Morocco and Mauritania on 14th November 1975 under which Spain would withdraw from the territory (but retain access to the phosphates at Bou Craa) and Morocco and Mauritania would partition the Western Sahara.

Within days of the agreement, Moroccan forces crossed into the Sahara to establish bases. By the end of November, Polisario was at war with both countries. Clashes occurred in the north and the south of the territory. Bou Craa was occupied by the Spanish in December 1975, Polisario being unable to prevent either the Moroccans or the Mauritanians from taking or holding the main towns. A protracted guerrilla war ensued. On 27th February 1976, the Saharan Arab Democratic Republic was founded by Polisario and its supporters. By this time, Polisario was based in the Tindouf area of Algeria and received strong Algerian as well as Libyan support. Both states supplied Polisario with modern, Soviet-made weapons – though there is no evidence of direct Soviet support for Polisario or even agreement that Libya and Algeria could pass weapons on to Polisario. Neither the Soviet Union nor any of its eastern European allies recognised or gave open support to Polisario or the SADR. The

Soviet Union supported the concept of self-determination in the Sahara, but limited its actions to diplomatic support for the UN referendum plan. Cuba, however, is suspected of giving some military training to Polisario fighters – it certainly gave educational and medical assistance to Polisario and recognised the SADR in 1980. No Cuban troops or advisers served in the SADR (Dominguez, 1989, p. 128).

The Saharawi forces proved most successful in raiding Mauritanian held areas and Mauritania itself. The country's armed forces were only 3,000 strong, with paramilitary forces of 2,000. The Polisario leader, El-Ouali, took a direct role in the fighting and was killed during an attack on the Mauritanian mining town of Akjoujt in June 1976. He was succeeded as Secretary-General of Polisario and effective leader by Mohammed Abdelaziz. The pace of the war did not slacken and ever greater pressure was put on Mauritania, while guerrillas kept up regular guerrilla attacks against the Moroccans, notably around Bou Craa. On 13th May 1977, Morocco and Mauritania signed a defence pact and Moroccan forces were flown to northern Mauritania by the French air force.

- The growing vulnerability of Mauritania led to an internationalisation of the conflict through the direct intervention of the French. Both Mauritania and Morocco sought French aid, the former seeking direct military assistance from French combat forces, and the latter seeking weapons and advisers. The French responded favourably to both countries. The last French troops had left Mauritania in 1966, but an air base was still operative at Atar and French advisers were attached to the Mauritanian army (Thompson and Adloff, 1980, p. 72). At first the main French effort was put into building up the Mauritanian armed forces. These were increased from 3,000 in 1975 to 15,000–17,000 in 1979 (Lynn Price, 1979, p. 44). In October 1977, the French launched Operation Lamartin. This involved the provision of direct air support to the Mauritanian armed forces from French Jaguar units based at Dakar, Senegal (which supported Mauritania and Morocco). Additional French special forces were sent to the base at Cap Vert, Dakar, and preparations were made for the use of French ground forces to strengthen the Mauritanians. In November 1977, the number of French officers and NCOs serving with the Mauritanians was increased to 105 (*ACR* 1977–8, p. B163) and an airlift operation was started to rearm the Mauritanians. The first air strikes by the French started on 2nd December 1977 following a Polisario attack on railway installations 75 kilometres north of Nouadhibou in northern Mauritania. The attack was coordinated with the Moroccans, who sent T-6 combat planes to attack the Polisario forces. Few doubt that the French took the major role in the operation, though the French Defence Minister denied any involvement. The air attacks on Polisario were devastating, with scores of fighters being killed. More attacks followed on 18th December after another Polisario raid. On 23rd December, the French admitted for the first time that their air force had been in action against Polisario (*Le Monde*, 24th December 1977). Just over a week later, President Giscard d'Estaing announced his intention of continuing direct military support for Mauritania. He declared that 'we cannot allow our African friends, especially the weakest among them, to be subjected to the threat of destabilisation . . . our friends can count on France's solidarity . . . France will not abandon the weak' (*Le Monde*, 4th January 1977). At the same time as increasing support for Mauritania, France started to supply Morocco with advanced Mirage aircraft and helicopter gunships. One French source said that French paratroops had been sent to a base at Benguerir, near Marrakesh, in readiness to support Morocco in the Sahara (*Le Canard Enchaine*, 2nd November 1977). There were also reports of the French secret service recruiting mercenaries to fight alongside the Moroccans and Mauritanians (*Le Matin de Paris*, 31st October 1977).

But the growing French role did not stop the Polisario raids, it only made the fighting more bloody. Attacks on the railway in northern Mauritania – which linked the Zouerate mining centre with the coast – were stepped up. By early 1978, there were 9,000 Moroccan troops in Mauritania and a squadron of Jaguars in addition to those operating from Dakar. On 5th May 1978, French Foreign Minister Louis de Guiringaud stated that France was continuing to carry out air strikes against Polisario 'within Mauritania's international borders and not in the contested territory of Western Sahara' (*Le Monde*, 9th May 1978). But the French support role was vital in maintaining the Mauritanian war effort and in ensuring that Polisario did not gain control of the southern part of the Western Sahara. French air strikes continued throughout the year, as did Polisario attacks on Moroccan and Mauritanian bases and installations. Polisario claimed in November 1978 that in the previous twelve months it had downed two Jaguars and killed 6,794 enemy troops. By that date, France was more or less running the Mauritanian armed forces and was also reportedly giving air support to Moroccan units (*ACR* 1978–79, p. B154).

French support to Mauritania continued after the military coup in Mauritania on 10th July 1978, which overthrew Ould Daddah and brought Colonel Mustapha Ould Salek to power. Polisario announced a cessation of hostilities against Mauritania following the coup, hoping for a change in direction. The Salek regime attempted at first to get Morocco to take part in an effort to end the fighting and reach a peaceful settlement, but this failed due to Moroccan intransigence (it still had 9,000 troops in Mauritania). In August 1978, the new military regime made contact with Polisario, but nothing substantial came of the talks. Polisario wanted unconditional withdrawal of the Mauritanians from the southern part of the Western Sahara. Further inconclusive talks were held in October. By then, Mauritania had obtained the withdrawal of about a third of the Moroccan military presence. Morocco was opposed to Mauritanian talks with Polisario, as was Senegal to the south. The Senegalese tried to influence the Mauritanian attitude by making scarcely veiled threats about giving help to black nationalist groups in Mauritania which opposed political domination by the non-African northerners. But further instability in Mauritania led to a 'palace coup' in April 1979, which led to the rise of Colonel Haydallah. On 30th July 1979, he announced the renunciation of all Mauritanian claims to the Sahara (Hodges, 1983, p. 273). The Mauritanian withdrawal led to the end of the overt and direct French role in the conflict. It continued to supply arms to Morocco and to train its armed forces, but it refrained from the use of its air power. Giscard d'Estaing even began to refer to the Western Sahara conflict as one of 'decolonisation'.

But if the fighting in Mauritania came to an end, the Moroccans kept up the fight, moving into the areas formerly claimed by Mauritania. Polisario achieved a major military success in August 1979, when one of its columns smashed a Moroccan armoured unit inside Morocco's southern border. The Moroccan armed forces suffered a major defeat on their own territory in October. In November 1979, the fighting escalated in the Sahara and Morocco was forced to commit 6,000 crack troops to the war in the south in order to prevent Polisario gaining control. Polisario was by now receiving extensive support from Algeria and still enjoyed the backing of the Libyans. Morocco accused Polisario of being an Algerian puppet and said that Algerian troops were fighting alongside Polisario, though it failed to substantiate the claims. Polisario's strength was such that in late 1979 and early 1980 it was able to keep a large Moroccan force bottled up at Zaag, in southern Morocco. One relief attempt involving 7,000 Moroccans was routed by Polisario and success was only only achieved when 20,000 Moroccan troops were dispatched to end the siege.

Although Polisario was in an increasingly strong position and Morocco was becoming increasingly isolated within the OAU and internationally after Mauritania's withdrawal from the fight, the Saharawis were nowhere near winning an overall military victory and needed diplomatic support and greater military help. Polisario and Algeria became increasingly impatient with Libya, which gave arms and political support to the SADR but did not recognise it until 1980. Even then, the Libyans still made reference to a desire to see the SADR integrated with Mauritania, with whom Libya had developed close relations. Libyan arms supplies increased after the recognition of the SADR, but Libya was never as reliable an ally as Algeria. Its ambivalence towards Polisario and its periodic flirtations with Mauritania and even Morocco destroyed its credibility as a radical state and a supporter of liberation movements. During 1980 and early 1981, Libya did make strenuous attempts to get African support for Polisario and in 1981 arms supplies from Tripoli increased to the extent that Libya was giving Polisario around 90 per cent of its weapons (*ACR* 1981–82, p. B11). But in mid-June 1981, as part of its attempt to get the OAU chairmanship for Qadhafi, Libya did an abrupt about turn and effected a rapprochement with Morocco, abandoning support for Polisario. But relations between Tripoli and Rabat did not last long. In October 1981, the Moroccans suffered a major military setback at Guetta Zemmour and once again accused Libya of aiding Polisario. King Hassan said that Libya had supplied Polisario with SAM-6 missiles which were used against Moroccan aircraft.

The war continued throughout the early 1980s, with Polisario increasingly dependent on Algerian support, as Libya vacillated between support and its flirtations with King Hassan. The Saharan issue effectively destroyed Libya's attempts to host OAU summits and was an obstacle to OAU operations throughout 1982, 1983 and 1984. On 16th June 1983, Libya renounced its role in supporting Polisario. Qadhafi said in a major speech on that date that 'Libya has finished carrying out its duty with respect to the Western Sahara. There is no longer any dispute between Morocco and Libya in this region.' (Tripoli home service in Arabic, 16th June 1983). A more prolonged rapprochement followed with Hassan visiting Tripoli and Qadhafi going to Rabat. The process culminated in the signing of the Oujda treaty between the two countries on 13th August 1984. This pledged them to working towards union. Most of the agreement was rhetoric and was unlikely to be implemented, but it did signal closer relations. It resulted from Morocco's desire to weaken and isolate Polisario and Libya's to end Moroccan hostility (particularly towards its role in Chad) and to break out of its increasing isolation. Both states were concerned about the rapprochement between Algeria and Tunisia and what this entailed for the balance of political forces in the region.

But the Oujda treaty did little to alter the political or military situation in the Sahara. By the end of the year, Morocco had an estimated 100,000 troops in the Sahara (against at most 20,000 Polisario guerrillas) and was suffering internal dissension because of the decline in the economy, caused partly by the cost of the war. The war could only be maintained and the economy kept from collapse through massive US military and financial credits. And far from being weakened by the defection of Libya to the Moroccan camp, Polisario gained in strength as Algeria greatly increased its aid to Polisario (including the supply of weapons to make up the shortfall following Libya's cessation of assistance) and enabled it to launch major attacks against Moroccan positions. In October 1984, the front's fighters launched an offensive in the Sahara and claimed to have killed 600 Moroccan troops and downed several combat aircraft (Tessler, 1988, p. 99).

The Moroccan response to Polisario in the 1980s was a chiefly defensive one. It was unable to do more than hold on to defensive positions and settled areas. The Moroccan strategy therefore became one of building a defensive wall around the economically important areas of the Western Sahara. The wall would enclose the Bou Craa deposits and the main areas of human settlement. The desert and semi-desert areas would be left to Polisario. By May 1982, the wall stretched from southern Morocco to Smara, then on to Bou Craa, reaching the Atlantic coast near Boujdour. Further wall building took place over the next two years – the construction operations being defended by tens of thousands of Moroccan troops backed by armour and air support. By mid-1984, the wall enclosed 17,000 square miles. This strong defensive ring enabled the Moroccans to restart operations at Bou Craa. Nevertheless, the Moroccans were forced to keep over 30,000 combat troops and tens of thousands of support troops in the Sahara to defend the wall. But Polisario was able to mount serious and damaging attacks on Moroccan defensive positions. Having an estimated 20,000 regular fighters, T-54 and T-55 tanks, mobile artillery and SAM anti-aircraft missiles, Polisario was able to pose a conventional military threat as well as being an effective guerrilla force. In mid-1983, the front launched a major offensive in southern Morocco in the Ouarkziz mountains, bombarding Moroccan positions with artillery and multiple rocket launchers (Soviet-made weapons supplied by Algeria). In early September, the attacks were extended to Smara, where tanks, rockets and artillery were used to smash Moroccan units. During that month, five Moroccan defensive positions along the wall were believed to have been totally destroyed (*Le Monde*, 3rd November 1983). In November, Polisario claimed that it had routed a major Moroccan column which had attempted to launch a counter-offensive beyond the wall (Algiers home service, 7th November 1983).

The war was still a huge drain on Moroccan resources and in the mid-1980s it was only US and French military and financial aid that prevented bankruptcy. US military credits for Morocco rose from $14m in 1975 to $65m in 1984. Much of the hardware supplied was used to strengthen and extend the wall. In 1984, it was lengthened with a line running from Zaag in Morocco to a point just north of the Mauritania–Western Sahara border. But Polisario actions increased in late 1984 and early 1985, forcing Morocco to reinforce its troops – by the middle of 1985, there were an estimated 120,000 Moroccans stationed in the Sahara (*ACR* 1985–86, p. A119). Further wall building was Morocco's only answer and by early 1987, five lines of walls had been built with a total length of 2,500 kilometres.

But the walls did not enable Morocco to relax its military posture or cut its defence budget. Polisario could still hurt Morocco militarily and wear it down through a war of attrition along the wall. Thus in early 1986, Morocco, under pressure from its allies and from the UN and OAU, agreed to 'proximity' talks in New York, but these were fruitless. Morocco remained intransigent over the holding of a referendum in the Western Sahara. Prior to Spanish decolonisation, it had supported the idea of a referendum as a political ploy and it had declared its willingness to let Saharawis vote on their future again in 1981 at the Nairobi summit of the OAU, but Polisario's growing strength and its admission to the OAU led him to change his mind and from 1984 onwards he rejected the idea. But the holding of such a vote was at the heart of the UN and OAU plans for an end to the war. Polisario accepted the concept and expressed its willingness to cooperate with both institutions, but a vote was impossible without Morocco's active involvement. The UN Secretary-General, Javier Perez de Cuellar, made repeated attempts during 1986 to bring both sides together, but as with past efforts they foundered on Morocco's refusal to hold direct talks with Polisario, claiming that it was Algeria that was behind the war in the Sahara, and because King Hassan still opposed a referendum (*Africa*, May 1986).

The shifting alliances in the Maghrib did nothing to assist the finding of a solution to the Saharan conflict. Algeria remained steadfastly in support of the claims of the Saharawis, while Libya, Mauritania and Tunisia changed position so many times that it was often hard to say at any one time which side they supported. The regional equation became more confused than ever in September 1986, when Libya renounced its two-year-old treaty with Morocco, over Morocco's links with Israel. But Libya did not automatically return to the Polisario fold. In early 1987, Morocco attempted to gain international sympathy by claiming that Iran was giving substantial help to Polisario and that Iranian military advisers were present in Polisario training camps in Algeria (Rabat home service in Arabic, 31st January 1987). The SADR government rejected the report totally and replied with a counter-accusation that Israeli officers were active in the Sahara and had given assistance to the Moroccans (*West Africa*, 23rd February 1987). Neither of these claims was ever substantiated. What was clear, though, was that without US financial aid and military supplies, Morocco would be hard put to maintain its defensive posture for a long period. The USA, despite its loathing for Qadhafi, was firm in its support for Morocco and continued to supply arms and technical aid in return for the use of bases at Sidi Slimane and Beguerir for its Rapid Deployment Force. The American Westinghouse company helped the Moroccan defence effort in the Sahara by installing sophisticated electric sensor systems and radar networks along the wall (*Africa Confidential*, 15th April 1987). But the technology was unable to prevent Polisario from remaining a military threat. In February 1987, on the eleventh anniversary of the founding of the SADR, a new offensive was launched by the front which led to a breaching of the wall and a Polisario incursion 20 kilometres behind Moroccan lines. Over 200 Moroccans were killed in the fighting (*Africa Now*, May 1987).

In 1988 and 1989, the moves towards unity among all the Maghrib states (including Morocco and Algeria) led to hopes that closer relations would lead to a greater Moroccan willingness to negotiate over the Sahara. Diplomatic relations were reestablished between Morocco and Algeria and greater economic cooperation envisaged, but over the Sahara, the differences remained. As the new decade approached, Morocco seemed ever more isolated over the issue and faced the threat, despite the Maghrib union initiatives, of being the odd man out in the region, as well as in Africa and, increasingly, at the UN. Even countries such as Saudi Arabia, formerly an important financial backer for Hassan, by the end of the 1980s were beginning to look more kindly upon the SADR and less sympathetically on Morocco's claims (*West Africa*, 7th–13th November 1988). The SADR's international position was strengthened in March 1989, when the European Parliament ended the EC's official position of supporting Morocco and passed a resolution stating that the Saharan problem was one of decolonisation.

To back up its strong diplomatic position, in late 1989, Polisario launched a new offensive against the wall. On 7th October, major attacks took place against Moroccan positions around Guelta Zemmour in which the front claimed to have killed 200 Moroccans and to have pushed the Moroccan defensive line back by 25 kilometres. Further attacks came at the end of the month and in early November, by which time Rabat acknowledged the attacks, though not the Polisario figures of 450 Moroccan dead and the shooting down of at least one aircraft. This offensive destroyed attempts being made during the year by King Hassan (which included a six page glossy advertising feature on Morocco's claim to the Sahara in 13th November's edition of *Time* magazine) to convince the world that the war was over and that it was time that Polisario and its supporters recognised this (*West Africa*, 20th–26th November 1989). In late November, Hassan announced the holding of a referendum in Morocco on delaying parliamentary elections. In his speech giving his reasons, he said that he was willing to hold a referendum on the future of the Sahara. But he continued to state that the Sahara was a province of Morocco and to reject direct talks with Polisario. He added, that if the UN failed to hold a referendum in the Sahara within two years 'then it will be time to deduce the proper conclusions from that procrastination' and he went on to say that no one should doubt that the Sahara was and would remain Moroccan (Rabat television in Arabic, 22nd November 1989). Not surprisingly, Polisario rejected Hassan's speech as meaningless and said that an advance towards peace and a proper referendum could only be made through direct talks. A statement by the front on Algerian television the day after Hassan's speech, said that it was not up to Hassan to set a deadline or arrange a timetable for the vote, this was to be the subject of direct talks under the auspices of the OAU and/or the UN. But in early December, the SADR Foreign Minister, Bachir Mustafa Sayed, said that Polisario was willing to take part in a referendum in 1990 as long as direct talks were arranged and that the referendum could take place in a Sahara free of the Moroccan military presence (Radio France International in French, 5th December 1989).

But despite these peaceful sounding words, peace seemed no nearer in 1990 than in 1980, with the fighting continuing, with Morocco refusing direct talks with Polisario and with Morocco and Algeria still hostile. Direct foreign military intervention seemed to have ended though the continuation of the war was made possible by external military and financial aid for both sides – US and French aid to Morocco and Algerian support for Polisario.

Uganda: Libya's East African safari

The close political and military relations forged between the Ugandan dictator Idi Amin and Israel in the period immediately before and after Amin's seizure of power did not last long. In the early 1970s, Arab states, and particularly Colonel Qadhafi's Libya, were making strenuous efforts to wean African states (notably the Muslim states or states with a large Muslim population, like Uganda) away from their relations with Israel. And they had two strong arguments to use against Israel. The first was that Israel was occupying African soil – it had invaded and occupied Egypt's Sinai peninsula during the 1967 war. The Arab states argued that Egypt was a member of the OAU and had been a victim of Israeli aggression. Fellow OAU members should not maintain relations with a state which had carried out aggression against a fellow member and had occupied African territory. The second argument was a financial one. From the early 1970s onwards, the burgeoning oil wealth of much of the Arab world, put it in a position to offer substantial aid and investment to friendly states – clearly a state which had diplomatic relations with Israel would not qualify as a friendly state.

Uganda was wooed by the Arabs in an attempt to end the Israeli presence there – Israel played a role in training Amin's army, as well as providing economic and technical assistance. Particularly after the end of the Sudanese civil war, Uganda had a lesser reason for ties with Israel, if more extensive aid could be found elsewhere. So Amin was vulnerable to the blandishments of Colonel Qadhafi. In 1972, he kicked out the Israeli military and economic advisers and started to

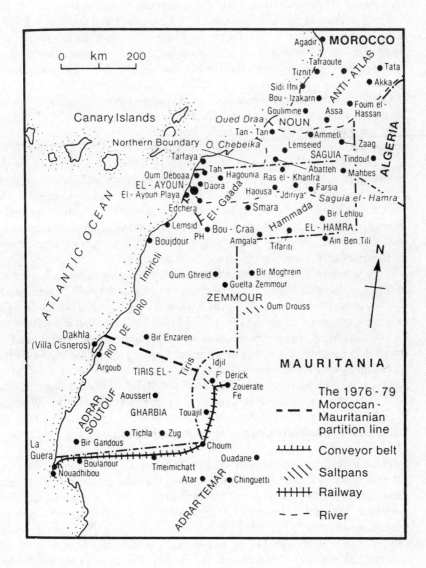

Map 5 The Western Sahara
Source: Richard Lawless and Leila Monahan, eds.
War and Refugees London, Pinter Publishers, 1987.

develop a close relationship with Libya. One of the channels for building up ties was the Muslim faith. Amin began to stress his adherence to Islam. In return for Libyan financial aid, Amin undertook a campaign to promote Islam within Uganda and to promote the Arab and Palestinian causes within Africa as a whole.

Israeli military advisers were replaced by Arab ones and a number of Palestinians were believed to have been brought in to serve with Amin's bodyguard. Amin also looked towards the Soviet Union for military equipment and training for his armed forces (though the British also continued to help him, despite growing distaste for his repressive policies and his open brutality).

Uganda was in need of political and military support from abroad, both to boost his own domestic standing and to guard against the threat posed by Ugandan exile movements based in Tanzania. Frequent border skirmishes occurred during the 1970s on the Tanzania–Uganda border, one following a failed incursion by pro-Obote exiles based in Tanzania. In the mid- and late 1970s, the tension grew as Amin became more and more isolated within Uganda and more and more inhuman in his crushing of all perceived sources of opposition. The 1976 Entebbe raid by Israel to rescue hostages seized by Palestinian guerrillas showed how vulnerable Uganda was to an organised and sophisticated enemy. It also showed the hostility of neighbouring states – as Kenya was strongly suspected of having assisted the Israeli commando force.

If the Israeli raid was a spectacular but one-off warning to Amin, the growth in the Ugandan exile movements and the increasing hostility of Tanzania (and a number of other OAU states) towards Amin was a signal that a concerted effort to remove him could be on the cards. The Ugandan leader therefore deepened his relations with Libya to the extent of allowing Libya to base several hundred troops in the country and to become the main foreign prop for the regime. When Amin left Uganda for foreign visits or summits, security was frequently left in the hands of Libyan advisers and troops. Between 400 and 700 Palestinian guerrillas were also stationed in Uganda to provide further military support. When the President was attending the Afro–Arab summit in Cairo in March 1977, 200 Libyan commandos were flown in specially to ensure against any coup attempt (*ACR* 1977–78, p. B77).

The test for Amin and for his relations with Libya came in October 1978 when a period of severe border tension ended with a Ugandan invasion of the Kagera region of Tanzania. The invasion followed mutinies at a number of Ugandan army bases. Members of an elite mechanised regiment at Bombo (50 kilometres from Kampala) rebelled in early October. Forty soldiers and NCOs attempted to capture Amin, but failed. The mutiny spread but was crushed by loyalists. As many as 200 mutineers fled across the border into Tanzania. Troops supporting Amin crossed the border in hot pursuit and continued as far as the Kagera river. The Ugandan dictator tried to cover up his invasion and the fact of the mutiny by claiming that Uganda had been attacked by Tanzania. Amin said that Tanzanian armoured units supported by Cuban troops had crossed the border and attacked. This account was plainly false and was denied totally by Tanzania and Cuba – the latter had no troops stationed in Tanzania. Once across the border, Ugandan forces pushed into Tanzania killing and abducting civilians as they went. Ugandan aircraft bombed the town of Bukoba, apparently without any military motive. At first, the Libyans were wary of supporting Uganda in open aggression against another OAU state. Military supplies were stopped and relations cooled dramatically.

Had the Ugandans withdrawn, the conflict might have ended there for the time being and Ugandan–Libyan relations might have remained cool. But Amin continued the invasion of Tanzania and on 1st November 1978 announced that he had annexed the Kagera salient in northern Tanzania (along the western shores of Lake Victoria). Kampala radio announced that the new Uganda–Tanzania border was the Kagera river (Kampala home service, 1st November 1978). The radio said that Uganda's military successes had added 1140 square kilometres to Ugandan territory. It added that 'all Tanzanians in the captured area up to the River Kagera must know that they are under the direct rule of the Conqueror of the British Empire, Field Marshal Amin'.

Tanzania's answer was swift. The day after the annexation announcement, President Nyerere told the nation, 'We have one task only – and that is to hit him. We have the ability to hit him. We have a reason to hit him – and the determination to hit him . . . This man is a savage' (Dar es Salaam home service, 2nd November 1978). Libya made a futile attempt to mediate in the dispute, but Uganda was unwilling to withdraw and Tanzania clearly could not accept occupation and annexation of its territory. International calls for Ugandan withdrawal and for negotiations were rejected by Amin. He referred to US condemnation of the invasion as interference 'in an African dispute with the aim of creating a second Vietnam' (*The Times*, 6th November 1978). But on 8th November, Amin said he would withdraw if Tanzania promised never to invade Uganda again. Not surprisingly, Nyerere refused to comply and said that 'I have a duty, and my duty is to kick this aggressor out' (*Guardian*, 9th November 1978).

On 11th November, Tanzania's counter-attack began. By 13th November, Ugandan forces were beginning to withdraw under heavy pressure. They were forced out before the end of November and the Tanzanians then began a military build up along the border with Uganda. Amin accused Tanzania of aggression. Uganda accused Tanzania of sending troops into Uganda in late November, this was denied by the government in Dar es Salaam.

The next move in the crisis came from former President Milton Obote. On 11th January 1979, Tanzania allowed him to broadcast an appeal for the overthrow of Amin over Tanzanian state radio. Obote called for an end to Amin's 'regime of death'. The Tanzanians also assisted with the arming of former Ugandan soldiers who had fled to Tanzania after Amin seized power. Around 950 of them were given uniforms, weapons and training. They were led by two officers who had commanded the abortive 1972 invasion by Ugandan exiles, Tito Okello and David Oyite-Ojok. Other Ugandan exile movements were able to come up with a few volunteers to join the anti-Amin force. By mid-January, the Ugandans were assembled near the border, as were 30,000–40,000 Tanzanian troops and members of the People's Militia. They crossed the border on 20th

January and advanced towards Entebbe and Jinja. The Tanzanian government openly announced that its troops were operating in Uganda, but said they were only there to answer the aggression by Amin's forces. Amin accused the Tanzanians of using white mercenaries to bolster their forces – this was totally rejected by the government in Dar es Salaam (Dar es Salaam home service, 30th January 1979). The radio said that the claims were those of 'a demented individual, the King of buffoons'. But Amin was becoming desperate. On 30th January, he publicly lamented that none of his Arab friends had come to his aid, though he did say that Israel had sent him some small arms and rocket launchers (*ACR* 1978–79, p. B430).

The Tanzanians and their Ugandan allies achieved rapid success and by 23rd February, the force was nearing Masaka. The Uganda leader then issued an appeal for aid to Arab countries. But Libya only responded once Amin's position was precarious in the extreme. The Tanzanians had almost reached Kampala by the time that Qadhafi dispatched Libyan troops and arms supplies to Uganda. Some arms began to arrive from Libya in late February and at least 1,500 Libyan troops were flown to Kampala in the first week of March. By that time Oyite-Ojok's forces were within 60 kilometres of the capital. Soon after the arrival of the Libyans, they took part in a fierce battle at Lukaya, where they suffered heavy casualties.

For a while, Amin was able to hold off the forces threatening the capital. This he achieved both through the use of the Libyans, but also because his forces had large quantities of Soviet-made 122mm artillery pieces with a 30 kilometre range. The delays and the increased use of the Libyans convinced Nyerere of the need to use Tanzanian troops to effect the capture of Kampala, something he had hoped to avoid in the interests of seeing a 'Ugandan' solution to the war. But with Libyans and Palestinians fighting on Amin's side, Nyerere decided that he was justified in using his forces to complete the overthrow of Amin. By 29th March, the Tanzanians and the Ugandan exiles were moving towards the capital. Amin then fled Kampala, using his forces to hold the road to Jinja open to enable him, the Libyans and the Palestinians to escape. The Libyans, meanwhile, tried another ploy to avoid disaster. On 26th March, Qadhafi sent a personal envoy to the Tanzanian government carrying a message that Libya would declare war against Tanzania if it did not withdraw its army from Uganda within 24 hours. Nyerere was unmoved by the threat. He issued the following response:

We will not change our stand on Amin. Amin is a murderer, a liar and a savage. We shall continue to fight those who threaten our security. Since the threats have increased, we shall also intensify our preparations to counter them . . . By threatening to send troops to Uganda, Colonel Qadhafi has declared war against Ugandans who have the right to remove any dictatorship (*International Herald Tribune*, 28th March 1979)

In early April, after the abandonment of the capital, more Libyan troops were sent into northern Uganda and a Libyan bomber attempted to bomb the Tanzanian lake port of Mwanza. But this did not stop the Tanzanian–Ugandan advance. Entebbe was captured on 5th April. But the following day, Amin returned to Kampala and swore he would stay to the end. By the first week of April there were between 2,400 and 2,700 Libyans fighting for Amin (*Guardian*, 2nd April 1979). Libyan arms supplies were still reaching Uganda, some by air but some by sea and then rail across Kenya. President Moi of Kenya refused Tanzanian requests to halt the delivery of arms via Kenya. But by the end of the first week of April, the end was near and the Libyan forces began to withdraw from Kampala along the open road to Jinja. On 10th April, Amin went back on his oath and fled the capital just before 800 men of the Ugandan exile forces, supported by the Tanzanian army moved in. On 11th April, a government was formed in Kampala by the Uganda National Liberation Front led by Yusuf Lule.

Amin fled Uganda via Libya and ended up in Saudi Arabia, where he remains, despite a bungled attempt to return to Uganda in 1989. The Libyans pulled their forces out after the fall of Kampala. They left behind some 500 dead (estimates of the total vary between 300 and 700) and 400 prisoners. Qadhafi tried to deny that his troops had fought and lost. He said in June 1979 that his aid to Amin had been limited to humanitarian and economic assistance. The Libyan leader accused Tanzania of conducting a 'crusade' against Uganda's Muslims. After mediation by OAU members, the relations between Tanzania, the new Ugandan government and Libya improved slightly. In November 1979, the 400 Libyan prisoners were released and fifty-two Ugandans and Amin's personal jet were returned to Uganda by Qadhafi. Not that relations between Tanzania and Libya improved greatly; neither did successive Ugandan regimes, until the seizure of power by Yoweri Museveni's National Resistance Army, show any signs of dropping their justified suspicions of Libya's intentions. In 1981, the then Ugandan Interior Minister accused Libya of trying to smuggle arms into Uganda to support anti-Obote forces in the imminent elections.

Obote strongly resisted attempts to hold the 1982 OAU summit in Tripoli and accused Qadhafi of giving arms and training to rebel guerrilla groups. There was some evidence that Libya supplied arms and financial help to Museveni's movement (*ACR* 1982–83, p. B51). In July 1982, Interior Minister John Luwuliza-Kirunda, told the Ugandan parliament that Libyan-supplied arms had been used by rebels in attacks on government forces in Kampala in February of that year. He added that NRA guerrillas were being flown to Libya to be given military training. But a partial rapprochement took place after a visit to Tripoli by Ugandan Prime Minister Alimadi in August 1982. As a result of the trip and the improved relations that followed, Qadhafi said publicly that he had been misled by Amin and that he would not assist Ugandan rebel groups. But Obote was not entirely convinced by Qadhafi's promises and in May 1983 warned strongly against any further Libyan interference in Uganda (*New African*, June 1983, p. 31).

Obote's overthrow by the military led to a further improvement in bilateral relations – Qadhafi was widely believed to have cut all relations with Museveni (though the warmth of Ugandan–Libyan relations after Museveni's victory in 1986 somewhat belies this belief) and was even said to have started assisting the Okello government. Kenyan newspapers reported in September 1985 that Libyan planes were flying arms to Entebbe airport for the Uganda armed forces

(*Kenya Times*, 26th September 1985). There was also evidence that Egypt was actively helping the military regime fight off Museveni (*ACR* 1985–86, p. B482).

Following Musevini's seizure of power, there was a dramatic improvement in relations with Libya. Qadhafi visited Kampala in September 1986 and promised expanded economic aid. He is also believed to agreed to give military assistance to the NRA. The visit was viewed as a success despite the virtual occupation of a Kampala hotel by hundreds of heavily armed Libyan security men who accompanied Qadhafi. At least one Ugandan was believed to have been killed by the Libyans during the state visit and Western journalists reported that the Libyans acted in a high-handed manner towards their hosts.

The Horn of Africa: full-scale war and massive foreign intervention

The 1974 revolution in Ethiopia was a turning point in the conflicts throughout the Horn of Africa. Far from removing some of the causes of the Eritrean rebellion and of the simmering discontent of other ethnic groups, it fueled their desires for secession or greater internal autonomy. With regard to the dispute with Somalia, the revolution and the ensuing chaos, combined with the construction of a large and well-armed military machine, made possibly by substantial Soviet aid, led to an increase in Somali calls for the return of the Ogaden and a revival of the WSLF. This, and the escalation of fighting between Ethiopian forces and the Eritreans and Tigreans, prompted a full-scale Somali invasion to try to achieve what backing for the WSLF had failed to achieve. A full-scale war resulted which in turn led to massive foreign military intervention that surpassed even the levels of external involvement in the Angolan civil war.

At the time of the Ethiopian revolution of 1974, the existing conflicts between Ethiopia and Somalia and within Ethiopia itself were simmering. The Somali military regime continued to espouse the cause of Pan-Somalism, even though it did little during its first five years in power to further that aim (apart, of course, from its massive military build-up). In Eritrea, the war continued. The Eritreans were secure in their liberated areas but were unable to advance or to take major towns or transport routes. The Ethiopians were able to hold on to the towns and the main roads to the Red Sea, but couldn't make headway against the rebel-held areas. But the conflict was a costly one – necessitating tens of millions of dollars of arms imports, vast expenditure on the maintenance of a large army in Eritrea, loss of agricultural output in battle zones and steady loss of life among the combatants.

The war in Eritrea was a steady drain on Ethiopia's human and material resources. As such, it was a factor in the growing discontent that led to the coup against the Emperor. It combined with dissatisfaction over the government's handling of the severe drought of the early 1970s and the resulting economic crisis. The drought was at its worst in 1973, with famine in many areas of Ethiopia. No solution was in sight in early 1974, and the whole economy was suffering. Increases in fuel and other retail prices led to increasing discontent in the main towns, while long-overdue but half-hearted attempts at educational reform led to extensive student protests.

The crunch came for Haile Selassie in mid-January 1974 when an army unit at Neghelle in south-western Ethiopia mutinied in protest over the inadequate water supplies at their desert garrison. The government sent envoys to the base but they were imprisoned by the mutineers. Before that crisis was solved another one reared its head, this time in the air force. Air force personnel at the Debre Zeit base near the capital mutinied over pay. The mutiny stirred up the students in Addis Ababa, who held a mass demonstration on 14th February. Ten days later, the second army division at Asmara, in sensitive Eritrea, mutinied. Soon military units around the country were joining in. Their immediate demands were over pay and conditions but they also called for the sacking of the government. The Emperor tried to relieve the pressure by replacing the Prime Minister. But the man he put in the job, Endalkatchew Mekonnen, filled the new cabinet with members of the aristocracy. This fuelled further protest from soldiers and students. Then the trades unions, led by the Confederation of Ethiopian trades unions (CELU), joined in.

The inability of the government to control events or retake the initiative and the increasing politicisation of the armed forces led to what has been described as a 'creeping coup'. First of all a section of the army calling itself the National Security Commission crushed the strikes by workers. The NSC appeared to rally some military support for the government (Halliday and Molyneaux, 1981, p. 85–7). But the rest of the army, particularly junior officers and NCOs, was becoming increasingly unwilling to accept a continuation of the status quo. Further mutinies took place in the army in June and a group of junior officers from the army and police came together to form a Coordinating Committee (known by its Amharic name, the Derg). The Derg held its first meetings in late June. Although it had no clear leadership structure, it came to be dominated by Atnafu Abate and Haile Mengistu Mariam. The 'creeping coup' gained pace after the formation of the Derg, which called for a new constitution and for the prosecution of ministers and officials who had engaged in corruption or had deliberately hidden the extent and effects of the famine. The Derg's programme was reformist but not socialist, let alone Marxist.

The ebbing away of the power of the monarchy and the government led inexorably to the abdication of the Emperor and the seizure of power by the Derg. Haile Selassie was forced to abdicate on 12th September 1974 and his government was replaced by the Provisional Military Administrative Council (PMAC) formed by the Derg. The Derg was supported in its actions against the monarchy and government by students, CELU and by the developing leftist parties. But they wanted the Derg to hand power over to the civilians. But the civilian groups were fragmented and constantly at each others' throats and were in no position to challenge the armed forces, who lined up behind the Derg. In October, the Derg made public its intention to hold on to power for the time being.

In order to retain support from wide sections of the army and to gain international credibility, the Derg appointed as its spokesman and effective leader General Andom (who had led the Ethiopian forces in the short war against Somalia in 1964). He was a moderate and attempted to slow the pace of change and prevent rash actions, such as the wholesale execution of members of the royal family. He also favoured negotiations with the Eritreans and other nationalities who wanted greater autonomy. The rest of the Derg disagreed. Andom was dismissed, arrested and then executed on 23rd November. After his death, fifty-seven members of the royal family were put to death by the Derg. The Derg then sought to continue the war in Eritrea and to entrench itself in power. But it also carried out sweeping reforms, particularly those relating to use and ownership of land. Old feudal land rights were swept away. The policy was part of a programme announced by the Derg in December 1974. The programme was known as Ethiopia Tikdem (variously translated as Ethiopian Socialism, Ethiopia First and Ethiopian Unity). It was a generally socialist programme including distribution of land, the formation of peasant associations and cooperatives, and the nationalisation of banks and major economic enterprises and institutions. The land reform was the single most important reform, as it destroyed the economic base for the land-owning elite and the aristocracy. It gave land to the peasants and led to the formation of 24,000 peasant associations. The land reform was also used as a means of getting militant students out of the Derg's hair. They were sent out to rural areas to assist in the formation of the associations and to launch literacy campaigns.

The Derg was keen to avoid open conflict with the civilian leftists, but was equally keen to hang on to power itself. But the use of students in rural areas and the links forged by some Derg members with political groups did not stop the growth of anti-Derg leftist groups or for the escalation of conflict between the armed forces and the civilian politicians. Throughout 1975, a fierce debate raged within and around the Derg over the role of both the military and the civilian movements. Mengistu (then deputy head of the Derg) called for dialogue. He led a faction which sought to form a political party from among the Derg members with support from selected civilian parties. Opposed to him were Derg members who wanted no links with the civilians and civilian parties, such as the Ethiopian People's Revolutionary Party (EPRP) which was opposed to military rule. One socialist group, known as Meison, did cooperate with the Derg and it helped Mengistu and his supporters in the Derg to set up the Political Office for Mass Organisational Affairs (POMOA), whose role was to organise an embryonic political movement. The Derg also set up urban dwellers associations known as kebelles. They were to become tools of the Derg when open warfare developed between the EPRP and Derg followers in late 1976 and 1977.

By April 1976, it was clear that the Derg was moving towards definite adherence to Marxism. On 20th April, it announced the Ethiopian National Democratic Revolution Programme. This was outlined by Mengistu as follows: 'elimination of feudalism, bureaucratic capitalism and imperialism . . . to build a new people's Ethiopia . . . a People's Democratic Republic will be established . . . under the leadership of the proletariat in close collaboration with the farmers, the petty bourgeoisie, anti-feudalist and anti-imperialist forces to guarantee to the Ethiopian people their right to freedom, equality, unity, peace and prosperity' (*Ethiopian Herald*, 21st April 1976). The programme also set out the aim of enacting a transition to socialism, in which all nationalities would have equality and rights. In the programme, the Derg promised to hand over power to the 'broad masses', but it continued in practice to accumulate power. It cooperated with and used Meison to increase its own power. Although civilians were appointed to ministerial positions and continued to play a role in POMOA, they did not participate in the work of the PMAC, which continued to be the fount of all wisdom and decisions.

As the Derg showed no signs of handing over power, the EPRP launched a campaign of urban guerrilla warfare. Derg supporters were gunned down and attempts were made to disrupt Derg programmes. The Derg fought back by launching its own urban war against the EPRP and its supporters. There was also growing conflict within the Derg. There was a massive rate of attrition within the Derg as a result of the level of political conflict; over a hundred members or high-ranking military officials were executed, including one of the Derg's Vice-Presidents, Sisay Habte. The internal power struggle came to a head at a meeting of the Derg on 3rd February 1977. The power struggle at the meeting became a shoot-out. This resulted in Mengistu's seizure of power and the deaths of the PMAC Chairman, Teferi Bante, and of his two closest supporters, Alemayehu Haile and Mogus Wolde-Michael. Mengistu became Derg and PMAC Chairman and commander of the armed forces. He merged the Derg and PMAC and kept tight hold on all the reins of political and military power. Mengistu proceeded to launch what has been described as a 'red terror' against the EPRP (Schwab, 1985, pp. 40–41; Halliday and Molyneaux, 1981). In November 1977, Mengistu himself announced that 'Red terror will henceforth engulf the quarters of reaction and counter-revolution throughout Ethiopia' (*Ethiopian Herald*, 18th November 1977). All the armed units available to the PMAC were used to combat the EPRP – the police, armed forces, people's militias and armed groups from the kebelles. The urban warfare lasted until the end of 1978 and claimed thousands of lives.

The level of domestic conflict and violence created conditions of instability that the Somalis and the discontented nationalities within Ethiopia exploited to advance their own causes. This led to civil war in many of Ethiopia's provinces and war between Ethiopia and Somalia.

Between the military coup of 1969 and the Ogaden war of 1977, the Barre regime in Somalia revived the claims to the Ogaden, NFD in Kenya and Djibouti but took no direct action to pursue them. Rather, with massive Soviet aid, it concentrated on building a large, well-equipped and well-trained military machine capable of using force to regain the territories. The size of the army was increased from 12,000 in 1970 to 23,000 in 1975. In the last two years before the Ogaden war it grew to nearly 30,000 men armed with 250 T-34 and T-54/55 tanks, 300 armoured personnel carriers/armoured fighting vehicles and 52 jet fighters/ fighter bombers (IISS, 1975–76 and 1977–78). The Soviets supplied the arms and also large numbers of military and civilian advisers. A former US diplomat in the Horn and adviser to the US National Security Council on the Horn of Africa has estimated that by 1976, there were 4,000 Soviet advisers in Somalia (Henze, 1981, p. 61) plus hundreds of Cuban military instructors and an unknown number of East German and Bulgarian advisers. The value of the Soviet military aid to Somalia in the 1969–77 period has been put at between $300m and $1bn (Ottaway, 1982, p. 67). Although the Soviet refrained from giving open support to Somalia's irredentist claims, it had created 'a war machine quite fearsome for that part of the world and well-equipped for making rapid advances into the "missing lands"' (ibid.). The Soviet role also included extensive economic aid. Conservative Western observers were convinced that Somalia had become little more than a Soviet colony and that even day-to-day government decisions were taken by Soviet advisers rather than by the Somali government (Crozier, 1975). But later events were to show that the Somalis took Soviet aid and bought Soviet weapons but made their own policies. The Soviet position in Somalia was dependent on falling in with Somali aims. True, the Soviets gained the use of Somali airfields for reconnaissance missions over the Red sea, the Gulf and the Indian Ocean and built up major naval facilities at Berbera, but they were not in control of Somali policy, least of all as regards the use of the armed forces to pursue basic national objectives.

The most basic of these objectives was the restoration of the Ogaden to Somalia. Barre remained committed to this and in the mid-1970s allowed the WSLF to resume political and then military activity. The growing domestic conflict in Ethiopia, the drought in the Ogaden and exodus of ethnic Somalis from the drought areas into Somalia created the ideal conditions for the resumption of the WSLF's fight against the Ethiopians. In 1975, Barre allowed the front to start operations from Somali territory and he began to give arms and training to WSLF guerrillas (Ottaway, 1982, p. 83). The Somali military helped the WSLF to reorganise its military units and to prepare for a major offensive. Small-scale attacks were launched in 1976 and early 1977. By 1977, the WSLF had convinced Siad of the need for a more vigorous military campaign backed by the Somali armed forces (Selassie, 1980, p. 111). In February, a major clash took place in the Ogaden when 1,500 Somali troops crossed the border and were confronted by Ethiopian forces. The army also helped the WSLF by allowing soldiers to fight with the front, ostensibly as guerrillas. Somali officials admitted that serving soldiers who were on leave were allowed to 'volunteer' to join the WSLF (*ACR* 1977–78, p. B374).

The pace of the conflict increased in July when WSLF units destroyed five bridges on the Addis–Djibouti railway. On 23rd July, a full-scale invasion took place, spearheaded by Somali armoured forces. The Ethiopians were unprepared and retreated hastily. In September, the Somalis and WSLF advanced far into Ogaden and on 12th September captured the key town of Jijiga. The next targets were Dire Dawa and Harer. If they fell, the Ethiopians would be in danger of losing the whole of the Ogaden. Luckily for the Ethiopians, the besieged forces in the two towns were able to hold out until a counter-offensive was launched.

The Somali attack was a desperate blow to the Derg. Its forces were engaged in major counter-insurgency campaigns in Eritrea and it was still at war with itself and with the EPRP. It needed large-scale military assistance and dependable allies. In the early years of the revolution, the Ethiopians had continued to receive and to rely on US military aid. They needed arms and ammunition to continue the war in Eritrea and to keep strong forces along the border with Somalia. Haile Selassie had received substantial (though not as substantial as Soviet deliveries to Somalia) US arms supplies in 1973 and 1974. Following his overthrow, the US government had no clear policy towards the Derg but it continued to supply large quantities of arms and to keep open the Kagnew base. In 1975, the Derg received military grants worth $12.5m, credits totalling $25m and it made purchases of military equipment totalling $20m. In February 1975, the Derg asked for a further $29m dollars worth of arms (US Congress, 1976, p. 121). The US government had protested against the executions of members of the royal family in Ethiopia and had doubts about the orientation of the Derg, but it was loth to give up its position in Ethiopia at a time when the Soviet Union seemed so firmly entrenched in Somalia. Paul Henze, who served as a US diplomat in Ethiopia in the early 1970s and later advised the National Security Council on developments in the Horn, believes that 'there can be no doubt that American policymakers confronted considerable dilemmas and confusion in this period' (Henze, 1981, p. 63). But instead of stopping military aid, they increased it. In 1976, grants and credits totalled $22m, but cash purchases soared to $100m – the highest level ever (US Congress, 1976, p. 121). The decision to supply huge quantities of arms 'was based purely on geopolitical considerations' (Ottaway, 1982, p. 101).

But during 1976, the start of the terror campaigns, the conflict within the Derg and signs of increasing links between the Derg and Moscow meant that the relationship was becoming an embarrassment. When Jimmy Carter, with his stress on human rights, became President, policy began to change. In early 1977, Carter made it clear that arms would not be forthcoming and that the level of military assistance would be scaled down. Mengistu, who was by then in command and who had developed new links with the Soviet Union, reacted by closing down the Kagnew base and expelling the US military assistance mission. But even after that, the US government still sold Ethiopia spare parts for combat aircraft.

The Soviet Union, though heavily committed to Somalia, watched developments in Ethiopia with great interest. Moscow was wary of making a commitment to improving relations, but was impressed by the Derg's attempts to form a pro-Marxist political movement and by its stress on anti-capitalism and anti-imperialism. During 1976, radical army and air force officers began to criticise the Derg for reliance on the US military aid and Mengistu began to put out feelers to the Soviet Union. But the Brezhnev leadership was cautious, clearly not wanting to alienate the Somalis if the Derg was not serious in its commitment to socialism and anti-imperialism. Talks were held between Derg representatives and the Moscow leadership; and the Soviet ambassador in Addis Ababa is said to have promised arms to the Ethiopians early in 1976. But until the end of the year no firm commitments were made. Bruce Porter believes that promises of arms were used by the Soviet Union to get the Derg to make plain its adherence to Marxism–Leninism (Porter, 1984, p. 192). But there is no evidence of this and it seems more likely that until Mengistu increased his power within the Derg and made clear his ideological position, the Soviet Union preferred to keep the Ethiopians at arms length.

The National Democratic Revolution Programme, adopted in April 1976, no doubt helped to increase Soviet interest in Ethiopia and in the summer educational and technical aid was given to the Derg (much to the Somalia's consternation). But the real change in attitude occurred at the end of the year when the head of the Derg defence committee visited Moscow and signed a secret arms deal worth $100m – chiefly for defensive arms such as anti-aircraft guns, artillery and anti-tank missiles. It is unlikely to have been a coincidence, given the later Soviet–Cuban military coordination in Ethiopia, that the arms deal was signed during a visit to Moscow by the Cuban Armed Forces Minister (and effective deputy leader) Raul Castro and Foreign Minister Carlos Rafael Rodriguez (*Pravda*, 16th December 1976). The Cubans had taken an early interest in the Derg – in early 1975, General Arnaldo Ochoa Sanchez, who was in command of the Cuban forces in both Angola and Ethiopia, visited Addis Ababa and in July diplomatic relations were established. The Cubans were said to have played a role in advising Mengistu in how to deal with the Soviets and in acting as a go-between in the development of relations between Moscow and the Derg (Dominguez, 1989, p. 158).

The developing relationship between the Ethiopian regime and both Moscow and Havana took a new turn following Mengistu's seizure of power in February 1977 following the shoot-out at a Derg meeting. His ascent to chairmanship of the PMAC was quickly welcomed by the Soviet Union. The month after the Derg battle, the first Soviet-supplied tanks reached Ethiopia. By April, several shipments of armoured vehicles had arrived as, it was strongly rumoured, had Cuban advisers (Ottaway, 1982, p. 108).

In March 1977, President Castro toured the Horn of Africa, visiting both Ethiopia and Somalia. Following his stay in Addis Ababa, Castro went on to Aden in the People's Democratic Republic of Yemen (PDRY), accompanied by Mengistu. There the two met President Barre of Somalia. According to a later account by Barre himself (*Washington Post*, 17th May 1977), Castro unveiled a Soviet-sponsored plan for a Marxist federation of Red Sea states – Ethiopia, Somalia and the PDRY. This was an attempt by the USSR and Cuba to prevent a war between Ethiopia and Somalia and to develop their ties with Ethiopia without destroying their existing relationship with Somalia. It was a naive plan based on the supposition that the adherence to socialism declared by both Ethiopia and Somalia would assist them to overcome their dispute over the Ogaden and the decades of hostility. Somalia rejected the plan and began to accuse the Soviet Union of one-sidedness in its policy towards the Horn.

The rejection of the federation plan and of the related Soviet and Cuban attempt to maintain peace in the region, prompted both Castro and Brezhnev to continue.developing close ties with Mengistu. In the spring of 1977, an Ethiopian military delegation visited Moscow and obtained a pledge of further arms supplies. In May 1977, Mengistu was received warmly during a state visit to the Soviet Union (*Pravda*, 5th May 1977) and another arms deal, this one worth $350–450m was signed; the deal included 48 MiG-21s, 200 T-54/55 tanks, Sagger anti-tank missiles and SAM-7 anti-aircraft missiles (Patman, 1982, p. 50). At the end of the meeting, the document signed by both delegations laid strong emphasis on 'the territorial integrity of states and the inviolability of state boundaries' (*Pravda*, 9th May 1977; Radio Moscow in English for Africa, 9th May 1977).

The evident signs of Soviet opposition to the Somali plans for recovery of the Ogaden did nothing to stop the Barre government from pushing ahead with its military offensive in the Ogaden. The invasion was initially a great military success and by mid-September most of the major towns and military garrisons in the Ogaden had been overrun by the Somali forces. But increased Soviet arms supplies (and the arrival of Soviet and Cuban advisers, though not combat troops) reversed the situation. Large numbers of tanks, 122mm rocket launchers and combat aircraft reached the Ethiopian forces around Dire Dawa and Harer in October and enabled them to turn the tide; in August, the Soviet Union had halted its military deliveries to Somalia.

The Soviet moves to reduce aid to Somalia and to help Ethiopia led inevitably to an acrimonious split. On 13th November 1977, Siad Barre repudiated the Treaty of Friendship and Cooperation with the Soviet Union and expelled all Soviet personnel. He said that Moscow had taken Ethiopia's side against Somalia (Mogadishu home service in Somali, 13th November 1977). This now gave the Soviet Union no excuse for holding back on total support for Ethiopia.

At the start of the Ogaden war, the Soviet Union avoided direct criticism of Barre. The officially-backed Soviet Committee for Solidarity with Afro-Asian Countries in August appealed for an end to fighting between Ethiopia and Somalia, saying that 'by fanning an armed conflict in the Horn of Africa, imperialism and reactionary regimes want to undermine the progressive governments of Somalia and Ethiopia' (*Pravda*, 7th August 1977). Not the most accurate account of the origins of the conflict but an obvious bid to sit on the fence and not alienate Somalia. Until the use of Cuban combat troops and Soviet advisers to mastermind the Ethiopian offensive against the Somali invasion force, the Soviets kept up this line of argument, that the Western powers and reactionary Arab states had engineered the conflict to protect their own interests and to weaken the growth of socialism in the Horn of Africa (see for example, Radio Moscow in English for Africa, 27th July 1977; and, *New Times*, no. 1, January 1978). The official Soviet international affairs weekly *New Times* said in February 1978 that 'there is no longer the slightest doubt that the present events in the Horn of Africa are the direct result of a compact between the imperialist powers, primarily the United States, and the reactionary Arab regimes – a compact spearheaded against the progressive forces in the Red Sea basin. The area has been allotted an exceptionally important place in the imperialist strategic plans because of its geographical location at the junction of two continents.' Rather ludicrously, given Moscow's extensive and high profile role in building and arming the Somali armed forces since 1963, in January, the Soviets accused the West of sending arms to Somalia in order to test them in battle conditions (Radio Moscow World Service in English, 28th January 1978). Moscow justified its own role in the conflict, more reasonably, pointing out that it had tried to prevent war, had in the end come down on the side of the victim of aggression and, perhaps less accurately, had not sought any gains for itself.

If Moscow's words were soft on Somalia, its actions were not. Between the start of the war and the end of 1978 an estimated $1–2bn worth of Soviet arms were airlifted or shipped to Ethiopia (Ottaway, 1982, p. 116). The massive Soviet airlift of arms, advisers and Cuban troops got under way on 26th November 1977. Between 15,000 and 17,000 Cuban troops were sent to Ethiopia between November and February 1978 (Patman, 1982, p. 53; and CIA, 1978, p. 4). The arms and troops enabled the Ethiopians to stabilise their position, repulse further Somali attacks and then begin a massive counter-offensive. The latter started around Jijiga in February and within a month had succeeded in pushing most of the Somalis out of the Ogaden, though mopping up operations against Somali and WSLF units continued until the end of the year. The Somalis officially announced their withdrawal from the Ogaden on 9th March 1978.

The Soviet operation was proof of an increasing Soviet ability to project its power into the Third World and to coordinate with its allies – notably the Cubans but also the Yemenis (the PDRY is believed to have sent several regular army units to Ethiopia to support the Ethiopians). Other friendly states also helped out with the delivery of arms, notably Libya and Mozambique. But Cuba played the major role. It built up its forces in Ethiopia from 1,000 in December to 17,000 in March. At least 100 Soviet advisers were in Ethiopia in late 1977, and this number grew as the offensive got under way. Bruce Porter estimates that there were 1,500 Soviet military advisers serving with the Ethiopian forces at the height of the counter-offensive. The Ethiopian response to the Somalis is believed to have been masterminded by the Deputy Commander of the Soviet General Forces, General Vasiliy Petrov, assisted by the former head of the Soviet military mission in Somalia, General Grigoriy Barisov (Porter, 1984, p. 204; and Legum and Lee, *ACR* 1978–79, p. A45). The Cuban forces were led by General Arnaldo Ochoa Sanchez, a veteran of the Cuban intervention in Angola. In addition to combat troops, the Cubans made a vital input to the Ethiopian war effort by supplying pilots and tank crews. East German military advisers are also thought to have played a role in the war.

The Soviet-supplied arsenal was an impressive one. It included 300–400 T54/55 tanks, 30–55 T-34 tanks, 200–350 armoured personnel carriers and armoured fighting vehicles, 55–60 MiG-21s, 30 Mi-8 helicopters, batteries of 122mm rocket-launchers, 300–400 100mm and 150mm artillery pieces, six mobile anti-aircraft batteries and SAM-3 and SAM-7 anti-aircraft missile systems. It gave the Ethiopians one of the most powerful armies in Africa and one far superior to that in Somalia. In the period following the Ogaden war, the Cubans and Soviets helped Mengistu to build a massive army. Including the people's militia units, the armed forces totalled 150,000 by 1979 (IISS, 1978–79).

During the hottest phase of the conflict, there was no US involvement. Having lost its foothold in Ethiopia, the USA was wary of risking intervention through support for Somalia. But once the split between Somalia and the Soviet Union widened and the extent of the Soviet–Cuban commitment to Ethiopia was clear, President Carter began to make overtures to the Somalis, though he didn't actually come up with any military supplies or direct support until 1980. President Barre claimed that the Americans had offered him military aid in return for expelling the Soviets and had then failed to fulfil their side of the bargain. Somalia was certainly in need of military aid following the expulsion of the Soviets, as the Ogaden defeat showed. After the war, there were signs of dissension within the army and among the competing clans. Those clans linked with the Ogaden Somalis were outraged at the military debacle and the withdrawal. Pressure from the army, the clans and the WSLF pushed Barre into another military adventure in the Ogaden in early 1980. Although fighting lasted until September 1980, the Somalis were no match for the new Ethiopian army, still backed by Cuban combat troops. Somali troops seconded to the WSLF (at least 1,000 men) continued to fight in the Ogaden late into the year.

The failure to make headway in Ogaden led Barre to approach the USA once more for aid. In August 1980, pushed on by his hawkish national security adviser, Zbigniew Brzezinski and by the shock of the Soviet intervention in Afghanistan, Carter gave his assent to an agreement under which the USA supplied arms and advisers for the Somali army in return for use of the Soviet-constructed facilities at Berbera. In the first two years of the agreement, the USA supplied military credits worth $40m. By 1980, Somalia was also receiving substantial military aid and arms supplies from China. Chinese military followed Barre's visit to Peking in April 1978 and was part of China's increasing hostility towards the Soviet role in Africa. The Chinese took the view that it was in their interest to side with the West and with conservative African regimes against the Soviets and Cubans rather than to follow the independent, radical policies that they had developed towards Africa in the 1960s.

The Soviet Union became Ethiopia's main source of political, military and ideological support following the Ogaden war. In November 1978, the two countries signed a twenty-year Treaty of Friendship and Cooperation. The Soviet Union played a major, by Soviet standards, economic role in Ethiopia, notably in the mining, power generation and industrial sectors. Cuba was also an important source of support. Even after the war was over in 1978, it kept anything up to 10,000 combat troops in Ethiopia and sent hundreds of civilian advisers to help in the medical, educational and construction sectors (Dominguez, 1989, p. 161).

Libya had assisted Ethiopia during the war, though not by sending troops. Libya was used as a vital staging post for Soviet arms deliveries and Colonel Qadhafi pledged $425m in credits and economic aid to the PMAC in June 1977. Both Libya and the Soviet Union supplied Ethiopia with oil at prices well below the world market rates. Libya also cut its longstanding links with the Eritrean rebels – though a minor Ethiopian–Libyan row in 1979–80 over Ethiopian backing for the Tanzanian role in Uganda led to Qadhafi sending financial aid worth $2.5m to the EPLF as a gesture of irritation with Mengistu.

The ethnic conflicts inside Ethiopia and in Eritrea became a more nagging problem for the PMAC than the war with Somalia and continuing tension over the Ogaden. The 1974 revolution had led to a blossoming of secessionist or pro-autonomy movements. They ranged from the Eritreans to the Tigreans, Oromos and Afars. The chaos created in Ethiopia and the hopes aroused by the overthrow of the Emperor contributed to the growth in ethnic unrest. The Eritreans used the revolution firstly to try to press their demands for self-determination. They were disappointed when in 1976, the PMAC made clear that although limited autonomy could be granted to provinces, there could be no secession. The EPLF and the weaker ELF then renewed their rebellions with greater vigour than before, despite further splits in the movements themselves.

The Derg launched an offensive in Eritrea in 1976 that made clear its intention to solve the Eritrean question by force. The offensive was a disaster as the Ethiopian force of 20,000 troops was outnumbered by 25,000 EPLF fighers and nearly 20,000 men from the ELF. After that failure, the Derg put together a huge attacking force made up of tens of thousands of hastily trained peasant militias plus regular units. As the massive force was concentrating to prepare for the offensive, the EPLF struck at it, smashing the army and preventing the offensive from getting under way. The peasant militias were then reassigned to serve as defensive units in peasant cooperatives. The Derg then looked around for foreign aid for the Eritrean war. It succeeded in getting Libya and the PDRY to drop their support for the EPLF and was able to use large quantities of Soviet-supplied weapons in Eritrea. During the Ogaden war, Ethiopia was able to hold off the EPLF and ELF, because the arrival of the Cubans in the Ogaden enabled thousands of Ethiopian troops to be retained in Eritrea. The conflict in Eritrea escalated in 1976–7 as the Eritreans sought to take advantage of the Ogaden war and as President Numayri of Sudan increased his support for the Eritreans. His motive was to hit back at the Derg, which he accused of cooperating with Libya in an attempt to overthrow the Sudanese ruler in July 1976. The bid failed and Numayri then became a firm supporter of the Eritrean and Tigrean liberation movements.

By early 1977, the Ethiopians had lost control of much of the Eritrean countryside and only controlled the major towns and garrisons. In mid-1977, an EPLF offensive cut the Ethiopian presence back to little more than garrisons in Massawa and Assab. At the time both the Soviet Union and Cuba (who during Haile Selassie's reign had sympathised with the Eritreans and given them limited financial and military aid) were trying to talk Mengistu into opening negotiations with the Eritreans. This attempt failed. The Soviets then effectively backed the Ethiopian campaigns against the EPLF, ELF, TPLF and other ethnic movements by supplying arms and advisers to the Ethiopian armed forces. The Cubans refused direct requests for Cuban troops to fight in Eritrea, though thousands of troops remained in the Ogaden area and instructors helped the army and air force. Mengistu was angered by the Cuban refusal and persistently pressed Castro. One Cuban government official has been quoted as saying that 'the Eritean problem is Ethiopia's, not Cuba's' (Dominguez, 1989, p. 160). But Mengistu failed to get his way, despite direct appeals to the Cuban people at rallies in Havana during state visits in May 1978 and again in 1979.

The conflict in the Horn in the late 1970s, had become very much an international one. But despite the large Soviet role in Somalia and then the Soviet and Cuban operation to support Ethiopia, the nucleus of the problem remained African. The massive Soviet and Cuban interventions determined the results of the fighting but 'Ethiopia and Somalia remained remarkably autonomous agents in this period, pursuing goals quite separate from the great powers' (Ottaway, 1982, p. 155). The Soviet Union and Cuba were willing to involve themselves deeply in the war and the political conflict in the Horn of Africa but they did so at the request of the Somalis and then the Ethiopians; they did not impose themselves on the conflict. The two outside powers were willing to support what they saw as revolutionary states and for the Soviet Union ideological interests went hand in hand with strategic ones – even though the stress on ideology led to the failed attempt to build a Marxist federation and ultimately to the expulsion from Somalia and the loss of the Berbera base. But the initiative in the relationship between the states of the region and the superpowers remained with the Ethiopians and Somalis. The regimes in both countries 'sought and welcomed the intervention of the great powers, even when they decried it publicly for political reasons. Both countries were willing to allow the development of military facilities in their territory when they thought they would obtain advantages by doing so' (Ottaway, 1982, p. 172).

6   The 1980s: a decade of destabilisation

If the post-1974 period saw the launching of foreign military operations in Africa on a huge scale, the 1980s witnessed the start of sustained campaigns of destabilisation. Foreign troops (Cubans, Libyans and French, plus advisers from countries as far apart as the USA and North Korea) remained in Africa in large numbers and played an active combat role in Angola and Chad. But the new factor in African military equations became destabilisation. South Africa made it the chief instrument in its southern African strategy, while Libya used it as a weapon against the states bordering the Sahel.

In the cases of both South Africa and Libya, destabilisation was supplemented by direct armed attacks on neighbouring countries. South Africa occupied a large part of Angola's southernmost provinces right up until the closing years of the decade and only pulled its army of occupation out of Namibia in November 1989. Libya continued to intervene to support selected allies in Chad and to militarily occupy the disputed Aouzou strip (see Chapter Four). France also played a combat role in Chad and used the military as an instrument of policy elsewhere in Africa. The Soviet Union continued to be the main supplier of arms to a number of friendly governments and had thousands of advisers serving with African armies. But as the decade wore on, its involvement in Africa waned and where it was involved it turned to diplomatic rather than military means of resolving conflicts.

Southern Africa: the total strategy

The victory of the MPLA in the Angolan civil war, the formation of a Frelimo government in Mozambique and the independence of Zimbabwe under the rule of a radical nationalist party redrew the political and strategic maps of southern Africa. Through cooperation with the Portuguese colonial rulers and through direct military participation in the struggle in Zimbabwe (not to mention military, political and economic pressure on other states in southern Africa), South Africa had sought during the 1970s to ensure its hegemony in the region and to protect its borders and its racist political system against the mounting challenge of African nationalism. By the start of 1980, this policy, and the idea of a 'constellation of states' in southern Africa based on South African political and economic power, had collapsed. The idea of regional domination had not been dropped nor had the intention to use any means available to stem the nationalist flood been diluted. The government of P.W. Botha – who had succeeded Vorster in the wake of the Soweto uprising of June 1976 and the later corruption crises (Muldergate as it became known) – was committed to what it termed a 'total strategy' to meet a 'total onslaught'.

The concepts of the total strategy and total onslaught had been first enunciated in the 1977 Defence White Paper presented to the South African parliament by the then Defence Minister P.W. Botha. They were ideas emanating both from Botha's own view of how to defend white political and economic supremacy and from the strategic thinking of senior military leaders such as the Chief of the SADF, General Magnus Malan, and his deputy, Jannie Geldenhuys. They saw the onslaught as a communist-inspired and sponsored campaign to destroy white supremacy in South Africa – though it is the author's view that the communist angle was often played beyond the actual belief in its of its proponents in order to attract Western support. Botha, speaking to parliament in Cape Town in January 1978, set out his view of the threat as follows: 'South Africa is experiencing unprecedented intervention on the part of the superpowers ... The Republic of South Africa is experiencing the full onslaught of Marxism and it must not be doubted that the Republic enjoys a high priority in the onslaught by Moscow.' This onslaught manifested itself in the armed struggle and political campaigns of the exiled ANC and SWAPO in Namibia, the high level of domestic political unrest and violence following Soweto, the growth of a militant black trades union movement inside South Africa, the radicalisation of independent states in southern Africa and their total opposition to apartheid and the activism of anti-apartheid movements around the world which called for economic sanctions against South Africa.

These combined threats were being orchestrated by Moscow and its allies in order to overthrow the whites, seize mineral resources and control the Cape sea route. The 1982 Defence White Paper emphasised Moscow's role –

the ultimate aim of the Soviet Union and its allies is to overthrow the present body politic in the Republic of South Africa and to replace it with a Marxist-oriented form of government to further the objectives of the USSR, therefore all possible methods and means are used to attain this objective. This includes instigating social and labour unrest, civilian resistance, terrorist attacks against the infrastructure of the Republic of South Africa and the intimidation of black leaders and members of the security forces. This onslaught is supported by a worldwide propaganda campaign and the involvement of various front organisations and leaders.

All methods were utilised, according to South African total onslaught theorists, to achieve these aims and therefore the South African state should utilise all weapons at its command to combat the onslaught.

The belief of P.W. Botha and his closest advisers in this theory led to the militarisation of South Africa's system of government and to the rise of a system of security management that brought military leaders, intelligence and security chiefs and the heads of major industries and private corporations together in bodies such as the State Security Council and regional management councils around South Africa (see Grundy, 1986, pp. 5–57; and Cawthra, 1986, pp. 32–40). The system that was built up at least partially superseded the existing institutions of government, notably the cabinet, and the ruling National Party. Botha succeeded in having a new constitution drafted that gave him the post of executive president and vastly increased his ability to bypass the cabinet and parliament in order to implement his total strategy through the growing security apparatus. This apparatus aimed to coordinate political, military, economic and social policies in the fight to defend apartheid. Cosmetic reforms of the apartheid system and divide and rule tactics aimed at splitting the Indians and Coloureds from the blacks and to create a black middle class to split the black community were a vital part of the whole offensive.

In terms of regional policy, the total strategy coordinated military, political and economic instruments. Where possible neighbouring states would be bribed into acquiescence to or even direct cooperation with South Africa's policies. States that would not comply would be battered into submission through the use of economic, political and, ultimately, military pressure. South Africa had intervened militarily in Zimbabwe to support the Smith regime, there had been clandestine military cooperation between the South African army and the Portuguese forces in Angola and Mozambique (unattributable interview with a former Portuguese officer who served in Mozambique and was responsible for liaison with the SADF), had launched the 1975 invasion of Angola, South African forces were occupying Namibia and force had been used to support an erstwhile ally in Lesotho in 1970. But the scale of military intervention and subversion through rebel forces in southern Africa in the 1980s were to increase massively under the total strategy.

The targets were states which did not fall into line with South African policies – and this could range from trying to destabilise or overthrow governments in Angola and Mozambique to which South Africa was totally opposed ideologically, to limited actions aimed at hitting particular targets (such as ANC or SWAPO offices) and even to sabotage attacks on one country's transport or infrastructural facilities that would in turn affect a third country by cutting its trade routes or restricting vital supplies (notably oil).

The use of such tactics started in the late 1970s (earlier in Angola's case) as it became clear that Zimbabwe was approaching independence and therefore that the last 'white' ally in southern Africa was about to disappear and be replaced by a radical, black nationalist government. South African police and paramilitary forces were directly involved in fighting the liberation forces in Zimbabwe (they did not pull out until early 1980) and so Pretoria could hardly expect any independent Zimbabwean government to be anything but hostile towards its regional activities. But immediately prior to the end of the Zimbabwean struggle, South Africa squeezed every last drop out of its relationship with the white minority regime in order to further its aggressive regional strategy. In March 1979, the South Africans launched a joint raid with the Rhodesians on a vital oil storage depot at Beira in Mozambique. Rhodesian special forces were landed at Beira by a South African submarine. They then destroyed the oil storage tanks and were taken off again. The raid was then claimed by the MNR. A later attack on fuel tanks at Maputo (following the same pattern as the Beira raid) failed. During 1979, South Africa used the Rhodesian connection to build up strong links with the MNR. When Zimbabwean independence came in 1980, the whole MNR HQ, including a radio station (the Voice of Free Africa, later called the Voice of the MNR), was transported to northern Transvaal.

Following Zimbabwe's independence, it too became a target for South Africa's regional policies. Party militias loyal to Bishop Abel Muzorewa and Ndabaningi Sithole (both of whom were defeated in the pre-independence elections, having been disgraced by their cooperation with Ian Smith) fled the country following ZANU's election victory and were taken in by Pretoria. Several thousand former militia members were trained in sabotage at bases near Phalaborwa in northern Transvaal. They were then used to mount sabotage raids in southern Zimbabwe. They became a serious problem for the Mugabe government during the period of instability in Matabeleland between 1982 and 1985. The basic problem arose from rivalry between ZANU and ZAPU. The latter was a junior member of the government but many of its members wanted to challenge ZANU militarily. This led to a bush war between government forces and disgruntled members of ZAPU's former guerrilla army. The South Africans took advantage of this to infiltrate former Muzorewa or Sithole supporters into the south to carry out attacks and to create even greater instability.

South Africa's capacity to intervene in Zimbabwe was strengthened by the exodus to South Africa of thousands of soldiers who had fought for the Rhodesian army (and particularly the special units such as the Selous Scouts, Greys Scouts and the Special Air Service). They provided a pool of experienced officers and men who had carried out commando style raids against neighbouring states during the liberation war and had engaged in sabotage, assassinations and other clandestine activities.

The various forces assembled in South Africa were soon put to use both in Matabeleland and in more finely targeted operations. On 3rd August 1981, a South African hit squad was used to assassinate the ANC representative in Zimbabwe, Joe Gqabi. Mugabe was convinced (and there is little reason to doubt his belief) that the attack was carried out by former Selous Scouts based in South Africa (*Herald*, 26th September 1981). Later the same month, a sabotage squad attacked Inkomo barracks, near Harare, destroying arms and military equipment worth $36m. On 18th December 1981, a bomb attack was carried out against the headquarters of the ruling ZANU party in central Harare – six civilians were killed and substantial damage caused to the building. The bomb explosion occurred to coincide with a planned ZANU Central Committee meeting. There was around the same time an attempt to destroy thirty tanks and armoured cars at an army base in Harare. Explosives with a sophisticated timing device were planted at the base but discovered before they exploded (Martin and Johnson, 1989, p. 65). The most successful sabotage attack against Zimbabwe occurred on 25th July 1982, when at least ten combat aircraft, including newly purchased Hawk fighter/trainer aircraft, were blown up on the ground at the Thornhill air force base near Gweru. The attack destroyed the main air defence units and the air force's strike and interception capabilities. It was not possible to pin down exact blame in these cases, but they all involved the use of sophisticated sabotage techniques and all conformed to the general pattern of South African attacks against neighbouring states.

At the time of the air force attacks, South African military leaders, notably Defence Minister Malan, were busy trying to convince the world that the frontline states of southern Africa were building up their armed forces, particularly air and tank numbers, in order to be in a position to pose a conventional military threat to South Africa. The idea of a conventional attack by the frontline states on South Africa's bigger and better armed and trained army was quite ridiculous, but it was a constant theme in Pretoria's propaganda effort – needless to say, the Soviet Union was repeatedly accused of building up the armed forces of southern African states in order to destabilise South Africa. At the time, though, Britain was the main supplier of weapons to Zimbabwe and it had a large military training team there.

The first direct clash between South African and Zimbabwean forces took place on 18th August 1982, when Zimbabwean army units intercepted a unit of South African troops which had crossed the Limpopo river into Zimbabwe. A skirmish took place in which three white South African soldiers were killed. The remainder of the South African unit escaped back across the border. The SADF command at first denied the Zimbabwean reports of the incident, but under pressure to get the bodies back for burial, SADF Chief Constand Viljoen was forced to admit on 26th August that the men had been killed (Johannesburg radio in English for abroad, 26th August 1982). The men had come from the SADF base at Phalaborwa, where former Rhodesian forces were based. Viljoen claimed that the raid had been unauthorised.

During late 1982 and the following two years, the Zimbabwean government frequently accused the South African government of complicity in guerrilla attacks by anti-government forces in Matabeleland. It believed that the weapons being used by former ZAPU guerrillas and by other insurgents operating in the region had been smuggled into the country via South Africa. Weapons captured were not former Zimbabwean army ones or from stocks dating back to the liberation war. The only likely source for them was South Africa (Martin and Johnson, 1989, p. 71). Guerrillas captured in Matabeleland by the Zimbabwean security forces during late 1982 frequently said they had received training in South Africa at SADF bases.

The success of the government in ending the dissident actions in Matabeleland and the political unity forged in the late 1980s by ZANU and ZAPU, prevented South Africa from being able to use the rebel problem in the way they had exploited UNITA and the MNR. The war though was a serious cause of instability in Zimbabwe and a serious obstacle to political reconciliation and economic development. But the Zimbabwean government did not have to call on foreign assistance to deal with the problem. Although British soldiers were involved in training members of the Zimbabwean armed forces in eastern

Zimbabwe and North Korean advisers trained the crack (and later notorious Fifth Brigade), no foreign troops took part in the fighting on Zimbabwe's side.

Zimbabwe also maintained a policy of diversification in arms supplies. Britain was a major source of arms – from aircraft and light armoured vehicles to communications equipment. Some weapons, including tanks, were purchased from China and North Korea. Relations with the Soviet Union were poor in the early years of independence, but improved in the mid-1980s. In the last five years of the decade, ties improved markedly. Mugabe began to look to the USSR for arms supplies around this time. His reasoning was not just connected with maintaining a diversified arsenal, but also to ensure that the Zimbabwean troops sent to fight in Mozambique against the MNR had equipment similar to their Mozambican counterparts – an obvious advantage when joint operations were launched and in terms of arms and ammunition supplies for units in the field.

On 19th May 1986, South African special forces mounted a two-pronged attack on Harare and Lusaka. The raids were ostensibly against ANC targets – the ones in Harare were the ANC officers in the centre of town and the house in the suburbs outside which Joe Gqabi had been killed in 1981. There was no attempt to hide the raids, even though they came at the time of a sensitive Commonwealth mission to southern Africa. President P.W. Botha congratulated the SADF on the attacks and threatened the frontline states that more would follow if they did not cease their support for the ANC. His words and the attack itself was clearly intended to bring to an end the Commonwealth attempt to mediate in southern Africa.

In April 1987, Zimbabwe was believed to have concluded a major deal with the Soviet Union for the purchase of sophisticated MiG-29 aircraft. These would give Zimbabwe the technical edge over South Africa in the air. The deal was at first denied by the Zimbabweans, but there were strong reasons to believe that the Soviet Union had agreed to supply twelve MiGs. One reason was the visit to Moscow in March 1987 by the head of the air force, Josiah Tungamirai, intelligence chief and Security Minister, Emmerson Munangagwa, and Finance Minister Bernard Chidzero.

South African destabilisation was not limited to Zimbabwe. Botswana, Lesotho and Zambia were also periodic targets for South African military and sabotage actions. Botswana because Pretoria believed that its long border with South Africa was used for infiltration by ANC guerrillas; Lesotho, for the same reason and because the government of Chief Jonathan refused to expel ANC representatives from Maseru; and Zambia because of its long-standing support for the ANC and SWAPO, both of which maintained their headquarters in Lusaka. Lesotho was the most vulnerable of the southern African states to South African military, political and economic pressure. It is completely surrounded by South African territory and relies totally on transport routes through South Africa for all its external trade. A large proportion of its imports come from South Africa. In the 1960s and 1970s, Pretoria gained great influence in the country both through its massive economic investments there (massive by Lesotho's standards) and through its open support for the government of Chief Leabua

Jonathan. In January 1970, the South Africans openly supported a coup by Chief Jonathan following his defeat in general elections – this action by Jonathan led eventually to the formation of a guerrilla army, the Lesotho Liberation Army, which was determined to overthrow him.

Relations with South Africa remained close during the early 1970s, but soured towards the end of the decade and at the start of the 1980s as Lesotho became a firm supporter of the SADCC and expanded its political support for the ANC, allowing the movement to set up offices in Maseru and to have transit facilities there for political refugees fleeing South Africa. These policies angered Pretoria, which wanted to ensure Lesotho's compliance with its regional aims and security needs. Pretoria put economic pressure on through its control of trade routes and began to nurture links with the formerly radical but strongly anti-Jonathan Lesotho Liberation Army (LLA) of Ntsu Mokhehle. The LLA started launching sabotage attacks and assassination attempts against government figures in May 1979. Many of the raids were cross-border ones from bases inside South Africa. Lesotho tried to end the row with South Africa in 1980, but there was only a temporary respite and 1981–2 saw a rapid escalation of LLA activity.

Relations with South Africa continued to worsen and on 9th December 1982 the SADF launched a vicious raid against houses used by South African refugees in Maseru. South African commandos supported by helicopters and armoured vehicles crossed the border into Lesotho and attacked a number of houses in the capital, killing forty-two civilians – thirty of them South African refugees and twelve of them Basotho bystanders. South Africa then warned Lesotho that it should end its relationship with the ANC or else. The following month there were further attacks on the eve of a meeting of SADCC ministers in Maseru. A series of bomb attacks occurred in the capital destroying water pumping installations. The Prime Minister, Chief Jonathan, told the SADCC meeting that the attack was the work of the South Africans, who were using the LLA as tools to destabilise his country. He said that at one time his country had been 'an island of peace within the raging sea' of southern Africa but that the sea had become so turbulent that 'its furious waves spill into our country' (*New African*, March 1983). In February 1983, bomb attacks caused severe damage to oil storage tanks in Maseru. Again the LLA was thought to have launched the sabotage raid from across the border in South Africa.

As the attacks continued, the South Africans called for Jonathan to stop supporting the ANC in return for improved relations. They made it abundantly clear that the LLA attacks and raids against the ANC and South African refugees were part and parcel of a deliberate policy of coercion. Pretoria never openly admitted helping the LLA, but the movement could not have carried out attacks inside Lesotho without having used South African territory as a rear base.

In an interview in 1983, Chief Jonathan said that he was absolutely convinced that LLA activity was part and parcel of overall South African policy towards his country and was aimed at making him a client of Pretoria. He was adamant that he was not helping the ANC to launch attacks into South Africa but that he would not stop helping refugees from South Africa or give up his total opposition to apartheid. He also revealed that South Africa had offered him a deal in October 1982 under which LLA attacks would end in return for the handing over of various ANC officials living in Lesotho. The Lesotho leader said the campaign against Lesotho was part of 'a deliberate policy of Pretoria to destabilise all the independent countries bordering on South Africa for the simple reason that they want to have puppet governments.' (*New African*, April 1983).

In May 1983, the South Africans used their control over road routes into Lesotho to restrict traffic entering and leaving the country. This caused immediate and severe economic problems. In return for lifting the blockade, the South Africans forced the Lesotho government to fly sixty South African refugees out of the country. But sabotage attacks continued and a prolonged campaign of guerrilla activity started in August 1982. The campaign was stepped up in 1983 and 1984 as the Lesotho government sought to strengthen its relations with the socialist countries as a means of increasing its ability to withstand South African pressure. China and Cuba opened embassies in Maseru and Cuba was believed to be helping to train a militia force linked with Jonathan's ruling Basotho National Party. During 1984, following the Nkomati accord between South Africa and Mozambique, Lesotho came under pressure to expel all ANC representatives from the country and to sign a non-aggression pact. When the government refused, South Africa increased the military pressure via the LLA and the economic pressure through the reimposition of transport restrictions along the borders. The situation worsened after the scandal and debacle surrounding the elections of September 1985. In the closing months of the year, South Africa tightened the trade blockade and rumours started circulating of a possible coup attempt against the government backed by South Africa. On 19th December 1985, South African commandos launched another attack against refugees in Maseru, killing six. The following month, the long-expected coup took place. On 20th January 1986, the leader of Lesotho's paramilitary forces, General Lekhanya, overthrew Jonathan and established a military regime – with Pretoria's blessing. The transport blockade was immediately lifted and cordial relations re-established. There seemed little doubt about South African complicity. Since the coup, Lesotho has ceased to be a safe haven for South African refugees.

Although Botswana did not suffer the same fate as Lesotho, it was also on the receiving end of the SADF on a number of occasions. Each time raids were carried out by the South Africans, it was claimed that Botswana was being used as a launching-pad for ANC military operations inside South Africa. The most serious raid took place on 14th June 1985, when South African special forces attacked ten houses and an office block in Gaborone. The attacks were ostensibly against ANC offices and officials, but Botswanan civilians were among the twelve people killed. Later in the day, the Chief of the SADF, Constand Viljoen, claimed that the targets had been members of the ANC military wing (Johannesburg radio in English for abroad, 14th June 1985). Although some of those killed were refugees connected with the ANC, none was an active member of Umkhonto we Sizwe. Further raids against Gaborone took place in 1986 and on

New Year's Day 1987. The aim was to intimidate Botswana into dropping its open condemnation of apartheid and its moral support for the ANC and for South African political refugees.

Serious though the South African actions described above were, they were minor events compared with the concerted campaigns of direct military action, support for rebels, sabotage and destabilisation launched against Angola and Mozambique.

Angola: occupation and destabilisation

Angola was a primary target for South African destabilisation for a number of reasons. Firstly, it was ruled by a party espousing Marxism which had the military support of tens of thousands of Cuban troops and received weapons, funding and military training from the Soviet Union. Secondly, the MPLA–Workers' Party government was committed to supporting the liberation war being fought by SWAPO against South Africa's illegal occupation of Namibia and the armed struggle being waged by the ANC against the apartheid system itself. Thirdly, South Africa had established close political and military ties with the UNITA movement of Jonas Savimbi during the Angolan civil war – it thus had to hand an indigenous movement which could serve to destabilise the MPLA, be a possible alternative government for Angola, which could be used as a buffer against SWAPO incursions from southern Angola, to camouflage South African raids into Angola and as part of the wider strategy of making southern Africa dependent on South Africa economically.

Support for UNITA had been maintained after the 1975–6 debacle and South African forces had carried out raids into Angola in 1977 and 1978 – ostensibly against SWAPO bases. In 1979, the destabilisation campaign against Angola was escalated by increasing South Africa's direct attacks and by expanding aid to UNITA. On 26th September 1979, the South African Air Force (SAAF) bombed the southern Angolan towns of Lubango and Xangongo. Lubango was the capital of Huila province and a major regional centre. The air raid destroyed factories and other economic installations. In November, South African forces carried out ground attacks, supported by combat helicopters, in which railway bridges and tunnels were destroyed. In the same month, a strong South African force backed by armoured vehicles moved 30 kilometres into Cunene province and occupied the town of Naulila. From then onwards, raiding into southern Angola became a frequent activity. Although the South Africans claimed to be in hot pursuit of SWAPO guerrillas, the attacks were clearly aimed at destroying the infrastructure in the south, at establishing a permanent military presence in Cunene and Cuando Cubango provinces and aiding UNITA by creating South African-controlled areas.

In mid-1980, the campaign was cranked up further when a large SADF column seized large areas of the two southernmost provinces and set up a zone of SADF control. The units involved were larger and better equipped than the armoured column which had been used to support UNITA in 1975. They used their 'liberated' territory to give logistical support to UNITA and to attempt to deny SWAPO access to northern Namibia. From the buffer zone they also carried out raids further into Angola. One such was the SADF attack on Mavinga (Cuando Cubango province) in September 1980 (People's Republic of Angola, 1983). The town, which housed a major Angolan army garrison, was more or less destroyed. The reasoning behind the attack was to destroy a base that could be used by the Angolan army as a jumping off point for attacks against UNITA's South African protected headquarters at Jamba, between Mavinga and the Namibian border.

The South African actions enabled UNITA to greatly increase its activities from 1980 onwards. UNITA groups, often supplied with weapons and other equipment by South African air drops, established operational areas for their guerrillas in Cunene, Cuando Cubango, Huambo, Bie, Huila and Moxico provinces. The Angolan army, FAPLA, carried out frequent counter-insurgency sweeps – killing over 600 guerrillas between December 1979 and April 1980 (*ACR* 1980–81, pp. B648–9). The success of the FAPLA actions pushed UNITA into acts of urban terrorism in Huambo and other parts of central Angola – UNITA strategies included placing mines in fields around the towns to prevent the production of crops. UNITA was also forced into ever greater reliance on the protection of the SADF.

The military pressure on Angola was stepped up in 1981. This was both part of the overall South African destabilisation campaign and a reaction to the election of Ronald Reagan as US President. Vehemently anti-Soviet and viscerally pro-South African, Reagan and his African Affairs Secretary, Chester Crocker, launched their 'constructive engagement' policy towards South Africa. P.W. Botha quite rightly took this as a green light to launch a new wave of attacks and proxy wars against states in southern Africa friendly towards the Soviet Union and supportive of radical African nationalist movements.

President dos Santos of Angola said on 1st January 1982 (Luanda home service in Portuguese, 1st January 1982) that between January and November 1981, the South Africans had carried out fifty three ground attacks and over a hundred air raids against targets inside Angola (see also Hanlon, 1986, p. 159; and Somerville, 1986, pp. 62–3). During the early part of the year, the raids included an assault by helicopter-borne troops on the town of Cuamoto, 38 kilometres inside the Angolan border. But the major attack during 1981 amounted to an SADF invasion of most of southern Angola. Operation Protea, as it was named by the South African defence chiefs, was launched in the last week of August 1981. Two South African armoured columns entered Angola on 23rd August. They cut the N'Giva-Lubango road and blew up the Xangongo road bridge, to hamper counter-attacks by FAPLA. They then advanced towards Lubango. Over 5,000 troops took part in the thrust and the majority of Cunene province came under South African control. The SADF expected to push on to Lubango to destroy the major army and air bases there (notably the radar and anti-aircraft defence network based in the town) and to attack SWAPO camps in the region. They reached Cahama, 110 kilometres north of the Namibian border, but there were blocked by a strong FAPLA force. Unlike in 1975, the Angolans did not need to call on any of the 17,000 Cubans based in the country. The FAPLA force put up a determined defence at Cahama and in spite of the town being more or less flattened by the SADF, the South African advance was stopped. During the advance, a Soviet warrant officer was captured by the South Africans. He was paraded before the press as proof of Soviet involvement in Angolan military operations. He was in fact a technician rather than part of a combat unit (*The Times*, 3rd September 1981).

The South Africans had been prevented from reaching Lubango, but FAPLA was unable to regain the areas occupied by the SADF and the SAAF retained air superiority in southern Angola. The two factors enabled them to continue a war of attrition in the south and to boost the fortunes of UNITA, which now had a large zone of southern Angola from which to launch raids and in which to build up a large guerrilla army.

Although there was still a large Cuban military presence in Angola, the MPLA government used only Angolan forces in fighting UNITA and the South Africans. The Cubans were a force of last resort but, more importantly, were used to guard the oil fields in the north and to free Angolan troops for the fighting in the central and southern areas. This fighting escalated rapidly following the 1981 invasion. The SADF occupied Cunene province in strength through until 1988. Despite an agreement on disengagement of forces reached by Angola and South Africa in Lusaka in February 1984 – a provision of which was the withdrawal of the South Africans – the South Africans continued to control large parts of Cunene and to have a presence in Cuando Cubango until the SA–Angola–Cuba agreement of December 1988. From this occupied zone, the SADF provided invaluable logistical help and a defensive shield for UNITA, enabling it to extend its operations and to seriously threaten government control throughout southern and central Angola. FAPLA was able to retain the main towns, but UNITA was active in rural areas. UNITA successes in 1983 and 1984 took its guerrillas right up to the diamond mines of Lunda Norte and the coffee producing areas of Uige province.

The Angolans launched repeated counter-offensives against UNITA. There was a clearly indentifiable pattern to the offensives and to South Africa's reactions. The Angolan army would start its offensives from the towns of Menongue and Mavinga and push steadily towards Jamba and the UNITA strongholds just north of the Namibian border. Still not having a conventional army (even though it had tens of thousands of guerrillas), UNITA would fall back. If UNITA was unable to halt the advance, the South Africans would then step in using air support, long-range artillery and, when necessary, SADF ground troops to turn back the FAPLA columns. The South Africans also continued to carry out air raids and helicopter-borne attacks deep into Angola. In April and May 1983, South African forces attacked Mulondo (200 kilometres inside the border), the iron mining centre at Kassinga and the railhead at Jamba (not Savimbi's base but an important junction further to the north).

The Angolan government launched a major political and military reorganisation exercise to cope with South African aggression and the growing threat from UNITA. The country was divided into nine military regions, each with a regional military council. The councils had the task of coordinating all military, political and economic activities as part of a concerted effort to defeat UNITA, fight off the South Africans and maintain MPLA control in war-effected areas. Speaking in Malanje, in the north, on 5th September 1983, President dos Santos outlined the political and military situation as he saw it:

Racist South Africa, with the support of imperialism, has established as a goal the destruction, by criminal actions, of our democratic and popular regime . . . But the links forged between the people and the MPLA–Workers' Party in the unyielding defence of the overriding interests of our fatherland and in the application of our revolutionary principles at home and abroad are solid and indestructible . . . This is why, in view of the impossibility of the UNITA puppets' task of subversion in the field of military operations, the regular army of this aggressor country finds itself increasingly compelled to intervene directly to create the false impression that the puppets control a vast area of Angola (Luanda home service in Portuguese, 6th September 1983).

Dos Santos's words about South Africa having to aid UNITA in its operations were immediately validated when a major UNITA offensive against the town of Cangamba ran into serious difficulties. A UNITA force estimated at around 3,000 men made a concerted effort to take the town but was repulsed with heavy casualties, but the South Africans were unwilling to see UNITA suffer such a serious reverse and the SAAF launched a bombing raid that reduced the town to rubble, forcing the Angolans to withdraw. UNITA then claimed to have captured the town single-handed. The following month, after the arrival of major shipments of modern Soviet weapons, including MiG-23 aircraft and a sophisticated radar defence system, FAPLA launched a huge offensive. By early November, the South Africans were again forced to step in and the Angolan forces came up against South African troops backed by Ratel armoured vehicles. But the Angolans claimed major successes in the fighting. Defence Minister Tonha Pedale said that 600 UNITA guerrillas had been killed at Mussende and that the whole area around the town had been liberated. UNITA more or less admitted government successes but claimed that the Angolans had been supported by 8,000 Cubans, 3,000 SWAPO guerrillas and 1,000 ANC fighters. The Angolans denied this and there was no evidence to support the UNITA claim.

Again South Africa decided that UNITA should not go unaided in the face of a major offensive. On 6th December, South African armoured units with artillery and air support launched an invasion of Huila province from the occupied areas in Cunene. The Angolans resisted and heavy fighting ensued during December and January with major engagements at Cahama and Cuvelai. On 29th December 1983, the South Africans bombed the town of Lubango, targeting air bases, radar stations and economic installations. The SADF Chief, General Viljoen said that the South African actions were aimed solely at SWAPO guerrillas. This was patently untrue. The operations were an attempt to prevent UNITA from being swept from central Angola and back towards the Namibian border. The South African action threatened a major escalation of the war and both the Cubans and Soviets decided that it was time to step in. On 6th January, the Soviet news agency Tass carried an official statement warning South Africa that it had better withdraw or else. Five days later, Soviet, Cuban and Angolan officials met in Moscow and issued a statement that made it abundantly clear that if the South African military action continued then the SADF would once again find itself fighting the Cubans. The statement said that the three states had agreed on measures 'providing aid to the People's Republic of Angola in the matter of strengthening its defence capacity, independence and territorial integrity'. South African sources reported that the country's diplomats at the UN in New York had been warned directly by Soviet representatives that Moscow would not stand idly by and watch the destabilisation or destruction of the Angolan government (Johannesburg radio in English for abroad 12th January 1984). The result of the threat was an end to the military operation and the start of negotiations between Angola and South Africa with the USA's Chester Crocker mediating. The product of the talks was the Lusaka disengagement agreement, which was never implemented by South Africa. Moscow had suspected that this would be the case all along. The party newspaper *Pravda* had warned on 5th March that the US role in the whole affair was part and parcel of 'imperialist aggression' in southern Africa. Certainly the USA could hardly have posed as a totally disinterested spectator over Angola. The Reagan Administration repealed the Clark Amendment, which banned US support for UNITA, and in 1986 started giving military and financial aid to UNITA. In late 1986, it started work to rehabilitate the Kamina air base in Southern Zaire for use as a staging post in sending arms and other equipment to the rebels. US aid for Savimbi continued throughout the decade, even after the December 1988 agreement on a Cuban withdrawal from Angola and the independence of Namibia. The main value to Savimbi of the US aid, apart from the obvious diplomatic advantage, was the supply of Stinger anti-aircraft missiles.

But the strengthening of UNITA did not enable it to withstand unaided FAPLA offensives. A major Angola sweep in September 1985 nearly ended in disaster for Savimbi. The Angolans took the town of Cazombo in Moxico and then Mavinga, which had fallen into South African – UNITA hands after one of Pretoria's offensives. The Angolans were then poised for a major advance towards the UNITA headquarters at Jamba. At that point another huge South African rescue operation was launched. Massive air strikes and attacks by helicopters and commandos destroyed a whole FAPLA column at a river crossing outside Mavinga. The SADF units involved included 32 Battalion, a special unit led by South African officers but containing a large number of foreign mercenaries (including British and American army veterans). The unit was frequently used for combat in Angola and northern Namibia (Marcum, 1986, p. 193). The South Africans smashed an armoured unit and scores of military vehicles. The government forces lost equipment worth over $100m, including twenty helicopters and MiGs destroyed on the ground by South

African air strikes and 150 tanks, armoured vehicles and trucks (ibid.). The attack prevented further FAPLA advances that year.

The extensive and frequent South African raids enabled UNITA to continue its large-scale guerrilla campaign. This prevented the use of the Benguela railway, destroyed the agricultural wealth of the central plateau (Angola's main grain producing area), wrecked the coffee industry and cut transport routes in rural areas throughout Angola. The economy, with the exception of the oil sector in the north and in Cabinda, was devastated. Attacks were claimed by UNITA on the Cabinda oil fields, but UNITA had no success there. One of the attacks claimed by UNITA turned out to have been a wholly South African operation when a South African officer, Captain Wynand du Toit, was captured during a South African special forces attack on oil installations in Cabinda in May 1985. On 21st May, a South African commando unit including Du Toit was discovered near an oil refinery. The Angolans attacked the raiders killing several and capturing Du Toit. Following his capture, the officer admitted having taken part in South African sabotage raids against Angola over a period of five years. His exploits included sabotaging the Luanda oil refinery in 1981, the mining of Soviet and East European ships in Luanda harbour in 1984 and the destruction of a number of road bridges in 1982 (*Africa*, July 1985, pp. 26–7). All these operations had been claimed by UNITA. Du Toit admitted that the South Africans frequently carried out sabotage attacks, leaving behind UNITA propaganda material, to give the impression that UNITA was capable of carrying out sophisticated operations throughout Angola.

South African raids continued into 1986, with South African naval forces attacking the Angolan port of Namib on 5th June. Merchant vessels were destroyed during the attack, involving frogmen and missile boats. Oil, tanks at the port – used to supply Angolan army units further inland on the Namib–Menongue railway – were a main target. The South Africans used Israeli-supplied boats and Gabriel-II surface-to-surface missiles during the attack (Luanda home service in Portuguese, 5th June 1986).

American support for UNITA increased during 1986, most of its routed via Zaire, though some went directly to South Africa. One report stated that the USA had airlifted 40 tons of machine guns from Connecticut to Johannesburg, a further 20 tons of rockets and launchers to Johannesburg and arranged for European air-freight companies to fly small arms from Belgium and Switzerland to South Africa, all for onward shipment to UNITA (*West Africa*, 22nd December 1986). In an interview in December 1986, President dos Santos said that his government was aware that UNITA was being armed by the USA using Zaire as a channel for arms supplies. He also accused Zaire of allowing its territory to be used by UNITA as a rear base for attacks into northern Angola. In the same interview, Dos Santos made it clear that the tens of thousands of Cuban troops (approximately 30,000 in 1986–7) would remain in Angola as long as South Africa continued its policy of aggression and destabilisation. He said both Angola and the Cubans wanted an end to the Cuban military role but added that 'they will leave when the aggression and all threats of aggression come to an end and when Namibia attains its independence' (Luanda home service in Portuguese, 22nd December 1986).

During early 1987, Angola stepped up its military efforts, supported by major shipments of arms from the Soviet Union (by early 1987, Angolan debts to the Soviet Union, mainly for arms purchases, totalled over $3bn). In February 1987, the Angolans deployed sophisticated Soviet MiG-23s in southern Angola as part of a major attempt to improve air cover in the south. Many of South Africa's incursions had been backed by or made possible by South African air superiority. The development caused alarm in South Africa. The commander of South African air units in Namibia, General van Heerden, said that the MiGs and the radar control systems being installed in southern Angola would give the Angolans the capability to reach as far south as Tsumeb in Namibia. For once, the South African claims about growing Angolan air strength appeared to be true. The Angolan Interior Minister, Alexandre Rodrigues Kito, told the BBC World Service on 5th February that the new equipment and planes would give the Angolans the edge in the air.

During early and mid-1987, contacts developed between the Angolans and the Americans in an attempt to find a solution to the two countries' differences and to start a wider search for reconciliation in south-western Africa. The Angolans were keen for peace to rebuild the shattered economy, while the Americans appeared to have a master plan for peace in southern Africa, the first step towards which would have to be Namibian independence and an end to the war in Angola. The Angolans expressed their willingness to hold talks and to make the withdrawal of the Cubans part of a peace deal involving the withdrawal of all South African forces from Angola, an end to South African destabilisation and support for UNITA and the implementation of UN resolution 435 on Namibian independence. But at that stage, neither the South Africans nor UNITA were willing to take part, they thought they were on a winning streak.

The South Africans and UNITA clearly thought that they had the upper hand militarily in the south and that they could make further advances against what they saw as a weakened FAPLA. They were totally wrong in their calculations. After the Mavinga setback, the Angolans, Cubans and Soviets had launched a major exercise to strengthen FAPLA and to build a modern air force, thus the supply of the MiG-23s. The air force and strengthened army units were based along a defence line from the major bases at Lubango through to Menongue and Cuito Cuanavale. The latter was the jumping off point for any offensives against UNITA and contained an important air base. By mid-1987, the Angolans were confident that they could use this defence line to beat off any new offensive and could gain air superiority (*Africa Confidential*, 27th May 1987).

The offensive was not long in coming. It followed another FAPLA push against UNITA. This attack was blocked by UNITA forces backed by South African long-range artillery. The South Africans then pushed ahead with a major attack, backed by thousands of UNITA troops. The Angolans were forced out of the Mavinga area (the recapture of the Mavinga being their initial aim) and retreated north-westwards. The combined force moved towards Cuito Cuanavale, with the intention of breaching the defence line and of destroying the air force network by destroying the air base there. A siege started with large

FAPLA units defending Cuito Cuanavale against infantry attacks by waves of UNITA guerrillas. The South Africans pounded the town with howitzers and mobile G-6 artillery weapons. Much of the town was destroyed, but the Angolans were not dislodged and the air base continued to operate. South African air attacks failed as they were countered by the Angolan air force. The South Africans at first denied any involvement but soon had to admit a heavy commitment. And they also had to admit heavy losses. By November 1987, there were signs that the South Africans were not going to succeed. They had lost an estimated 230 men (far more than in any other operation since the Second World War) and, more importantly, a large number of combat aircraft. The South Africans would only admit to a couple of planes being shot down. The Angolans said forty-three had been destroyed. The real figure is probably twelve-twenty. But the Angolans had clear air superiority and used it to defend the town, to attack UNITA concentrations and to hit back at the South Africans.

The South Africans refused to admit defeat. They threw thousands of UNITA troops against the Cuito Cuanavale defences and stepped up their role. By early 1988, there were believed to be as many as 9,000 SADF personnel in southern Angola, at least 3,000 at Cuito Cuanavale, 3,000 in Huila province and more in southern Cunene and Cuando Cubango provinces. Every indication was given of a full-scale South African campaign to capture Cuito Cuanavale. At this point President dos Santos decided it was time to call for Cuban support. President dos Santos warned in the first week of December 1987 that he would call on Cuba for increased military support and for Cuban troops to play an active role in the fighting around Cuito Cuanavale. The commander of the Cubans in Angola in 1975 and in Ethiopia in 1978, General Ochoa Sanchez, was recalled to Angola to head the crack 50th Cuban division. It was reported on 7th December that the division was heading south for Cuito Cuanavale (Maputo home service in Portuguese, 7th December 1987). Both Dos Santos and Castro made it clear that they would match force with force to beat the South Africans and UNITA (*Independent*, 14th December 1987). The Angolans also went to the UN Security Council, which set a deadline for South African withdrawal in December 1987. The deadline came and went with no international response. The Angolan President said that as the deadline had been ignored he would unleash the Cubans against the SADF (*New African*, February 1988, p. 23). By mid-December, the Cubans were said to have reached Menongue prior to deployment around the threatened town.

But the siege continued well into 1988. A total of four major attacks were launched by the South Africans and UNITA. The last, in spring 1988, ended in disaster for the South Africans with a tank unit becoming trapped in a minefield. The unit suffered heavy casualties, including the loss of several of South Africa's most modern tanks – variants of the British Centurion tank updated with assistance from Israel. The South Africans and UNITA had to abandon the attack and pull back in that sector (*West Africa*, May 16th 1988).

The result of the failure of the attempt to take Cuito Cuanavale and the clear determination of the Angolans and Cubans to strengthen their forces and push the South Africans and UNITA out, forced South Africa to rethink its strategy. It had 3,000 men and large mechanised units south of Cuito Cuanavale. But the Cubans and Angolans had forces in the town and a column to the south-west of the SADF concentration. The danger was that with the rains coming, the armoured units could become bogged down and the South Africans would be in the humiliating position of being trapped in southern Angola and of becoming targets for the Angolan air force and the Cuban–Angolan reinforcements. Unconfirmed reports said that in some parts of southern Angola, the Cubans had pushed right up to the border with Namibia.

The effective military defeat of the South Africans and the loss of air superiority were a crushing blow to the whole of South Africa's military policy in south-western Africa. It could no longer be assured of success in operations to support UNITA, it had suffered losses that were unprecedented and were unacceptable domestically, and it was faced with the possibility of an escalation of SWAPO attacks in Namibia, with SWAPO rear bases well-protected by Angolan and Cuban forces. The basing of MiG-23s and Soviet-supplied Frog missiles in southern Angola gave the Angolans the capability of striking deep into Namibia.

The military setback coincided with serious attempts by the USA to get UNITA to drop its South African connection and to base itself in Zaire and set up a new headquarters at Quimbele in northern Angola. The Americans did not want to drop UNITA but neither did they want to become involved in a long and costly war between Angola and Cuba on one side and UNITA and South Africa on the other. They wanted a peace settlement that would get the Cubans out of Angola, would provide a chance to water down the Marxist nature of the Angolan government and end the long-running problem of Namibia's independence. In the latter objective they were supported by the USSR, which under Mikhail Gorbachev was committed to solving regional disputes through negotiations rather than continuing with military means which could lead to a wider conflict and to superpower confrontation.

The combination of all these factors led to the London meeting between Angolan, Cuban, South African, Soviet and American delegations in May 1988, which started the peace process in south-western Africa. This led directly to the withdrawal of all South African forces from Angola and the start of a phased withdrawal by the Cubans.

It did not, though, end the war between the Angolan government and UNITA. UNITA continued to receive arms and financial aid from the USA; and South Africa had given it sufficient supplies to keep going for months. The Soviet Union pushed for peace but did not halt arms deliveries. By late 1989, it was clear that despite mediation efforts by President Mobutu of Zaire (backed by other African leaders) peace was not going to be found easily. Ceasefire attempts failed and the war between UNITA and the Angolan army escalated. At one stage Mobutu stopped US arms reaching Savimbi via the Kamina base in Zaire, but supplies resumed after Washington put heavy pressure on Mobutu. However, one major change had taken place in the fighting, little consolation though it must have been for the Angolans, and that was that despite continued foreign arms supplies to both sides, the conflict no longer involved foreign military forces. A large proportion of the Cuban contingent had left or was withdrawing north-wards, and the South Africans were no longer playing a combat role in Angola.

Mozambique: the proxy war

The independence in Zimbabwe in 1980, which brought to an end the long liberation war on Mozambique's western borders, brought not peace to the former Portuguese colony but the start of a new and more deadly struggle for the Mozambican people. In the first five years of independence, Mozambique had suffered from Rhodesian raids and the sabotage activities of the Rhodesian formed and sponsored Mozambique National Resistance movement (MNR). The attainment of independence and the destruction of white minority rule meant the end of the Rhodesia–MNR relationship. But, sadly for Mozambique, it did not mean the end of the MNR. Instead, the movement had a rebirth, with South Africa as the midwife.

The whole MNR operation was moved from Zimbabwe to South Africa. The rebels became a serious threat to Mozambican peace and stability. The South Africans used them to destabilise the Frelimo government, to destroy the rural economy and to cut regionally and nationally vital transport routes running through the country. MNR leaders and guerrillas based in Zimbabwe were moved into the northern and eastern Transvaal and a new MNR radio station established at Phalaborwa.

The move to South Africa coincided with serious defeats for MNR forces inside Mozambique. In October 1979, the rebels had been forced out of their mountain stronghold at Gorongoza and in June 1980, they lost their new base at Sitatonga in southern Manica province. But with extensive South African assis-tance, new bases were set up in central Mozambique and South Africa started an operation to airlift arms and other supplies to the rebels. The South African navy was also used to take supplies to contact points along the Mozambican coast. The logistical aid, arms supplies and direct assistance from the South African special forces enabled the MNR to greatly extend its area of operations to cover ten out of the country's eleven provinces. The MNR was encouraged by the South Africans (and South African commandos participated in some of the operations) to attack the rail, road and pipelines routes from Zimbabwe to the port of Beira and, after Malawi showed enthusiasm for SADCC projects and hosted an SADCC summit in Blantyre in November 1981, the road and rail routes from Malawi to Beira and Nacala. The first successful attack was in November 1980 against the Mutare–Beira pipeline (one of Zimbabwe's major sources of fuel). The line was cut and not eventually reopened until January 1983. Attacks were also carried out against the Cabora Bassa power lines, which took power from the generating station at Cabora Bassa to South Africa. Some observers believe that the attacks were carried out to hide the MNR–Pretoria link (Metz, 1986, p. 495).

The sabotage attacks were frequently carried out by South African special forces. In October 1981, a former British soldier serving with the SADF, Alan Gingles, was killed while trying to mine the Beira–Zimbabwe railway (Hanlon, 1986, pp. 136–8). He was involved in a series of attempts by the South Africans to destroy transport routes from Malawi and Zimbabwe to the Indian Ocean which passed through Mozambique and were a source of earnings for the Mozambicans as well as vital trade links for the landlocked states. The attacks were timed to precede the SADCC annual conference in Malawi. The attacks were on the railways, the roads, river bridges and navigational buoys at Beira harbour. They put particular pressure on Malawi by drastically reducing fuel supplies; as the author, who was living in Malawi at the time, found out when fuel rationing was introduced and some consumer goods imported via Mozambique became scarce.

The attacks marked the beginning of a campaign to put pressure on Malawi, once South Africa's loyal ally, but after Zimbabwean independence a country torn between increasing cooperation with its black neighbours through the SADCC and maintaining its existing links with South Africa and the MNR (some of whose leaders were close to President Banda). Ironically, South Africa helped the MNR to set up bases and transit routes in Malawi at the time that the sabotage attacks were used to bring economic pressure to bear on the country. Right up until 1987, Malawi continued to allow the MNR to use its territory to mount attacks into Mozambique and as a safe sanctuary during Mozambican counter-insurgency operations.

But the South Africans also carried out direct and well-publicised attacks against targets inside Mozambique. These were aimed at forcing the Mozambican government to cut its support for the ANC and to stop the ANC from using Mozambique as a route for the infiltration of guerrillas and political activists into South Africa. Between 1981 and 1984, the SADF carried out at least a dozen raids into Mozambique. The first was on 30th January 1981, when a strong force of commandos crossed into Mozambique and attacked houses used by ANC members living in Mozambique. Three houses were destroyed, thirteen ANC members and a Portuguese passer-by killed and many others wounded. One SADF member, another British ex-soldier, was killed (Maputo home service in Portuguese 30th January 1981). The Mozambican government protested to the South Africans, to Western governments and to the UN but to no avail. It was no coincidence that the attack occurred within a month of Ronald Reagan, who had open sympathy for the South African regime, taking over as US president. The only real support came from the OAU, the frontline states and the Soviet Union. The latter dispatched two warships to Maputo for a 'goodwill' visit and openly warned South Africa not to go too far. The Soviet Ambassador in Maputo said, 'we are not threatening anyone, but if anyone attacks our friends we will give an appropriate response' (*ACR* 1980–81, pp. A18–9). Such attacks by the South Africans and the rapid increase in MNR activity, led President Machel to seek increased arms supplies and military training assistance from the USSR. Following talks in Moscow between Machel and the then Soviet leader Yuri Andropov in March 1983, the Soviet Union agreed to help Mozambique in 'the

tasks involved in defending the achievements of the Mozambican revolution'
(Moscow home service 5th March 1983).

In 1982 and 1983, South African sabotage raids continued. On 23rd August,
commandos carried out a raid on Namaacha, near the border, killing two
Mozambicans and a Portuguese aid worker. In December of that year,
commandos attacked and destroyed fuel storage tanks at Beira, burning $20m
worth of oil and disrupting fuel supplies to the rest of Mozambique, Malawi and
Zimbabwe. In May 1983, South African aircraft carried out a raid on the Maputo
suburb of Matola. It was ostensibly aimed against ANC targets, but one of the
buildings hit was a food processing factory. The SADF claimed that forty-one
ANC 'terrorists' had been killed in the raid (Johannesburg home service in
English 23rd May 1983); but the Mozambican government said that three factory
workers had been killed and forty other Mozambicans injured (Maputo home
service in Portuguese 23rd May 1983). On 17th October 1983, South African
commandos again raided ANC targets in Maputo. One of those who took part in
the raid was Captain Wynand du Toit, who was later captured by the Angolan
army in Cabinda.

Damaging and humiliating though the raids were, the real menace from South
Africa came from its massive support for the MNR. By the end of 1983, the
MNR had become active in a large area of Mozambique – notably Zambezia
(along the border with Malawi), Manica, Inhambane, Nampula, Sofala and Gaza
provinces – and had destroyed much of the economic, health and educational
infrastructure in its areas of activity. By 1984, its guerrillas had wrecked a
thousand rural shops, hundreds of villages, much of the rural transport fleet, forty
trains, twenty sawmills, cotton gins and tea factories and most of the health
centres and schools in rural areas. The rural economy in guerrilla areas and the
health and education services in the countryside were destroyed. Rural transport
and transport routes from Zimbabwe, Zambia and Malawi to the coast were cut.
This had a devastating effect on the rural population. Tens of thousands were
forced to flee to safer areas, others stayed in rebel-infested regions and suffered
the consequences during the droughts and floods of 1984 and the later droughts
of 1986 and 1987. With the food distribution and transport networks in tatters,
the droughts brought famine on a large scale. When Western aid organisations
such as Oxfam and the Save the Children Fund tried to take in aid, the MNR
(using South African supplied mines) attempted to destroy relief convoys.
Famine was used as a weapon by South Africa and the MNR against the
Mozambican government and people (information on disruption of aid from
officials of aid organisations and aid workers who wish to remain anonymous).

The relief efforts and the publicity surrounding the man-made disaster led to
a rethink by Western governments concerning the Frelimo government.
President Machel and then Joaquim Chissano after him, were able to convince
the British, French and Portuguese governments that Mozambique was not a
doctrinaire Marxist state and that it was pursuing a genuinely non-aligned policy.
This, and a British desire to help states like Malawi and Zimbabwe with their
transport problems, led to a military and political support operation. British

military advisers in Zimbabwe started to train Mozambican as well as Zimbabwean forces and the British government permitted private organisations to send ex-military personnel, effectively mercenaries, to Mozambique to assist in training the security forces involved in protecting the Nacala and Limpopo transport corridors.

The suffering and instability caused by South Africa's proxy war forced Mozambique into negotiations with South Africa which led to the Nkomati accord of 16th March 1984, under which South Africa agreed to stop supporting the MNR and Mozambique to cut the ANC presence in Mozambique down to a limited number of political representatives. This led to an exodus of ANC personnel from Mozambique and an end to ANC infiltration across the border. But the South Africans did not keep their side of the bargain. Substantial aid supplies continued to be sent to the MNR, much of it via Malawi. The war between the Mozambican forces actually escalated after Nkomati. There was also evidence of continuing South African participation in MNR attacks during 1985 and 1986. In December 1985, the Mozambican government accused the SADF of assisting the rebels to destroy vital railway bridges.

Following the Nkomati accord, President Machel visited Malawi but despite assurances from Banda about an end to aid and bases for the MNR, the country continued to be a vital channel for the rebels supplies from South Africa and a safe rear base. The Comoros were also used by South Africa as a staging post for supplying the MNR. The South African supply operation and maintenance of close ties with the MNR were revealed after the Mozambicans, by then supported by thousands of Zimbabwean troops, captured the MNR's Gorongoza base in August 1985. Diaries and log books were found indicating visits by South African military personnel and by government minister Louis Nel to MNR bases inside Mozambique. The data captured showed that the SADF had not stopped air drops to the MNR or weapons supplies. On 18th September, South African Foreign Minister Pik Botha admitted that South Africa had 'technically' violated the accord (Johannesburg radio in English for abroad 18th September 1985). But the violations were far from technical. The South Africans had extended the landing strip at Gorongoza, had flown large quantities of arms into Mozambique and had used submarines to drop and pick up MNR officials from points along the Mozambican coast (Hanlon, 1986, pp. 149–50).

After the Gorongoza disclosures, South Africa once more pledged that it had stopped aid to the MNR. But Mozambique remains suspicious that this is not the case and that some supplies still get through. Experienced observers of the situation are convinced that aid still gets through and that even if the South African Foreign Military is sincere about the accord, the SADF isn't (conversations with Joe Hanlon, Eddie Cross of the Beira Corridor Group and Paul Fauvet of the Mozambique Information Agency).

The level of fighting during the mid-1980s and the effect on regional transport routes led to an internationalisation of the conflict. It was deliberate policy by South Africa to disrupt road and rail links and thereby to force states like Malawi and Zimbabwe into direct dependence on South African-controlled routes. This made the states concerned more vulnerable to pressure and cost them tens of millions of dollars in extra transport costs. As a result, Zimbabwe decided in 1985 to give direct assistance to the Mozambican government. Several thousand (by 1987 over 10,000) troops were deployed by Zimbabwe along transport routes and crack units took part in Mozambican operations against the MNR.

In September 1986, President Machel and Prime Minister Mugabe of Zimbabwe are believed to have directly threatened President Banda of Malawi that if he did not stop supporting the MNR, they would act to blockade his borders and, though this threat was implicit rather than explicit, overthrow him. The threat had an immediate effect and in October 1986, Malawi expelled thousands of Mozambican refugees and MNR supporters from camps inside the Malawian border. They flooded into Mozambique causing havoc in Zambezia province. This was followed by the death of President Machel in a still unexplained plane crash inside South African territory. He was returning from a frontline states summit. Mozambique and the other frontline states accused South Africa of deliberately bringing the plane down through the use of false navigational signals. The South Africans denied this and said months later that an investigation had proved pilot error. This account is not believed by the frontline states. At the time of the crash, the Tanzanian Foreign Minister, Ben Mkapa, told the author that the frontline states held South Africa responsible for the death of Machel. He also said that Tanzania was prepared to send troops to Mozambique to fight the MNR (interview with author in Dar es Salaam, 22nd October 1986). By early 1987, 2,000–3,000 Tanzanians troops were fighting in Mozambique against the MNR.

The shock of Machel's death and the pressure brought to bear by the frontline states then forced President Banda of Malawi not only to publicly agree to end support for the MNR but also to send troops into Mozambique to guard the Malawi–Nacala railway (which was being rehabilitated). Between 500–700 Malawian troops (quite a large unit given the small size of the Malawian army) were sent into Mozambique, where they became involved in combat with the MNR along the railway route. In March 1988, President Chissano of Mozambique confirmed that he had received assurances of Malawian good faith and he confirmed the active role of the Malawian troops in Mozambique (answer to author's question at a press conference in London in March 1988).

The war continued into 1988 and 1989, despite further talks between the Mozambican and South African leaders in September 1988 and the start of peace talks in Nairobi between the MNR and Mozambican church mediators during 1989. Despite continued South African assurances that it had cut all links with the MNR, the Mozambicans and many of the frontline states remained convinced that Pretoria was still playing a direct role in the military, political and economic destabilisation of Mozambique. On 17th November 1989, the Mozambican Army Chief of Staff, Antonio Hama Thai, reported continuing fighting in a number of provinces between the Mozambican.armed forces and the MNR (Maputo home service 17th November 1989). On the same day, government officials in Maputo said that they had evidence that the MNR was once again using Malawian territory to infiltrate and attack border towns, notably Milange (Maputo home service 17th November 1989). In early December 1989, the official Zimbabwean news agency cited President Mugabe as saying that the large contingent of Zimbabwean troops would stay in Mozambique until peace was achieved. He reaffirmed their role in assisting the Mozambican forces and in protecting transport routes to the sea.

Unlike in Angola, the internationalisation of the Mozambican conflict, itself a war started by Rhodesia and continued by South Africa in order to destabilise the Frelimo government, did not lead to direct involvement by non-African powers other than as suppliers of arms and other support to the Mozambicans – though it was frequently rumoured that the CIA had at one stage helped the MNR, particularly in the setting up of its radio station. South Africa's direct involvement and its use of the proxy war in Mozambique to bring pressure to bear on other southern African states, led not to Cuban involvement in the fighting but a partly successful effort by Tanzania (which withdrew its forces for economic reasons in 1988), Zimbabwe and Malawi to give direct aid to Frelimo through the provision of combat forces. The Soviet Union, and to a lesser extent Britain, France and Portugal, played a part in the war through their provision of military equipment and training for Mozambican forces.

Sudan: *déjà vu*

In 1983, the south of Sudan once more became the scene of a bloody civil war. Peace, of a sort, had lasted for over a decade. But a decision by President Numayri to redivide the south into three provinces – Bahr al-Ghazal, Upper Nile and Equatoria – was seen by many southerners as an attempt to divide and rule. Their perceptions were not far from the truth, as Numayri had launched a programme of what he called decentralisation. In fact, it meant splitting up larger administrative units within the country with the obvious aim of rendering them more vulnerable to pressure from the centre. In the south, the move was seen as a direct blow to the gains made through the Addis Ababa treaty.

The discontent engendered led to mutinies by southern troops and the birth of a new southern guerrilla movement – Anyanya 2. Southern resentment at northern dominance was worsened by Numayri's unilateral reinstatement of Arabic as the official language throughout Sudan, by moves to cement a closer union with Egypt and by the commencement of substantial oil exploration operations by the US Chevron company in the south. The latter was seen by many southerners as an attempt by the Khartoum government to exploit the south's riches for their own benefit – the same could be said of the start of work on the Jonglei canal, which would channel much-needed water northwards (Heraclides, 1987, pp. 227). The final straw was the decision by the Numayri government to introduce Islamic sharia law in September 1983. The law would apply to the whole of the Sudan and to non-Muslims as well as Muslims.

Anyanya 2 started operations in 1983, pledging to resume the war for the secession of the south from the north. But many of its new recruits and even more of the southern soldiers who deserted or mutinied sought a democratic change in Sudan as a whole rather than the creation of a separate southern state. These elements came together in a movement which became known as the Sudan People's Liberation Army (SPLA), with a political wing called the Sudan People's Liberation Movement (SPLM). Broadly socialist in outlook, the movement claimed to be acting not as a southern movement (though its membership was southern and mainly Dinka) but as a national one.

Anyanya 2 received relatively little external support and was very quickly supplanted by the SPLA, which received arms and logistical support (including it is thought rear bases across the border) from Ethiopia and financial and some arms supplies and training from Libya. Despite constant accusations by Numayri, there was no evidence of direct Ethiopian military assistance to the SPLA (such as bombing raids by Ethiopian aircraft) or by the Libyans.

The main targets of the initial stages of the insurgency were Sudanese garrisons, the Chevron oil camps and the Jonglei canal operations. The rebels succeeded in halting oil and canal construction work and in seizing the military initiative from the Sudanese army, which soon became restricted to populated and urban areas. Occasional counter-insurgency operations were launched, but with little success. One reason for the early success of the SPLA, as opposed to Anyanya, was that many of its cadres had mutinied from Sudanese army units taking with them modern weapons and a good knowledge of military skills and the tactics of the amry. The SPLA leader, Colonel John Garang de Mabior, mutinied, taking with him 2,000–3,000 southern troops loyal to his command – a very strong nucleus for a guerrilla force.

The war in the south was one of guerrilla attacks and of blockade of the garrisons and urban areas. There were few pitched battles and the Sudanese army appeared to have little desire to escalate the scale of individual engagements. The war was a huge drain on government finances at a time of economic decline and severe drought. Numayri, with Egyptian support and US financial backing, was committed to winning the war. But his refusal to reconsider the unpopular sharia laws and the failures of the army led to his downfall.

Popular discontent with his regime and with the appalling state of the economy led to riots and demonstrations in early 1985. The government seemed powerless to cope with them. Therefore the army stepped in and on 6th April 1985, Numayri was overthrown in a coup and replaced by General Muhammad Hasan Siwar Al-Dhahab. He made initial moves to placate the southerners, though without meeting all their demands for a more equitable political system, and also sought to mend fences with Libya. The former move had little success, but as Qadhafi's hostility towards Sudan had been very much directed against Numayri and his personal support for Egypt and for the Camp David agreement with Israel, the Libyan leader was willing to end his feud with Sudan. In fact, in a move reminiscent of his actions in both Chad and the Western Sahara, he not only ended his hostility towards Sudan, but ended military aid to the SPLA and instead started supplying arms to the new military regime. He loaned the regime two

Soviet-supplied bombers for use in the south and is believed to have supplied pilots as well; in late 1985, the Libyans certainly started training Sudanese pilots (*ACR* 1985–86, p. B593). In the mid- to late-1980s, during both the period of military rule and that of Sadiq al-Mahdi, there were reported to be thousands of Libyan troops in Sudan's Darfur province – this was denied by Colonel Qadhafi, who said that the troops in Darfur were members of Acheikh Bin Oumar's Chadian rebel forces.

The initial reaction of the SPLA to the coup was to accuse the military of hijacking the popular uprising against Numayri but then to assure the new government of the SPLA's commitment to national unity and to call for a return to the provisions of the Addis Ababa agreement which had ended the earlier civil war. Nothing came of the SPLA contacts with the government after the coup and the war continued, with Ethiopia continuing to use bases in Ethiopia (as a tit-for-tat move because Sudan was given similar support to the EPLF and TPLF).

In May 1986, the army handed power back to the civilians. The new government was headed by Prime Minister Sadiq al-Mahdi. Although when in exile and opposition he had attacked Numayri over the sharia laws and had called for peace in the south, he did little actively to promote it. Negotiations for an end to the war started by Siwar al-Dhahab and supported by the SPLA's backer Ethiopia, had led to a statement of intent and basic prerequisites for peace known as the Koka Dam agreement. But Sadiq did not follow up the initial moves and instead the SPLA and the Prime Minister developed almost as strong an antipathy as between the SPLA and Numayri. Attempts at serious negotiations were helped by dissension with the governing coalition over sharia, the south and the economy and by indications of in-fighting within southern forces – with regard to the latter, by 1986, the SPLA and Anyanya were at war, with the government reportedly supplying arms to Anyanya.

The war continued throughout the 1986–90 period, despite catastrophic famines, whose effects were worsened by the closure of roads and other transport routes by both warring parties. The Sudanese army clung on to the main towns, but was unable to make any headway against the core Dinka areas occupied by the SPLA. The SPLA for its part, could hold much of the countryside and some smaller towns, but was unable to push the army out of the south, let alone succeed in pushing north to overthrow what it saw as a series of northern-dominated government.

In 1989, Sadiq al-Mahdi went the way of Numayri. He had proved incapable of solving the problems of the south or of the economy. Recurrent splits within the government and factionalism with the northern parties led to increasing impotence. On 30th June 1989, the army seized power and installed Lt-General Omar Hasan Ahmad al-Bashir as head of state. The coup had been about by Al-Mahdi's refusal to listen to complaints from the army that the war had to be brought to an end. On 20th February 1989, the army command had sent a memorandum to the Prime Minister demanding an end to the war or a massive increase in the resources available for the armed forces. Neither was forthcoming. Between February and the coup, various parties within Sudan made attempts to start talks with the SPLA, but Al-Mahdi opposed and tried to wreck them. This was finally too much for the army. The new regime set up by it was broadly representative of the armed forces, though of course could not be said to in any way represent the south.

Soon after the coup, the army declared a ceasefire, which the SPLA adhered to for some months, until it became clear that the army was using it to resupply its bases (*Africa Confidential*, 28th July 1989) and to play for time by throwing out peace initiatives which it must of known would be rejected immediately. One such initiative was the offer by Bashir to agree to the secession of the south. This was totally rejected by the SPLA, which repeated its aim of bringing about democratic change in a unitary Sudan rather than establishing a southern state. Therefore, as with other ceasefires, this one broke down and fighting resumed.

A serious attempt towards peace was made by the former US President, Jimmy Carter, in the closing months of 1989. Following some success in initiating talks between the Ethiopian government and both the Eritreans and Tigreans, he tried to repeat this in Sudan. Peace talks began in Nairobi in early December and the fact that they continued for several days was seen as an advance; but on 4th December, the Sudanese government announced, to no one's great surprise, that no agreement had been possible on the issues of sharia law and the state of emergency in Sudan (Radio Omdurman, 4th December 1989). The SPLA also reported the failure to agree on these issues, adding that they were a precondition to further talks on a future constitution, a ceasefire and the formation of a more broadly-based government (Radio SPLA, 4th December 1989). The talks then broke up in disarray and at the time of writing, January 1990, no further meetings have been planned and the war continues.

The Horn of Africa: from inter-state to intra-state war

The abortive Somali incursion into Ogaden in 1980 marked the effective end of the Barre regime's attempts to use armed force to gain control of the region. Although low-level support was maintained for the WSLF, no major offensives were launched and the WSLF guerrilla attacks were little more than an irritant to the Ethiopians.

Threats to both governments from internal forces and the need to end the state of simmering hostility led to serious moves towards accommodation in the latter half of the decade. In response to the urging of other African leaders, notably President Hassan Gouled Aptidon of Djibouti and President Moi of Kenya (both of whom had a strong interest in regional peace and in an end to Somali irreden-tism), Mengistu and Barre met on 17th January 1986 and agreed to set up an ad hoc ministerial committee to work on a peace settlement. But this did not end lingering suspicions on both sides. The Ethiopians periodically accused Somalia of continuing aid to the WSLF, while in June 1986, the Somalis accused the Ethiopian air force of carrying out bombing raids on north-western Somalia in support of Somali rebel groups (the northern-based Somali National Movement and the Democratic Front for the Salvation of Somalia). A further meeting between the two leaders took place at an international anti-drought and desertification meeting in Djibouti in February 1987. There further progress was made towards a rapprochement, though no peace agreement or border demarcation was finalised. In April 1988, Ethiopia and Somalia resumed diplomatic relations, though still without a definitive solution to the Ogaden question. But for the time being, the threats posed to Barre's regime by the continuing war against it in the north waged by the Somali National Movement and the insurgency south of Mogadishu led by members of the Ogadeni tribe have prevented Somalia from even considering further military attempts to recover the Ogaden or even serious diplomatic efforts to reach a final solution. The regime is too concerned for its own survival.

Much the same can be said for President Mengistu in Ethiopia. The decline of the Somali threat in the 1980s did nothing to reduce the military pressure on the Derg (and later the Workers' Party of Ethiopia) regime. In Eritrea, Tigre and, to a lesser extent, in Oromo areas of southern and western Ethiopia, the liberation fronts representing the respective populations stepped up their armed struggles.

If the Ethiopians had been able to just about hold their own against the rebels in the late 1970s, but without making headway in regaining control of the countryside or suppressing the revolts, in the 1980s, the government forces were hard pressed to hold on to the urban areas and garrisons in which they based their forces. They launched repeated offensives in both Eritrea and Tigre, but only succeeded in losing more men and equipment and in destroying the morale of the armed forces. The Cubans still steadfastly refused to send troops into Eritrea and there is no strong evidence that they were active in Tigre either. Instead, there was a gradual withdrawal of Cuban forces from Ethiopia. In 1982, there were around 10,000 Cubans there, most of them combat troops based in the Ogaden, but around 2,000–3,000 of them instructors, advisers and technicians. Because of the decline in the Somali threat, they played little if any role in fighting during the decade but did enable the Derg to redeploy its own forces to fight elsewhere. By early 1990, the Cubans had pulled out all but 2,800 troops, most of whom were advisers and technicians.

The Soviet Union still remained the Ethiopians' most reliable ally. It continued to supply huge quantities of modern arms to the Ethiopian army and supplied advisers to enable the Derg to integrate the new weapons systems into the existing armoury. It is also widely believed (certainly by the EPLF and TPLF, whose London representatives assured the author that this was the case) that Soviet generals were closely involved in planning and directing Ethiopian counter-insurgency sweeps in both Eritrea and Tigre. If they were, the total lack of success despite overwhelming numbers and arms says little for Soviet counter-insurgency skills and the effectiveness of the Ethiopian army. In 1990, there were believed to be around 1,700 Soviet advisers and technicians aiding the Ethiopian army – this number had remained constant during the decade (although there were unconfirmed reports that in April 1986, between 3,000 and 5,000 Soviet military personnel had arrived at Asmara to support a massive offensive – the offensive failed and the Soviets were withdrawn, if they were ever there in the first place (*ACR* 1985–86, p. B292). The Soviet forces played no combat role – though they may have operated radar systems and flown transport planes for the Ethiopians. There were also around 500–600 East German advisers and 200 North Koreans present in Ethiopia throughout the decade and into 1990 (IISS, 1989–90).

But despite the continuing military support from the Soviet bloc and access to sophisticated weaponry, the Ethiopians were, by January 1990, being sorely pressed by the rebel movements. Successive offensives had ended in defeat and sometimes total disaster. The huge Red Star offensive in Eritrea and Tigre in February 1982 was repulsed by the rebels and in December 1982, the EPLF (by then 35,000 strong and receiving support from Sudan and a number of Gulf states) routed three Ethiopian brigades at Halhal. The Ethiopians were equally unfortunate in Tigre, despite TPLF claims that Cuban combat troops were involved in the fighting there. By early 1983, there were 50,000–60,000 Ethiopians fighting in Tigre against at most 20,000 TPLF guerrillas. Fighting was also in progress in Wollo and Gondar against forces of the Ethiopian's People's Democratic Movement (which in 1988 joined forces in a loose alliance with the TPLF). The Oromo Liberation front also kept up the fight, notably in Sidamo province.

At the end of 1983, the Ethiopians controlled only by the major towns and roads in Eritrea and little more than 20 percent of Tigre province (*ACR* 1983–84, p. B132). Early in 1984, the Derg's forces suffered serious blows to their military position and morale when they lost Tessene and Ali Gider to the EPLF. A major offensive in Eritrea to recapture lost towns and territory ended in defeat with the EPLF claiming to have taken 10,000 prisoners. Fighting escalated in 1985, and the EPLF again claimed major victories over the Derg. EPLF battle reports put out by the Voice of the Broad Masses of Eritrea radio station said that during the year 29,000 Ethiopians had been killed or wounded and 392 captured. The Ethiopians had temporary success in capturing some of the Red Sea coastal plains in late 1985 only to lose control of them again in 1986. In Tigre, the situation was desperate for the government and in February 1986 it lost the town of Mekelle to the TPLF.

In 1987, Ethiopia introduced its new socialist constitution, which included sections on autonomy for provinces. But the level of independence that the WPE was willing to allow was not enough to meet the demands for secession by the EPLF or for autonomy and national democratic reform put forward by the TPLF and the EPDM. So the wars went on. In March 1987, a government offensive in Eritrea failed when the EPLF smashed four brigades in a major battle on 20th March. A similar result was obtained in Tigre, where the TPLF had been able to utilise captured equipment and foreign financial aid to build a large conventional army. This enabled it to carry out brigade-sized attacks on Ethiopian units and to launch an offensive aimed at pushing all Ethiopian forces out of the province. In the spring of 1988, the TPLF armies had defeated the Ethiopians in a series of engagements, capturing Axum and a number of other towns. The pressure was then stepped up and in February 1989, a TPLF Central Committee member Yamane Kidane told the author that the whole of Tigre was in TPLF hands – this was confirmed to the author by journalists who had visited Tigre and surrounding areas of Ethiopia in early 1989. As the TPLF's aim, in common with the objectives of the EPDM, was to overthrow the WPE and Mengistu, rather than to secede, the war continued into 1990. By the start of the new decade, the Tigreans had advanced to within 100–200 miles of Addis Ababa. In November 1989, the forces of the two movements had moved south through Wollo province and were threatening the town of Dese, whose capture would endanger vital supply routes from the Red Sea ports to Addis Ababa.

In Eritrea, the Ethiopians were in a marginally stronger position, but could not seriously contemplate regaining any lost territory or threatening the EPLF militarily. In Oromo areas, guerrilla warfare continued. In January 1990, the Oromo Liberation Front claimed the capture of a Cuban medical team in western Ethiopia.

The continuing state of war had led to a series of disasterous famines, the worst in 1983–4. The war was costing Ethiopia thousands (if not tens of thousands) of lives annually and billions of dollars. Economic development was stalled and discontent rife. Discontent was growing within the army, as shown by the bloody but unsuccessful coup of 17th May 1989, in which eight senior army and air force commanders were killed (including the deputy commander of the Ethiopian forces in Eritrea, Brigadier–General Kumlachen Djene, and the air force chief, Major–General Ameha Destra) (*New African*, July 1989).

The combination of the military, political and economic pressures on Mengistu forced him to agree to peace talks with both the Eritreans and the Tigreans. The Soviet Union, a vital backer if Mengistu is to survive, supported the talks, having for some time been pushing towards a more flexible position (*Economist*, 18th November 1989). Talks between the government and the EPLF opened in Nairobi on 30th November. The two sides were brought to the negotiating table by Jimmy Carter, who somehow kept the peace process going despite serious disagreements during the talks in Kenya. But both sides for once seemed intent on taking the talks seriously (according to Dale Powers, Carter's personal assistant, in a telephone conversation with the author during the talks). Further talks were scheduled for early 1990. The TPLF also started talks with the WPE in late 1989. An initial round of negotiations was helped in Rome at the end of the year, and the process was expected to continue in 1990. But in the meantime, the fighting continued; though without any direct foreign role – the Cubans having refrained from involving themselves in Eritrea and having withdrawn all but advisers and technicians by 1990. The Soviet Union was involved as the main source of Ethiopia's weapons and in an advisory capacity, but not a combat one.

7 Why do states intervene?

It is obvious from the foregoing analysis that there has been no shortage of foreign states willing and able to intervene militarily in Africa's domestic and inter-state conflicts. Interventions have varied in size from a few dozen advisers or mercenaries to the commitment of tens of thousands of combat troops supported by armour and air cover. Some of the cases mentioned have lasted a matter of weeks, others decades. But why do states intervene, some with great regularity?

The motivations for intervention vary from state to state and from conflict to conflict and do not necessarily all share common characteristics. Libya, for example, intervened in Chad as a result of a mixture of security, territorial and hegemonistic concerns; while Cuba's involvement in Angola did not result from any direct threat to Cuba's national security, was not linked to any attempt to seize territory and clearly has not been part of a strategy aimed at gaining control or hegemony over central or southern Africa. On the other hand, there are similarities between the French role (hangover from the colonial period though it is) in supporting certain allied African states and the Soviet decision to give substantial military backing to Angola, Ethiopia and Mozambique – they have both sought to maintain in power governments whose political programmes are favourable to the intervening state's wider interests continentally and globally.

Clearly, some states have been more inclined to intervene in force and with a certain regularity than others. Britain, for example, came to the aid of beleaguered governments in Tanzania and Kenya in the immediate aftermath of independence and has more recently assisted Zimbabwe and Mozambique in training their armies but has not sought to play the same military role on the continent as France.

The United States has been a major supplier of arms and military expertise to a number of African states (notably Ethiopia up to 1976, Somalia since 1980 and to Morocco), but other than seeking the use of naval and air bases in Kenya, Somalia, Morocco and Egypt (and of course use of the Kagnew base in Ethiopia for over 20 years), it has not sought to play a direct military role. During the Angolan conflict, the CIA provided money and arms for Holden Roberto's FNLA movement, but did not become involved militarily itself – instead using mercenaries, support for Zairean intervention and covert backing for the abortive South African invasion to try to achieve its aims. Since the Angolan debacle, the United States has been content to use its financial strength and its ability to support actions by other states or groups to further its interests; such as support for the Moroccan military role in Shaba, the French and Belgian expedition after the second Shaba invasion, UNITA's guerrilla war in Angola and the French and Zairean actions to support Habre in Chad. The deputy Assistant Secretary of State for African Affairs, James Woods, told Congress in April 1987, that the United States had no major military goals in Africa but had an interest in maintaining access to military facilities in a number of African states, particularly on the Indian Ocean coast (Lewis, 1987). It is also clear that during the first six years of the Reagan presidency, constructive engagement in southern Africa effectively meant tacit support for South African destabilisation of pro-Soviet states in the region, notably Angola and Mozambique.

Morocco has been involved militarily in Africa in two ways – firstly, as an expansionist power seeking to add the former Spanish Sahara to its national territory, and secondly as an intervening force to back up President Mobutu of Zaire during the first Shaba crisis. The first and most substantial commitment needs little explanation. It is the action of a monarch seeking both to enlarge national territory and resources and to bolster his own popularity at home by seeking to appeal to very basic nationalist sentiments. As far as Shaba was concerned, the intervention was not unconnected to the Sahara. Zaire was a strongly conservative state which was automatically opposed to socialist-inclined movements such as Polisario. Furthermore, there was strong backing for it during the Shaba crises from conservative Francophone states (all of whom supported Morocco over the Sahara), France and the United States. By sending troops (with French and US assistance), the Moroccans were accumulating goodwill with states which they hoped would continue to back King Hassan over Morocco's claims to the Western Sahara. More generally, it was seen as a major effort by conservative forces to thwart the progress of radical forces in a sensitive and strategically important region.

During the 1960s and early 1970s, China was an important external actor on the African stage. Its initial policies were strikingly revolutionary and Peking came out in support of the Congolese rebel movements, of the emerging radical regimes in West Africa (Ghana, Guinea and Mali) and of the African socialist leaders in Tanzania and Zambia. China offered limited aid, endless political and ideological advice and arms and training for the armed forces of leftist states and for liberation movements. Military advisers were sent to Africa for the purpose of training guerrillas – notably in Tanzania – but they played no direct role in combat. In the 1970s, Chinese policy became more conservative, with a stress on combatting the Soviet role in Africa. Arms, training and economic aid were then offered to conservative states such as Zaire and to states like Sudan and Somalia which had turned against the Soviet Union. Major, by Chinese standards, commitments were made by sending several hundred military advisers to Zaire in 1974 to train the Zairean armed forces and to help Holden Roberto's FNLA oppose the Soviet and Cuban-backed MPLA. But the Chinese have not played a really significant, active military role in Africa and during the 1980s have greatly reduced their involvement in Africa.

France and Africa: an enduring presence

Although the dismantling of the French colonial empire led to a sharp decline in the French military presence in Africa it by no means signalled an end to France's military role in the continent's affairs. Since 1960, France has been the most regular and consistent foreign military intervenor in Africa. It has launched at least twenty different military operations in the last thirty years – all of them, with the exception of the French role in the second Shaba conflict, concerned with former French territories (Luckham, 1982, p. 61; and Chipman, 1985, p. 50). And France maintains the largest network of military bases and other facilities in Africa. In 1990 it had the following deployments in Africa – naval and maritime reconnaissance units at Mayotte and Reunion, where a total of 3,300 combat troops (marine infantry and the Foreign Legion) were based; 3,650 men at Djibouti (marine, Foreign Legion and artillery units) in addition to air transport units and one squadron of Mirage III combat aircraft; 1,700 men in Chad (infantry, artillery and anti-aircraft units) plus an unknown number of combat aircraft and helicopters; 1,200 infantry in the Central African Republic; 920 marines plus helicopters in Cote d'Ivoire, where France enjoyed the regular use of naval facilities; 1,150 men in Senegal (including a marine regiment and marine reconnaissance and air transport units); and 550 men (chiefly marines) plus a Jaguar combat squadron and transport aircraft in Gabon (IISS, 1989–90, p. 63). France also had military training and assistance teams in another 18 states and during the 1980s there were on average 2,600 African soldiers annually receiving training in France (Afrique Defense, 1982).

But why has France chosen to play such a lasting role in Africa? One primary reason is that it has established closer and more cooperative relations with many of its former colonies than any of the other former colonial powers. By 1986, there were more French people living and working in Africa than at the time of independence (50,000 in Cote d'Ivoire alone) and France continued to play a vital economic and technical role in many of her former colonies as well as in the former Belgian colonies of Zaire and Rwanda. France's policies were to maintain close political relations, too, with states willing to confer closely with successive French governments on African and international issues. Thus many former colonies still have an intimate relationship with France. Some of them (notably Cote d'Ivoire and Senegal) support strongly a continuing French political, military and economic role in Africa and have frequently encouraged France to intervene militarily this was certainly the case during the Libyan invasions of Chad in the 1980s.

The French desire to remain an important political and military force is linked both to France's view of its position in the world and to the large economic stake it has in many African states. France is the principal source of imports for Cameroon, Congo, Cote d'Ivoire, Gabon, Guinea, Burkina Faso, Mali, Mauritania. Niger, Central African Republic, Senegal and Togo. It provides financial backing to its former colonies which have chosen to remain in the franc zone and to use a common currency linked to the franc. To a great extent, France has enjoyed a monopoly over arms sales and military training in its former colonies (Guinea under Sekou Toure, Mali, Congo and, under Sankara, Burkina Faso being the only exceptions). Overall, it is hard to avoid agreeing with Le Vine that 'a patron-client relationship most closely approximates the realities of present Franco–African ties' (Le Vine in Duignan and Jackson, 1986, p. 118).

This patronising relationship, combined with immense economic power and influence in Africa, has given France a strong incentive to maintain military forces in Africa to protect the regimes which it sees as vital to the maintenance of French dominance over the economic and external relations of its former colonies and to give direct security assistance to those allied regimes requesting it; or, as the case of the Central African Republic, intervening unilaterally to replace a regime whose existence had become an embarrassment to France and which was cultivating close ties with a major French competitor in the region – Libya.

The French presence in Africa has varied according to the different priorities and perspectives of successive governments – though none has suggested a major diminution of the French role. After an activist five years after the granting of independence to the colonies, De Gaulle cut France's military presence on the continent and diversified interests there to ensure a lasting political and economic role as well as a military one. For a period, France was 'wary of using force to preserve regimes . . . favourable to France' (White, 1979, p. 245). But in the mid-1970s, France took on a more active political and military role under Giscard d'Estaing. He launched interventions in Chad, Mauritania, Djibouti (against separatists), Zaire and the Central African Republic. At first President Mitterrand scaled down the direct French military role – notably in the aftermath of the overthrow of Bokassa, but then reacted strongly to the Libyan interventions in Chad, committing large French forces and cooperating closely with the USA, Egypt, Sudan and Zaire in giving substantial support to President Habre. In the late 1970s and early 1980s, France saw itself (and was supported in this view by conservative Francophone states) as the chief bulwark against Libyan intervention and subversion in sub-Saharan Africa, notably the central Sahara and Sahel regions. Under Mitterrand, the already substantial forces available to France for direct military intervention, were strengthened when Defence Minister Charles Hernu announced the formation in 1983 of the Force d'Action Rapide – it totalled 47,000 men with an air-mobile division equipped with 250 helicopters. This enabled France to react quickly to events in Chad in 1983 and 1986 (Wells, 1988, pp. 67–8 and 72–3).

Chad was clearly a major milestone in France's military policies in Africa. Certainly, France had a major responsibility for the conflict, having created a state with no internal coherence or unity and with a government initially reliant on French economic and military support. Its role in the 1970s and 1980s, was one of supporting basically pro-Western and anti-Libyan forces against domestic opponents and, increasingly, against the Libyan islamic Legion and the Libyan armed forces. Chad was decisive for France in reaffirming its willingness to give direct military support to friendly governments, to maintaining a strong sphere of influence in central and west Africa, to forestalling the Libyan southward thrust and, not an insignificant objective, to ensuring that its influence was paramount to that of the other regional power, Nigeria (Thompson and Adloff, 1981, p. 130).

When considering the motivations of French policy in Africa, economic, political and strategic interests in the continent play a decisive role along the support for the French role given by conservative states in West Africa. But one should not forget the symbolic role played by the actions in Africa and the role that Africa plays in France's attempts to maintain its position as a world power in the rank immediately below that occupied by the superpowers. An independent role in Africa (even if that role is generally in support of conservative, pro-Western forces and occasionally played in conjunction with the United States), also serves as a reminder that France seeks to steer an individual course in world affairs, not entirely divorced from NATO but not entirely bound up with it either. As John Chipman has pointed out:

the ability of France to act with considerable freedom in her ex-colonies in Africa serves to justify a foreign policy that is written in large terms. In general, the French have believed that for France to maintain her position as a medium power the state must undertake a degree of activity which has implications for those living outside its borders . . . a medium power, such as France, must try to preserve for itself a certain exclusive influence in a region (Chipman, 1985. p. 1).

Libya: revolutionary expansion and destabilisation

For the purposes of this study it is Libyan policy since 1969, when Colonel Qadhafi seized power, which is of interest. Because of the dominant role played by one man during that period, particularly in the development and implementation of foreign policy, this will be very much an examination of why Libya under Colonel Qadhafi has adopted a highly interventionist policy in sub-Saharan Africa that has led to Libyans fighting in Chad and Uganda and to charges that Libya has supported the destabilisation of Niger, Mauritania, Sudan, Burkina Faso and a number of other states.

Reviewing Libyan policy over the last twenty-one years, one cannot fail to see a certain pattern and lasting broad aims – that the Libyans have been willing to pursue using all possible means. If one course of action or set of alliances fails to achieve the aims or advance Qadhafi's causes, then he has not hesitated to reverse policies totally, dropping allies and even turning on them militarily (as has been the case in Chad). This has given the impression that Libyan policy is purely adventurist, unprincipled and unpredictable. His policies have been described by Western opponents as 'the stuff of madness' (*Economist*, 11th–17th January 1986) or in President Reagan's strange but colourful language as 'flaky'. But in the view of this author, Libya under Qadhafi has had a number of core aims that motivate his military and other interventions in Africa: the security of his regime and the territorial integrity of Libya, Arab and Islamic unity, anti-imperialism and the desire to spread, by force if necessary, Qadhafi's own personal ideology (a synthesis of Islam, socialism, anti-colonialism and Libyan hegemony) as set out in the *Green Book*.

The intervention in Chad must be seen clearly as a combination of the above factors, but with security playing a major part. Shortly after seizing power, Qadhafi's revolution was threatened by a coup attempt launched by exiles basing themselves in Chad with the effective support of President Tombalbaye. The coup failed but left a lasting fear that Chad could be used as a springboard for the destabilisation or destruction of the Libyan regime. That this is not an example of flakiness or madness is witnessed by persistent reports in the late 1980s that Libyan exiles, notably the National Front for the Salvation of Libya, were being given massive US and Israeli aid to set up bases in Chad and Cameroon to train and create a force of anti-Qadhafi Libyans which could be used to weaken or overthrow the Libyan leader. Libyan prisoners-of-war seized by Chad during the offensive in northern Chad and Aouzou in 1987 were to form the nucleus of the force. Gabon was also said to be involved in the plot (*Africa Confidential*, 6th January 1989). Of course, it is a chicken-and-egg situation – which came first, Libyan destabilisation of Africa or the use of Africa as a base from which to destabilise Qadhafi. Whichever is the case, Qadhafi certainly perceives a security threat to his regime from Chad. In 1981, he openly expressed the view that Libya's security was dependent on Chad (Wright 1989, p. 143). This view was elaborated by the Libyan ambassador to Paris in 1983, when Libya was being criticised for its active military role in Chad. Sa'id Hafi'ana said that 'we consider the stability and security of Chad are linked to our stability and security . . . This means that there must not be a political regime in Chad that is hostile to Libya and which could allow Chad to be used as a base for direct action' (*Le Monde*, 13th July 1983). Clearly, Libya feels that it has the right to intervene in Chad militarily as well as politically to enhance its own security. The implication is that Libya views the sovereignty of neighbouring states as of little or no importance in relation to core aims of the regime. If Libyan security or a feeling of security requires the invasion or destabilisation of another country, so be it.

But security is not the only motivation. The Arab and Islamic unity aims of the government and anti-imperialism are also closely woven into policy. With all three factors they are as perceived by Qadhafi rather than as an outside observer might perceive them. So, Libya has been willing to take the side of Polisario against a fellow Arab League member, Morocco, because at certain times, Qadhafi has believed that the policies pursued by King Hassan have been in con-tradiction to Libya's idea of a radical Arab unity aimed against Western influence in the Middle East and having the objective of the destruction of Israel and the establishment of unions between Arab states on the basis of the ideas of the Libyan revolution. This motivation explains Libya's support for pro-socialist rebel groups (backed by non-Muslim Ethiopia) against the Muslim Siad Barre government in Somalia and periodic support for the SPLA in Sudan against an avowedly Muslim regime in Khartoum.

Libya's anti-imperialism has led to implacable hostility towards regimes such as those of President Mobutu of Zaire which have followed pro-Western policies and have been active (through the sending of troops to Chad) in backing other pro-Western and anti-Qadhafi leaders. Qadhafi's anti-imperialism has within it a desire 'to change the Libyans into actors, rather than those who are constantly acted upon' and to avenge the former exploitation of Libya, the Arab world and Africa for the exploitation by the former colonial powers (Harris, 1986, pp. 2 and 84). The revenge aspect and the intention to act rather than be acted upon explains much of the militant and interventionist stance taken by Qadhafi – his desire to destabilise rather than be destabilised. But this has led him into the subversion of neighbouring governments (such as support for several failed coups in Sudan, backing for Touareg dissident movements which have carried out military actions in Niger in 1982, when a uranium mine was attacked, and the raid against the outpost at Tchin Tabaraden in 1984) and open calls for the overthrow of governments that oppose him.

But these elements in Libyan policy are not constant factors, they vary in intensity according to Qadhafi's perception of particular situations. Thus the willingness to do deals with pro-Western Morocco at the expense of Polisario or to support Christian southern Sudanese or Chadians against Muslim northerners at times when it is expedient to do so in pursuit of long-term aims (security coming before all the other objectives).

The target areas for Libya's intervention and destabilisation have been decided by geography, the history of north African contacts with the states bordering the Sahel, Libyan hostility towards Egypt under Sadat and Sudan under Numayri and the Libyan leader's perception of which states make up the true Islamic and Arab worlds – he includes Chad, Niger, Mali, Mauritania and the Horn of Africa as well as more 'traditional' Arab states. He expressed his views on the common fate of all these areas and therefore the need for a Libyan hand in their future in an address to the nation on 21st June 1987:

if the Arab homeland came to an end, Ethiopia would come to an end, all these nations – Uganda, Kenya, Chad, Niger, Mali, Senegal and a number of other countries . . . would come to an end . . . here is Sudan, it is Arab, here is Somalia, it is Arab . . . we should remove the hate which the West planted in the minds of black Africans towards their Arab brothers . . . there should be a barrier which prevents both the French and the Americans from reaching Libya . . . naturally, this should not prevent us from extending a helping hand to our brothers in Africa (Tripoli television in Arabic, 21st June 1987).

But unfortunately for the Africans, being labelled an Arab by Qadhafi seemed to mean becoming a target, and the extended hand of help usually had a gun in it.

And the helping hand was often accompanied by a loud voice calling on Africans to overthrow regimes of which Qadhafi did not approve – regimes which Libya was believed to be involved in destabilising. During a visit to Burkina Faso in 1985, to cement the friendship which grew up between Qadhafi and Sankara when Libya backed Sankara's attempts to seize power (which succeeded in August 1983 and were followed by the Libyan dispatch of weapons to Sankara, which he returned as uncalled for and unwarranted), Qadhafi made this call to the people of Africa: 'We have decided not to reckon with the enslaved regime in Zaire, the agent regime in Liberia . . . we are warning all those who offer their hands to the Zionists [Israel] . . I am calling on the youth of Africa both in free and independent as well as reactionary countries to prepare for the final struggle against racism and African reaction . . . I call on the youth of Africa to rebel, to revolt and to seek vengeance' (Ouagadougou home service in French, 10th December 1985). But such calls embarrassed and annoyed his hosts, as did his belief that he could speak for and direct the actions of Africans. Sankara took Qadhafi's patronising behaviour during the visit and his high-handed attitude towards Africa as an insult (this was the version told to the author in Ougadougou in November 1987 by a former aide to the late Thomas Sankara).

But, despite temporary alliances between Libya and various factions in Chad, short-lived friendships between Libya, Ghana, Burkina Faso and Benin and Libya's military role in Uganda and Chad, Qadhafi's policies of intervention, destabilisation and attempted leadership in Africa have not succeeded. The seeming inconstancy towards allies, the high-handed attitude towards friends and Africans in general and the subordination of African interests to Libyan security and Qadhafi's crusades have created a 'legacy of distrust . . [which] is likely to persist within and among African states' (Lemarchand, 1988, p. 13). Furthermore, the views of many Africans towards Libya are coloured by suspicion, fear and a perception of Arab racism. Africans who have worked in Libya (unattributable interview with a Ghanaian migrant worker in Accra, November 1987) have suffered from prejudice and discrimination and many see Libya's intervention in Africa as a reversion to the policies of the Arab raiders who seized Africans as slaves. This may not be an accurate view of Libyan policies, but it is a widely held one. This perhaps explained the attitude of many Ghanaians and Burkinabes who expressed to the author their joy at Habre's victories over Libyan forces in 1987 – they saw them as African victories against an Arab invader. This was even the case at high levels in the Burkinabe and Ghanaian governments. A former aide to Thomas Sankara said that Sankara, although a friend of Libya and an opponent of Habre because of his reliance on French and US aid, was proud of Habre's victories over an essentially foreign army.

Cuba: revolutionary commitment

Ever since the massive Cuban intervention in Angola in 1975, Cuba's involvement in Africa and the motivations of its military and political actions have been the subject of wide and controversial debate among Western analysts. Evidence of Soviet and Cuban cooperation and coordination in Angola and later Ethiopia has led to the labelling of Cuba as a mere proxy of the Soviet Union in Africa. Its actions have been seen as those of a Soviet directed surrogate rather than an independent, self-motivated state (see Rees, 1977; Crozier, 1978). Some commentators have seen Cuba as self-motivated in its African policies but limited in its freedom of action by 'the parameters of Soviet political and strategic interests in Afria'.

But the view of this writer is that although coordination and cooperation with the Soviet Union were important aspects of Cuban policy, they were not determinants and that Cuba followed a strongly independent policy, though one that clearly advanced Soviet aims (but as a by-product rather than a main objective).

Cuba has followed a consistent, revolutionary and highly active policy towards Africa ever since the Cuban revolution. Initially, Castro was a revolutionary and anti-imperialist leader rather than a Marxist–Leninist one. In line with this early stance, in 1960, he offered political support and small quantities of arms to the FLN in Algeria (Volsky, 1981, p. 58) and then sent troops to Algeria to support the newly-established government in its border war with Morocco. Castro saw Cuba as a revolutionary force within the Third World and believed that one of its core objectives, both from the point of view of bolstering the revolutionary government in Cuba and as a means of spreading the revolutionary word, should be to assist revolutionary movements elsewhere in the developing countries. This commitment was enunciated by him in an address to the UN General Assembly on 26th September 1960: 'The case of Cuba is not an isolated one . . . it is the case of all underdeveloped countries . . . like that of Congo, Egypt, Algeria . . The problems of Latin America are similar to those of . . . Africa and Asia.' Castro's adoption of Marxism–Leninism and his alliance with the Soviet Union did nothing to diminish his belief in or commitment to Third World revolution. Rather it added to his belief that Cuba should be an active revolutionary state. Speaking in Havana on 2nd February 1962, he announced his conversion to Marxism and set out what path he thought Cuba should follow internationally: 'Our problems form part of the problems engendered by the general crisis of imperialism and the struggle of the subjugated peoples – the clash between the world that is being born and the world that is dying . . . The duty of every revolutionary is to make the revolution. It is known that the revolution will triumph in America and throughout the world, but it is not for revolutionaries to sit in the doorways of their houses waiting for the corpse of imperialism to pass by' (Castro, 1969, pp. 143 and 164).

And under his leadership, Cuba went out to fight for revolution and against what it saw as Western imperialism. Guevara and 200 Cuban volunteers from the army went to Congo to support the leftist rebels and they moved on to Congo-Brazzaville to support the left-wing government there and to give training and other help to the MPLA. The Cuban Communist Party and government developed good relations with radical and socialist governments and movements in Africa and gave material aid and training to liberation movements.

The response to requests for help from the Angolan government in 1975 followed on naturally from the policies developed over a period of fifteen years. There is no evidence at all that the Soviet Union pushed Cuba into Angola, if anything, the Cuban intervention led to an escalation of the Soviet role. The only difference between Angola and previous operations was the size and the eventual coordination with the Soviet Union over arms deliveries. In Ethiopia, Cuba made very early contacts with the Derg and Mengistu and, as set out in the sections on the Horn of Africa, may well have played a role in bringing Ethiopia and the USSR closer together. The military operation in late 1977 and 1978 was a joint one with the Soviet Union but again was decided upon by Cuba as a natural development of its existing policies in Africa. The Cuban refusal to fight the Eritreans was consistent with the pattern of Cuban policy.

In 1987, Cuba was willing to increase its already large military presence in Angola as a result of the growing threat of South African–UNITA forces around Cuito Cuanavale. The quick Cuban response helped the Angolans to prevent the loss of the town and to force the South Africans to negotiate. The Cubans were then willing to take part, with the Angolans, in peace talks which led to a Namibian settlement and to the phased withdrawal of Cuban forces from Angola. There has been no evidence of any attempt by the Cubans to prolong their stay. By late 1989, Cuba had reduced its presence in Angola substantially, with over 15,000 of the estimated 50,000 troops have been withdrawn and the reminder due to be out by 1st July 1991. Cuba was estimated to have between 30,000–40,000 personnel in Angola in 1989, 2,800 in Ethiopia, 600 in Mozambique and 500 in Congo. Prior to Thomas Sankara's death in October 1987 an unknown number of Cuban troops were serving with his personal bodyguard, though they were withdrawn after his murder. An unknown number of Cuban advisers are believed to be serving with the Ghanaian army.

Throughout its history of involvement in Africa, Cuba has been seen to stick to the letter of its agreements with host countries and to respect their wishes, though not to do their bidding if this was against basic policy (as in Eritrea). In the 1990s, Cuban policy is likely to be less interventionary, purely because of the situation on the ground in Africa. As long as there is no breakdown of the Namibia agreement, Cubans will be out of Angola in 1991. Elsewhere their presence has been much reduced and they are playing no discernable combat role. This could change if the peace processes under way in Africa are reversed, as there is no indication that Cuba has dropped its commitment to revolution.

The Soviet Union: an evolving policy

There is no quick and easy answer to what has motivated the Soviet Union in its policies towards Africa and in its willingness to become involved in military conflicts there. All too often when examining Soviet policies, analysts have opted for an all-encompassing explanation – whether it be expansionism, opportunism, defence of Soviet interests or a desire to control Africa's minerals and sea-lanes. The expansionist explanation, which can go hand-in-hand with the others, is a common one (Luttwak, 1983, Seton-Watson, 1978; and Greig, 1977). This interpretation has had a great effect on Western, particularly United States, policies towards the Soviet role in Africa. President Reagan's main African policymaker, Chester Crocker, presumed that a 'grand design' of some sort was behind Soviet policy in Africa (Crocker, Fontaine and Simes, 1979). Other analysts have rejected the idea of a grand design or that Marxism–Leninism has a strong influence over Soviet policy, arguing instead that the Soviet Union has taken advantage of opportunities that have presented themselves in Africa and have acted on the basis of realpolitik rather than ideology (Porter, 1984).

The author's view, and one that he believes is supported by the foregoing narrative, is that you cannot divide ideology from national interest – that the latter is perceived through the prism of ideology – and that the Soviet approach to Africa and the reasons for Soviet interventions can be found in the overall Soviet ideological approach. Furthermore, the tendency to interpret Mikhail Gorbachev's reform programme and his foreign policy initiatives, whether in Africa or elsewhere, as moves away from Marxism are based on the same misconception of ideology and its role in policymaking that in the past saw ideology and pragmatism/national interest as mutually exclusive. Ideology should not be seen as static or an inflexible set of ideas that leads to the rigid channelling of policy in a particular, inevitable direction. In Soviet policymaking, there is no distinction between the interests of Marxism–Leninism and the interests of the Soviet state, what advances one is seen as automatically advancing the other. This is not to say that this leads to sensible or effective policies (Brezhnev's policy towards Zimbabwe, for example, was based on a poor understanding of the Zimbabwean situation and on an ossified adherence to long-standing interpretations of Marxism–Leninism).

As far as Soviet policy is considered, ideology is the 'link between the generalised values of society and institutionalised actions of the state. It is both a set of assumptions about the nature of social reality and a system of guidance. This does not imply that any given ideology must be tightly woven or logical. It is the case that ideology, like those people who formulate it, will adapt itself to the capabilities and constraints of the operational environment at a given time' (Dawisha, 1972).

The making of Soviet policy on the basis of the ruling ideology involves assessing the balance or correlation of forces involved in each particular area of concern and using that to guide the direction which the Soviet Union should take. The correlation of forces involves the sum total of political, economic, military, class and cultural factors involved in a given crisis or area of policy and the alignment of those factors, this 'serves as a methodological basis for the definition of the main trends of Soviet foreign policy' (Kapchenko, 1977). The policies derived from this process will be as effective as the understanding of the policymakers involved – thus in 1977, the Soviet Union perceived it as being in its interest to combine military support for both Ethiopia and Somalia. Success in this would obviously have strengthened the Soviet position in the Horn of Africa. However, the policy decisions were based on a misinterpretation of the nature and level of conflict between Ethiopia and Somalia and an incorrect belief that Somalia's adherence to Marxism was stronger than its nationalist motivations regarding the Ogaden. Soviet policy suffered a setback as a result of an incorrect calculation of the forces at work in the Horn of Africa, it was not an example of the Soviet national interests being at odds with ideology.

Soviet aims in Africa are not part of a grand design, though they do fit into an overall view of the world and of the directions in which policy should be heading. During the main period of Soviet activism in Africa (from 1975 to the early 1980s), the aim was to give support to states and movements perceived to be pro-Marxist and anti-imperialist. They were worthy of support, in the Soviet view, as they weakened the position of the West in Africa and were part of a world revolutionary movement, whose interests were broadly in line with those of Soviet policy. This led to a commitment to provide arms and training for liberation movements fighting against colonial or white minority rule in southern Africa and to give massive help to the MPLA in Angola to prevent its defeat by groups supported by the USA and China.

In Ethiopia, aid to the Derg was seen as supporting a progressive regime whose existence was threatened by the Somali invasion, which had been condemned by most African states, and which had requested Soviet aid after Soviet mediation attempts had failed. The Soviet and Cuban intervention sought to maintain a regime in power and to enable it to develop and implement its policies rather than as an attempt to expand Soviet influence. The war with Somalia stopped at the border and did not involve the replacement of the Somali regime with a pro-Soviet one.

A common explanation of Soviet policy in Angola and the Horn has been to stress purely strategic issues, such as access to minerals and the control of sea-lanes. This ignored the fact that the Soviet Union had no vital interest in Angolan oil and has made no attempt to stop oil sales to the West and that any attempt to disrupt international shipping around the Cape or in the Horn Area would itself be an act of war. Any major conflict between the superpowers sparked off by such an incident would reach a level where the control of resources or sea-lanes would be irrelevant. And it must be noted that in the cases of Soviet involvement in African conflicts, the initiative has been with the African state or movement involved. Neto and Mengistu sought Soviet aid, it was not foisted upon them. Similarly, when Somalia, Sudan and Egypt decided to end their military links with the Soviet Union, there was no Soviet attempt to stay in the host country.

Looking at the development of Soviet policy towards Africa and Soviet involvement in the continent's conflicts, a number of basic aims can be identified (under Gorbachev these are in a process of evolution, though they held true for most of the period reviewed in this book):

1. The establishment of political and economic relations with as wide a variety of states as possible. Even in cases where Soviet political or military policy was in direct contradiction to the policies of a given state, as in the case of Zaire, every effort was made to maintain diplomatic and trade relations. This policy is being further developed under Gorbachev.
2. Opposition to the expansion of Western power and influence in Africa. It was clearly the Soviet view that in the long term – though it was clearly impossible to achieve in the short term because of the weakness of socialist economies and the pervasive power of the world capitalist economy – that the interests of African

states would be best served by cutting their dependence on the capitalist market system and by developing closer political and economic links with the socialist countries. This would help increase the strength of the socialist economic system and reduce the ability of the West to bring economic and political pressure to bear on African states to obtain their conformity to Western policies.

3. Support for national liberation movements in colonised countries or in ones ruled by white minority regimes. This was seen as a vital part of developing a world revolutionary movement opposed to imperialism and capitalism (see Brutents, 1977, Ulyanovskiy, 1974; and Solodovnikov and Bogolovskiy, 1975). Part and parcel of support for the liberation movements came the policy of giving political, economic and military assistance to states adhering to Marxism–Leninism. It was expected by the Soviet leadership that successful liberation struggle would lead to the establishment, as in Angola and Mozambique, of socialist governments which would eventually develop into fully socialist states. This area of policy is evolving under Gorbachev in the face of the massive military and economic problems suffered by many of the socialist-inclined states in Africa.

4. Opposition to Chinese influence and intervention in Africa. This was particularly intense following the Sino–Soviet split in the 1960s, when the Soviet Union and China engaged in an ideological struggle for the loyalties of Third World revolutionaries and then in the mid to late 1970s and early 1980s, when China adopted a pro-Western and violently anti-Soviet stance in Africa – most obvious in Chinese aid to the FNLA and UNITA in Angola and to Somalia following the 1977–8 war.

The current Gorbachev line of seeking a peaceful end to regional conflicts (such as in Afghanistan, Angola and Cambodia) and of encouraging political and economic reforms in Angola, Ethiopia and Mozambique is part of the global policy of creating an environment in which the Soviet Union can reform its own political and economic systems and of promoting 'national' solutions to the problems that have afflicted socialist states, including those in Africa. This complex task requires a safe international environment, the reduction of military spending and coexistence with the West. The settling of conflicts, such as the one in Angola, does not amount to a renunciation of past policies but a recognition of current realities. This new phase of policy requiring, to quote from a key Gorbachev speech to the CPSU Congress in February 1986, 'tactical flexibility, a readiness for mutually acceptable compromises and an orientation on dialogue and mutual understanding rather than on confrontation' (*Soviet News*, 26th February 1986). These compromises and flexibility have contributed to growing cooperation between the superpowers in an attempt to solve major regional conflicts, such as in Angola. But again this does not presume a Soviet abandonment of allies like Angola. As Kurt Campbell has stated, 'it is not unreasonable to assume that the USSR will continue to persevere there as the Angolan settlement is put into effect, even in the face of challenges from UNITA, South Africa and the United States. If the settlement fails and the MPLA's position is severely damaged, it would be difficult for the USSR to remain aloof'

(Campbell, 1989, p. 230). In line with this view, there is no evidence to suggest that despite the Cuban withdrawal and the Namibian settlement, the USSR has cut its level of arms deliveries to Angola, that are vital for the continuing war against UNITA.

Soviet policy towards the Third World and Africa is still evolving (Campbell, 1989, p. 263), but the current direction is away from military intervention and towards political dialogue. The progress in this direction will be decided both by Soviet priorities and, more directly, by development of the conflicts that are continuing in Africa. It is also likely to be formulated in a less secretive manner with more open debate among academics and policymakers about the best courses of action and concerning the real situation in Africa, rather than a false image brought about by adherence to outdated beliefs about the political, social, economic and class structures in Africa.

8 The roots of intervention: invitation or invasion?

In the introduction to this book, I asked why foreign intervention has proved so lasting a feature of the African landscape. That it is so has been amply demonstrated. It is also beyond doubt that there have been and still are sufficient foreign states willing and able to intervene for the phenomenon to persist. But this still has not answered the question, why is Africa the subject of such interventions?

In seeking an answer, one must look at two basic factors – long-term structural factors, and shorter term, political, social and economic factors. It is obviously not possible to make a clear divide between the two or to isolate the decisive factor in each individual case. It should, though, be possible to draw up broad categories of factors that have led to conflict and foreign military intervention.

Structural factors

It would be simple, and some analysts of African affairs have chosen such simplicity, to ascribe all the examples of conflict and interference to external causes and to the colonial inheritance. One leading commentator has written that the parameters of conflict in Africa 'are defined primarily by the global superpower struggle . . . it follows that the primary cause of the threat to peace in Africa stems from this superpower rivalry for hegemony, and that all other causes are secondary' (Tandon in Hansen, 1987). Other writers have sought to refute the argument that colonialism and external influences are to blame – 'one of the mythologies of contemporary Africa is that the continent is the victim of exploiting foreign powers . . . this belief is a post-colonial hangover from the days when Africa was indeed the passive victim of the major powers. The situation today is that foreign intervention occurs because African governments . . . are ready to engage external support (Legum, 1979, p. 54).

But life and African politics are not so simple. It is impossible to say that superpower rivalry is behind or responsible for all conflicts or threats to peace; and it is just as impossible to argue that a belief in the idea of foreign exploitation is purely a 'post-colonial hangover'.

Rather, I would argue that a primary, but not exclusive, cause for conflict in Africa is the geopolitical map of Africa drawn up by the colonising powers and bequeathed to Africa during decolonisation. The map has an amazing number of straight lines that cut across ethnic, cultural, religious and physical boundaries.

States were created, originally as colonies, that have no ethnic, religious, cultural, political, economic or social coherence. They jumble together ethnic communities which were polities in their own right prior to colonisation or were in the process of nation-building but which had minimal contact with each other; they throw together communities which were in competition with each other or were at war with each other prior to colonisation; they try to mix customs, beliefs and social structures which are totally incompatible; and they cut across ethnic groups and polities, dividing them up between two or more states. These are all primary causes of conflict, and without conflict there is little opportunity for intervention.

The map of Africa, with its straight lines and meaningless divisions, encompasses at least a hundred border disputes or ethnic cleavages (Asiwaju, 1987, has identified 103). One need only look at the history of Somalia and the Horn or of Chad to see how the creation of artificial boundaries that bear no relation to the people they seek to divide or incarcerate within borders has engendered conflict. Somalis have sought to regain what are seen as lost territories. Not surprisingly, those from whom they have tried to wrest the territories have resisted. War has resulted. In Chad, an artificial nation if ever there was one, the French ruled the territory as two distinct units. Even after independence, the French retained military control of the north. When the two were joined under one administration, who can be surprised that there was hostility, resentment and war. Chad's northern border with Libya was unclear – both states had strong historical claims. Is it surprising that Libya, with its own security concerns and political objectives, sought to use its claim as a pretext for intervention?

The primary structural factor behind conflict and intervention is clearly the nature, shape and ethnic make-up of the states formed as a result of colonisation. If Africa had not been colonised, the political map of the continent would be very different. It might still be troubled by conflict and subject to foreign influence, but the pattern would be different. The conflicts and forms of foreign interference we see now cannot be divorced from the colonial inheritance. As a former Ugandan cabinet minister, one who has seen and tried to cope with the legacy of imperialism, has said: 'The first cause lies in the manifest defects of the colonial legacy to each of these states. Most notable was the total failure of colonisation to combine within a given colony ethnic groups with compatible characteristics; instead, the colonial frontiers were drawn purely on the basis of alien strategic and economic interests' (Ibingira, 1980, p. xi–xii).

And colonialism introduced other factors which have been causal factors in conflict. In southern Africa, colonialism took a variety of forms. Some ended sooner than others. Attempts by the Portuguese and by the whites of South Africa and Zimbabwe to outlive the colonial period were bound to lead to political strife and eventually military conflict. African nationalists and revolutionaries within those regions would not be satisfied with less than what their brothers across the Zambezi or the Congo rivers had gained in terms of political power and independence. That Guinea Bissau, which achieved independence following the 1974 revolution, has not experienced the systematic destabilisation and war that has affected Angola and Mozambique is not because it has adopted a more effective political system, but because it was not situated in a region where white settlers had tried to create permanent colonies and to perpetuate minority rule through the use of force.

A factor also linked to colonialism, though one combining the effects of the sudden onrush of African nationalism of the 1950s and 1960s, is the inadequate process of transition from full colonial rule to independence. There was no systematic process of decolonisation in Africa. Even within states, such as Uganda and Nigeria, different regions and peoples were given a different path to independence. States became independent without the political infrastructure and experience that would enable their new leaders to cope with the strains of nation-building, inter-state relations and economic development. Many of those who succeeded the colonial rulers were, to use Franz Fanon's words, the spoilt-children of colonialism. They were not representative of their populations and had been placed in power by the departing governors. These rulers had little legitimacy and relied on the former colonial power for political, military and financial support. France used its armed forces to support a number of such rulers in the early years of independence. Some have even survived decades in power (usually with substantial foreign support); others were overthrown in coups or as a result of widespread discontent.

States achieved independence with only the inherited administrative and military infrastructure. Armies were frequently little more than small, ceremonial forces or were just the 'native' component of the colonial armies given a new name. They often had European officers (some still do) and no clear loyalty or allegiance to the new, independent government. They wanted the privileges of power that had been the preserve of their colonial predecessors. Such factors lay behind the mutinies in the Congo and East Africa. The mutinies in turn led to foreign interventions. The Belgian intervention was anachronistic and uncalled for. It exacerbated the political chaos in Congo (a result of minimal preparation for independence in a multi-ethnic state with no history of domestic political activity or compromise) and led to civil war and ever greater foreign intervention. In East Africa, the new governments requested limited military aid to quell the mutinies. They used the breathing space provided by foreign aid to build new armies and to seek to establish legitimacy. To a great extent they succeeded, even if they failed to shake off the economic effects of colonialism. Tanzania and Kenya have hardly been models of political development, but they have succeeded in creating systems that have a measure of legitimacy and have not succumbed to persistent violence and foreign intervention. Yet they, too, are examples of the way in which the structures inherited from the colonial period were vulnerable to disintegration and conflict – the two vital components of intervention.

Consequential factors

If the structure of the African state, its borders and its population are primary causes of intervention, why then have not all states been victims of foreign military aggression or intervention? The answer is clearly that the structural factors create a vulnerability to conflict and therefore intervention, but that alone they do not cause intervention. One needs a power willing to intervene and circumstances that open the way for intervention. These are provided by the political, economic and social developments in Africa since independence. They are consequent upon the colonial inheritance but take different forms according to the diverse systems developed by and varying problems experienced by different states.

A major cause of conflict has been the failure of African regimes to legitimise or popularise their rule. Many African leaders and movements sought not to build nations or develop economies but to reap whatever rewards they could from independence. What Ibingira has called the 'winner-takes-all' system developed (Ibingira, 1980, p. xii). Far from seeking to alleviate the problems of ethnic multiplicity and conflict, regional rivalries, economies dependent on a few export crops and therefore on foreign markets, heads of state and whole governments tried to use the inheritance to entrench themselves in power and to enrich themselves. It was the political in-fighting and corruption that led to the military coups in Nigeria and to the civil war. Yes, the basic divisions did spring from the effects of imperialism, but it was not inevitable that they should take the forms that they did and have the results that they did.

Other manifestations of the failures to find the basis for a coherent political system and for a path to nation-building, are attempts to externalise domestic problems by seeking a target or an objective outside the state that can be used to legitimise a government or at least divert attention from its failures. This can be clearly seen in Somalia, where generally the only factor uniting the different clans has been the attempt to regain territories believed to be intrinsically Somali that were allotted to other states under the colonial division of Africa. Throughout the early 1960s unstable coalitions of competing parties, none of which had any overall national legitimacy, ruled Somalia. All they could agree on was the irredentism. The failure of the party system led to the military coup, but the military leaders failed to establish any other source of legitimacy, be it through Marxism–Leninism, economic development or authoritarian political rule. Irredentist aims remained the cement that bound the Somali bricks together. Thus the search for arms and for help in building a modern army to achieve the objective of regaining the lost territories. The refusal of Ethiopia to give up what it saw as its rightful territory made war inevitable. The timing and the resulting need for Ethiopia to seek foreign military support came about as Ethiopia's monarchy finally succumbed to its own failure to cope with the need to establish a popular and representative form of government and to embark on a path that would lead to viable and equitable economic development – the monarch-takes-all system did not work. Ethiopia's vulnerability in the wake of the revolution and in the face of demands for secession or autonomy by different ethnic groups within the country meant that it was in no position to face the Somali invasion alone. The regime's survival depended on eliciting immediate and massive foreign support.

Survival was the imperative which led the MPLA in Angola to seek Cuban combat assistance and massive Soviet aid. Following the Portuguese revolution, independence was on the cards for Angola. But the three competing movements, each appealing to different sections of the population, could not agree on a workable system of power-sharing that would avert conflict. Attempts were made, with the assistance of other African states, to form a viable coalition. But efforts by the FNLA to take advantage of factionalism within the MPLA to put itself into a commanding position led to war. None of the movements was strong enough alone to win a decisive victory. To ensure its own paramountcy, the FNLA called on Chinese aid (in the form of arms and advisers), American financial help and Zairean troops. The use of Zairean regular forces to support FNLA troops gave the FNLA military advantage over the MPLA, which turned to Cuba and the USSR. The escalation of the conflict developed further when South Africa, the strongest regional power, intervened to prevent the MPLA from coming to power. The South Africans acted in the interests of the maintenance of white minority rule, the FNLA to seize power and the MPLA to survive and then to ensure that its implacable enemies would not challenge its supremacy.

In Chad, successive regimes have sought foreign military aid (French or Libyan) to retain power and to exert control over a fragmented country. The ethnic and political diversity of the country has made unity impossible, something which Libya has used to its advantage and which France has utilised to exert continued influence in the region. Survival or the seizure of power have been the objectives sought through the use of foreign forces, while the intervening forces have sought security, hegemony and influence. Africa's relative military weakness and its dependence on imported arms and expertise have made worse the problems of survival and security for African governments.

Economic factors have also played a vital role in African conflicts. Continued poverty, competition for land, water and scarce natural resources and the overall effect of dependence on world markets and financial systems that African governments are powerless to influence have all exacerbated conflicts and increased instability. One of France's primary aims has been to protect its economic stake in the continent. And African politicians have been equally keen to protect their stakes. The prevalent winner-takes-all system has involved the conflict over who reaps the economic benefits of political power – individuals, parties, clans, ethnic groups and regions have all sought power and the economic benefits that flow from it. One of the causes of the second Sudanese conflict was opposition to northern attempts to use the Jonglei canal to divert water north for irrigation, another was the start of oil exploration, which southerners saw as northerners once more plundering southern resources. Morocco sought the Western Sahara not just to expand national territory but because the territory contained large mineral deposits. France intervened in the conflict not just to protect Mauritania's integrity and regime, but to ensure the security of its mineral resources. Cuban troops were used to defend the MPLA government, but also to protect the vital Cabinda oilfields.

But not all African conflicts have led to foreign intervention. The Nigerian civil war, one of the bloodiest conflicts in Africa was fought almost solely by Africans. A few mercenaries were used by Biafra and the federal government relied on Soviet and British arms. But no foreign forces fought in the war. The answer would appear to be that both sides needed arms but the federal government had no need to call on foreign troops because of its overwhelming advantage in terms of numbers and arms, while the Biafrans were losers almost from the start and it was inconceivable that any foreign power would intervene in such a hopeless cause. The Horn of Africa conflict during the 1980s saw a declining level of foreign intervention. This was not because the Ethiopians did not want it – they repeatedly called on the Cubans to fight in Eritrea and Tigre – but because the Cubans refused to fight in a conflict in which they had divided loyalties. The Soviet Union continued supplying arms to the Ethiopians along with advisers but their troops were never openly involved in combat in Africa and Moscow certainly did not intend to set a precedent in Eritrea.

If a conclusion is possible, as wars are continuing and intervention is not over and may assume new forms, it is that the geopolitical, social and economic structures inherited from colonialism have rendered Africa vulnerable to political fragmentation, regime instability and armed conflict. The military weakness of African states (particularly in the first years of independence), dependence on foreign sources of arms and military expertise, the growth of the winner-takes-all political system, the failures of many governments to build national unity and political legitimacy, the readiness of governments and movements to utilise foreign military aid to survive attack or to seize power rather than to seek political solutions to conflicts, the existence of strong military powers willing to commit aggression and to engage in systematic destabilisation (South Africa and Libya), the willingness of foreign powers to intervene when their interests dictate it have all led to repeated foreign military interventions and to the fostering of military and political independence (to complement to the massive economic dependence) on external support.

Only major structural changes within or between states (the latter being unlikely given the OAU's commitment to retaining existing borders) can reduce vulnerability. But changes in political attitudes and objectives could reduce the opportunities for unwarranted intervention and the need of governments or opposition movements to seek foreign support. In southern Africa and the Sahel, only the removal of the apartheid system and of the crusading aspect of Libya's policies will end those particular threats – though of course new ones may take their place.

The cure for the cancer of conflict and intervention lies primarily in Africa. Whatever the causes of the wars, intervention has usually come at the request of one or both of the combatants. As Olusegun Obasanjo, then the President of Nigeria, said at the OAU Heads of State Conference in July 1978: 'We African leaders must realise that we cannot be asking outside powers to leave us alone, while in most cases it is our actions which provide them with the excuse to interfere in our affairs. We can no longer hide behind real or imagined foreign machinations for our own failing.'

Bibliography

In the text all references to *ACR* are to the annual volumes of the yearbook, *Africa Contemporary Record* (London and New York, Holmes and Meier); references in footnotes to IISS refer to the annual publications of the International Institute for Strategic Studies, *The Military Balance* and *Strategic Survey*. All radio, television and news agency sources are taken from the BBC Monitoring Service *Summary of World Broadcasts* (Parts 1 and 4).

Adefuye, Ade, 1987, 'The Kakwa of Uganda and the Sudan: The Ethnic Factor in National and International Factors' in Asiwaju (ed), 1987.

Allen, Chris, 1989, 'Benin' in Allen, Baxter, Radu and Somerville (eds), 1989.

Allen, Chris, Baxter, Joan, Radu, Michael and Somerville, Keith (eds), 1989, *Benin, The Congo and Birkina Faso* (London, Pinter).

Asiwaju, A.I., (ed), 1987, *Partitioned Africans: Ethnic Relations across Africa's International Boundaries, 1884–1984* (London, Christopher Hurst).

Beshir, Mohammed Omar, 1975, *The Southern Sudan from Conflict to Peace* (Khartoum, The Khartoum Bookshop).

Blundy, David, and Lycett, Andrew, 1986, *Qadhafi* (London, Weidenfeld and Nicolson).

Bridgland, Fred, 1986, *Jonas Savimbi: A Key to Africa* (Edinburgh, Mainstream Publishing).

Brogan, Patrick, 1989, *World Conflicts* (London, Bloomsbury).

Brutents, Karen, 1977, *National Liberation Movements Today* (Moscow, Progress).

Campbell, Kurt M., 1989, 'Soviet policy in Southern Africa: Angola and Mozambique' in Kurt M. Campbell and S. Neil MacFarlane, 1989, *Gorbachev's Third World Dilemmas* (London, Routledge).

Carter, Gwendolen, and O'Meara, Patrick, 1979, *Southern Africa: the Continuing Crisis* (London, Macmillan).

Castagno, A.A., 1964, 'The Somali-Kenyan Controversy: Implications for the Future', *Journal of Modern African Studies*, vol 2, no. 2, 1964.

Castro, Fidel, 1969, *Fidel Castro Speaks*, edited by M. Kemer and J. Petras (Harmondsworth, Middx, Penguin).

Cawthra, Gavin, 1986, *Brutal Force: The Apartheid War Machine* (London, IDAF).

CIA, 1978, *Communist Aid in Sub-Saharan Africa* (Washington D.C., Central Intelligence Agency).

Chipman, John, 1985, *French Military Policy and African Security* (London, IISS, Adelphi Paper, no. 201, Summer 1985).

Clapham, Christopher, 1986, 'The Horn of Africa', in Duignan and Jackson (eds), 1986.

Crocker, Chester, Fontaine, Roger, and Simes, Dimitri, 1977, *Implications of Soviet and Cuban Activities in Africa for US Policy* (Washington D.C., Georgetown University, Centre for Strategic and International Studies).

Cronje, Suzanne, 1972, *The World and Nigeria: The Diplomatic History of the Biafran War, 1967-70* (London, Sidgwick and Jackson).

Crowder, Michael, 1987, 'Whose Dream was It Anyway? Twenty-Five years of African Independence', *African Affairs*, vol. 86, no. 342, January 1987.

Crozier, Brian, 1975, 'The Surrogate Forces of the Soviet Union', *Conflict Studies*, no. 92.

Crozier, Brian, 1978, 'The Soviet Presence in Somalia', *Conflict Studies*, no. 54.

Davidson, Basil, 1978, *Africa in Modern History* (Harmondsworth, Middx, Penguin).

Davidson, Basil, 1981, *The People's Cause: A History of Guerrillas in Africa* (London, Longman).

Davidson, Basil, Slovo, Joe, and Wilkinson, Anthony R., 1976, *Southern Africa: The New Politics of Revolution* (Harmondsworth, Middx, Penguin).

Dawisha, Karen, 1972, 'The Role of Ideology in the Decision-Making of the Soviet Union' *International Relations*, vol. 4, no. 2, 1972.

Dominguez, Jorge, 1989, *To Make a World Safe for Revolution: Cuba's Foreign Policy* (Cambridge, Mass., Harvard University Press).

Dudley, B.J., 1973, *Instability and Political Order: Politics and Crisis in Nigeria* (Ibadan, Nigeria, University of Ibadan Press).

Duignan, Peter, and Jackson, Robert (eds), 1986, *Politics and Government in African States, 1960-85* (London, Croom Helm).

Dziak, John J., 1971, *The Soviet Union and the National Liberation Movements: An Examination of the Development of a Revolutionary Strategy* (Georgetown, PhD Dissertation, Georgetown University).

El-Khawas, Mohammed, and Cohen, Barry (eds), 1976, *The Kissinger Study of Southern Africa: The National Security Memorandum 39* (Westport, Conneticut, Lawrence Hill).

Firebrace, James, and Holland, Stuart, 1984, *Never Kneel Down* (Nottingham, Spokesman).

Foltz, William J., and Bienen, Henry S. (eds), 1985, *Arms and the African: Military Influences on Africa's International Relations* (New Haven, Yale University Press).

Green, Reginald H., and Seidman, Ann, 1968, *Unity or Poverty: The Economics of Pan-Africanism* (Harmondsworth, Middx, Penguin).

Greenfield, Richard, 1965, *Ethiopia: A New Political History* (London, Pall Mall).

Greig, Ian, 1977, *The Communist Challenge to Africa* (London, Foreign Affairs Publishing Co.).

Grundy, Kenneth W., 1968, 'On Machiavelli and Mercenaries' Journal of *Modern African Studies*, vol. 6, no. 3, 1968.

Grundy, Kenneth W., 1986, *The Militarization of South African Politics* (Oxford, Oxford University Press).

Halliday, Fred, and Molyneaux, Maxine, 1981, *The Ethiopian Revolution* (London, Verso).

Hanlon, Joseph, 1984, *Mozambique: The Revolution Under Fire* (London, Zed).

Hanlon, Joseph, 1986, *Beggar Your Neighbours: Apartheid Power in Southern Africa* (London, James Currey/CIIR/Indiana University Press).

Hansen, Emmanuel (ed), 1987, *Africa: Perspectives on Peace and Development* (London, The UN University/Zed).

Harris, Lillian Criag, 1986, *Libya: Qadhafi's Revolution and the Modern State* (Boulder, Colorado, Westview).

Henze, Paul B., 1981, 'Communism and Ethiopia' *Problems of Communism*, May–June 1981.

Heraclides, Alex, 1987, 'Janus or Sisyphus? The Southern Problem of Sudan', *Journal of Modern African Studies*, vol. 25, no. 2, 1987.

Hodges, Tony, 1983, *Western Sahara: The Roots of a Desert War* (Westport, Conneticut, Lawrence Hill).

Ibingira, Grace Stuart, 1980, *African Upheavals Since Independence* (Boulder, Colorado, Westview).

Jaster, Robert J., 1983, *A Regional Security Role for Africa's Frontline States: Experience and Prospects* (London, IISS, Adelphi Paper no. 180).

Kanza, Thomas, 1972, *Conflict in the Congo* (Harmondsworth, Middx, Penguin).

Kapchenko, N.I., 1977, 'Scientific Principles of Soviet Foreign Policy' *International Affairs* (Moscow), October 1977.

Kirk-Green, Anthony, 1971, *Crisis and Conflict in Nigeria: A Documentary Sourcebook, 1966–69* (Oxford, Oxford University Press).

Klinghoffer, Arthur J., 1980, *The Angolan War* (Boulder, Colorado, Westview).

Lefebvre, J.A., 1987, 'Donor Dependency and American Arms Transfers to the Horn of Africa' *Journal of Modern African Studies*, vol. 25, no. 3, 1987.

Legum, Colin, 1961, *Congo Disaster* (Harmondsworth, Middx, Penguin).

Legum, Colin, and Lee, Bill, 1979, 'Crisis in the Horn of Africa', (London, Resc Collins).

Legum, Colin, 1979, 'Communal Conflict and International Intervention in Africa' in Legum, Zartman, Langdon and Mytelka (eds), 1979, *Africa in the 1980s* (New York, Council on Foreign Relations/McGraw Hill).

Lemarchand, Rene, 1976, 'The CIA in Africa: How Central, How Intelligent' *Journal of Modern African Studies*, vol. 14, no. 3, 1976.

Lemarchand, Rene (ed), 1988, *The Green and the Black: Qadhafi's Policies in Africa* (Bloomington, Indiana, Indiana University Press).

Lewis, I.M., 1963, 'Pan-Africanism and Pan-Somalism' *Journal of Modern African Studies*, vol. 1, no. 1, 1963.

Le Vine, Victor, 1986, 'The State of Formerly French West Africa' in Duignan and Jackson (eds, 1986).

Lewis, William H., 1987, 'US Military Assistance to Africa' *CSIS African Notes* (Washington D.C., CSIS).

Low, D.A., 1974, *Lion Rampant* (London, Cass).

Luckham, Robin, 1970, 'The Nigerian Military: Disintegration or Integration?' in Panter-Brick, Keith, (ed), 1970, *Nigerian Political and Military Rule* (London, Institute of Commonwealth Studies).

Luckham, Robin, 1971, *The Nigerian Military: A Sociological Analysis of Authority and Revolt, 1960–67* (Cambridge, CUP).

Luckham, Robin, 1982, 'French Militarism in Africa' *Review of African Political Economy*, no. 24.

Luttwak, E.N., 1983, *The Grand Strategy of the Soviet Union* (New York, St Martin Press).

Lynn Price, David, 1979, *The Western Sahara* (Beverley Hills, California, CSIS/Sage, Washington Papers).

MacFarlane, S.F., 1983–4, 'Intervention and Security in Africa', *International Affairs*, Winter 1983–4.

McLane, Charles B., 1974, *Soviet African Relations* (London, Central Asian Research Centre).

Madiebo, Alexander A., 1980, *The Nigerian Revolution and the Biafran War* (Enugu, Nigeria, Fourth Dimension).

Mangold, Peter, 1979, 'Shaba I and Shaba II' *Survival*, May/June 1979, vol. xxi, no. 3.

Manning, Peter, 1988, *Francophone Sub-Saharan Africa, 1880–1985* (Cambridge, CUP, 1988).

Marcum, John, 1969, *The Angolan Revolution: Vol 1: The Anatomy of an Explosion (1950–1962)* (Cambridge, Mass., IT Press).

Marcum, John, 1978, *The Angolan Revolution: Vol 2: Exile Politics and Guerrilla Warfare (1962–1976)* (Cambridge, Mass., MIT Press).

Marcum, John, 1979, 'Angola: Perilous Transition to Independence' in Carter and O'Meara (ed), 1979.

Marcum, John, 1986, 'Angola: Twenty-Five Years of War' *Current History*, vol. 85, no. 511.

Markakis, John, 1988, 'The Nationalist Revolution in Eritrea' *Journal of Modern African Studies*, vol. 26, no. 1.

Marquez, Gabriel Garcia, 1977, 'Operation Carlota' *New Left Review*, no. 101–2, February–April 1977.

Martin, David, and Johnson, Phyllis, 1981, *The Struggle for Zimbabwe* (Harare, Zimbabwe Publishing House).

Martin, David, and Johnson, Phyllis, 1989, *Frontline Southern Africa* (Peterborough, Ryan Publishers).

Mazrui, Ali, and Tidy, Michael, 1984, *Nationalism and New States in Africa* (London, Heinemann).

Meredith, Martin, 1980, *The Past is Another Country: Rhodesia, UDI to Zimbabwe* (London, Pan).

Meredith, Martin, 1984, *The First Dance of Freedom: Black Africa in the Post-War Era* (London, Hamish-Hamilton).

Metz, Stephen, 1986, 'The Mozambique National Resistance and South African Foreign Policy' *African Affairs*, vol. 85, no. 341, October 1986.

Minter, William, 1972, *Portuguese Africa and the West* (Harmondsworth, Middx, Penguin).

Mondlane, Eduardo, 1983, *The Struggle for Mozambique* (Zed, London).

Moose, George E., 1985, 'French Military Policy in Africa' in Foltz and Bienen (ed).

Morrison, Godfrey, 1976, *Eritrea and the Southern Sudan* (London, Minority Rights Group Report, no. 5).

Muhammadu, Tiri, and Haruna, Mohammed, 1979, 'The Civil War' in Oyediran (ed).

Nkrumah, Kwame, 1968, *Neo-Colonialism: The Last Stage of Imperialism* (London, Heinemann).

O'Ballance, Edgar, 1977, *The Secret War in the Sudan, 1955–72* (London, Faber and Faber).

Ogunbadejo, Oye, 1976, 'The Impact of the Civil War on Nigerian Foreign Relations' *African Affairs*, no. 75, January 1976.

Oliver, Roland, and Crowder, Michael, 1981, *The Cambridge Encyclopaedia of Africa* (Cambridge, CUP).

Ottaway, Marina, 1982, *Soviet and American Influence in the Horn of Africa* (New York, Praeger).

Oyediran, Oyeleye, 1979, *Nigerian Government and Politics Under Military Rule* (London, Macmillan).

Patman, Robert, 1982, 'Ideology, Soviet Policy and Realignment in the Horn' in Dawisha, Adeed and Karen (ed), 1982, *The Soviet Union in the Middle East* (London, Heinemann).

Payton, Gary D., 'The Somali Coup of 1969: the Case for Soviet Complicity' *Journal of Modern African Studies*, no. 18, 1980.

People's Republic of Angola, 1983, *White Paper on Acts of Aggression by the Racist South African Regime Against the People's Republic of Angola* (Luanda).

Porter, Bruce D., 1984, *The USSR in Third World Conflicts* (Cambridge, CUP).

Radu, Michael S., and Somerville, Keith, 1989, 'People's Republic of Congo' in Allen, Baxter, Radu and Somerville (eds), 1989.

Ray, Ellen, Schaap, W., Van Meter, Karl, and Wolfed, L. (ed), 1980, *Dirty Work: The CIA in Africa* (London, Zed).

Rees, David, 1977, 'Soviet Strategic Penetration of Africa' *Conflict Studies*, no. 77, November 1977.

St John, Ronald Bruce, 1988, 'The Libyan Debacle in Sub-Saharan Africa, 1969–87' in Lemarchand (ed), 1988.

Samatur, Said, 1987, 'The Somali Dilemma' in Asiwaju (ed), 1987.

Schwab, Peter, 1985, *Ethiopia: Politics, Economics and Society* (London, Pinter).

Selassie, Bereket Habte, 1980, *Conflict and Intervention in the Horn of Africa* (New York, Monthly Review Press).

Seton-Watson, Hugh, 1978, *The Imperialist Revolutionaries* (Stanford, California, Hoover Institution Press).

Shaw, Timothy, and Heard, Kenneth A. (ed), 1979, *Politics of Africa: Dependence and Development* (London, Longman).

SIPRI, 1975, *The Arms Trade with the Third World* (Harmondsworth, Middx, Penguin).

Sitole, Ndabaningi, 1968, *African Nationalism* (Oxford, Oxford University Press).

Solodovnikov, V., and Bogolovskiy, V., 1975, *Non-Capitalist Development* (Moscow, Progress).

Somali Ministry of Foreign Affairs, 1965, *The Somali People's Quest for Unity* (Mogadishu).

Somerville, Keith, 1984, 'The USSR and Southern Africa' *Journal of Modern African Studies*, vol. 22, no. 1, March 1984.

Somerville, Keith, 1984, 'Angola: Soviet Client State or State of Socialist Orientation' *Millenium: Journal of International Studies*, vol. 13, no. 3, Winter 1984.

Somerville, Keith, 1984, 'The Soviet Union and Zimbabwe: The Liberation Struggle and After' in Mark V. Kauppi and Craig Nation (ed), 1984, *The Soviet Impact in Africa* (Lexington, Mass., D.C. Heath).

Somerville, Keith, 1986, *Angola: Politics, Economics and Society* (London, Pinter).

Stevens, Christopher A., 1976, *The Soviet Union and Black Africa* (London, Macmillan).

Stockwell, John, 1978, *In Search of Enemies* (London, Andre Deutsch).

Tessler, Mark, 1988, 'Libya and the Maghreb' in Lemarchand (ed), 1988.

Thompson, Virginia, and Adloff, Richard, 1980, *The Western Sahara* (London, Christopher Hurst).

Thompson, Virginia, and Adloff, Richard, 1981, *Conflict in Chad* (London, Christopher Hurst).

Thompson, W. Scott, and Silvers, Brett, 1979, 'South Africa in Soviet Strategy' in Bissel, Richard, and Crocker, Chester A. (ed), 1979, *South Africa Into the 1980s* (Boulder, Colorado, Westview).

Tordoff, William, 1984, *Government and Politics in Africa* (Bloomington, Indiana, Indiana University Press).

Ulyanovskiy, R., 1974, *Socialism and the Newly-Independent Nations* (Moscow, Progress).

US Congress, Senate Committee on Foreign Relations, 1970, *United States Security Commitments and Agreements Abroad, Part 8, Ethiopia* (Washington D.C.).

US Congress, Senate Committee on Foreign Relations, 1976, *Ethiopia and the Horn of Africa, 94th Congress, 2nd Session, 4th–6th August 1976, Senate Report* (Washington D.C.).

Volsky, George, 1981, 'Cuba' in Henriksen, Thomas (ed), 1981, *The Communist Powers and Sub-Saharan Africa* (Stanford, California, Hoover Institution Press).

Wai, Dunstan (ed), 1973, *The Southern Sudan: The Problem of National Integration* (London, OUP).

Weissman, Stephen R., 1974, *American Foreign Policy in the Congo, 1960–64* (Cornell, Cornell University Press).

Wells, Samuel F., 1988, 'Mitterrand's International Policies' *The Washington Quarterly*, Summer 1988, no. 67).

White, Dorothy Shipley, 1979, *Black Africa and De Gaulle* (University Park, Pennsylvania and London, Pennsylvania University Press).

Wolfers, Michael, and Bergerol, Jane, 1982, *Angola in the Frontline* (London, Zed).

Woodward, Peter, 1979, *Condominium and Sudanese Nationalism* (London, Rex Collings).

Wright, John, 1989, *Libya and the Sahara* (London, Christopher Hurst).

Young, Crawford, 1986, 'Zaire and Cameroon' in Duignan and Jackson (ed), 1986.

Index

[NOTE: *passim* means that the subject so annotated is referred to in scattered pages throughout the pages indicated.]